ROUTLEDGE LIBRARY EDITIONS: POLICE AND POLICING

Volume 21

POLICING BY THE PUBLIC

POLICING BY THE PUBLIC

JOANNA SHAPLAND
and
JON VAGG

Routledge
Taylor & Francis Group

LONDON AND NEW YORK

First published in 1988 by Routledge

This edition first published in 2023
by Routledge
4 Park Square, Milton Park, Abingdon, Oxon OX14 4RN

and by Routledge
605 Third Avenue, New York, NY 10158

Routledge is an imprint of the Taylor & Francis Group, an informa business

British Library Cataloguing in Publication Data
A catalogue record for this book is available from the British Library

ISBN: 978-1-032-41114-9 (Set)
ISBN: 978-1-032-41773-8 (Volume 21) (hbk)
ISBN: 978-1-032-41776-9 (Volume 21) (pbk)
ISBN: 978-1-003-35968-5 (Volume 21) (ebk)

DOI: 10.4324/9781003359685

Publisher's Note
The publisher has gone to great lengths to ensure the quality of this reprint but points out that some imperfections in the original copies may be apparent.

Disclaimer
The publisher has made every effort to trace copyright holders and would welcome correspondence from those they have been unable to trace.

Policing by the Public

Joanna Shapland and Jon Vagg

R

Routledge

London and New York

First published in 1988 by
Routledge
11 New Fetter Lane, London EC4P 4EE

Published in the USA by
Routledge
in association with Routledge, Chapman and Hall, Inc.
29 West 35th Street, New York NY 10001

Photoset by Mayhew Typesetting, Bristol, England
Printed in Great Britain by Biddles Ltd, Guildford

British Library Cataloguing in Publication Data

Shapland, Joanna, 1950–
  Policing by the public.
  1. Great Britain. Crimes. Prevention.
  Role of Public
  I. Title II. Vagg, Jon
  364.4'4

  ISBN 0-415-00691-0

Contents

Acknowledgements

This book is about the links between formal and informal social activities. It is somehow appropriate, then, that its origin lies in one of those professional social occasions at which criminologists, criminal justice practitioners, and Home Office officials meet. One of us (JS) was talking to a chief constable. Unfortunately we cannot name him, for to do so would make the areas we studied, some of their inhabitants, and many of the police officers we interviewed identifiable. The chief constable was intrigued that criminologists always study high-crime areas. Why not, he said, look at rural areas – if they have such low official crime rates, either they are doing something right about preventing crime, or their social structure inhibits it, or they suffer it in silence. Whatever it is, it is worth knowing about. Thus was born the idea of looking deliberately at low-crime areas and informal social control, as well as at high-crime areas and policing. We want, particularly, to thank that chief constable and his officers. We hope he is still pleased that he had the idea.

We should like to thank the Home Office for funding, from January 1983 to October 1985, the research study on which this book is based. Our ideas have also benefited tremendously from the more recent research conducted by JS with Dick Hobbs, *Policing on the Ground*, funded by the Economic and Social Research Council (ESRC) under grant no. E0022209. But responsibility for the finished product, including of course all its faults, rests with us. The views we express are entirely our own.

The study was based at the Centre for Criminological Research, Oxford University, and everyone at the Centre deserves thanks for help in ways too numerous to list. Many people have contributed to the effort of getting the research off the ground, doing it, and writing this book. We should like to mention, in particular, John Andelin, Andrew Ashworth, Vivienne Chamberlain, Ron Clarke, Richard Fries, Dick Hobbs, Roger Hood, Mike Hough, Velia Johnson, Valerie Johnstone, Janet Larkin, Carol McCall, Georgina Marson, and Hilary Prior.

The research entailed lengthy periods away from home and writing the book squeezed family life into the background for many months. Our respective spouses (Ian and Mary) and offspring (Alastair and Christopher) not only put up with all of this but actually supported it uncomplainingly.

Lastly, but in a way firstly, our thanks must go to the anonymous villagers, city-dwellers, business people, and police officers – especially the village constable at Southton – who answered silly questions, explained obvious things at length, and tolerated our presence with great good humour; without them neither research nor book would have happened.

1
Introduction: the soft underbelly?

> At a time when serious crime seems indivisible from metropolitan blight, a new breed of criminal is preying on the soft underbelly of society – the shires and villages whose only protective shield of community trust is wearing dangerously thin.
>
> ('The villains' new target', *Daily Mail*, 8 November 1985)

The scene is conjured up in a sentence. According to the *Daily Mail*'s feature writer, crime, that distinctively urban problem, is moving out to the countryside. Villages and rural areas, previously the epitome of the well-ordered society, are suddenly found to be victims of a new lawlessness. It is no longer possible to leave the milk money on the doorstep, and the neighbours live in their big city *pied-à-terre* during the week, so no one will see the burglar at the kitchen window. Trust is breaking down, and the attitudes and hardware of self-defence fragment the community and will ultimately destroy it. The local bobby is, says the same article, an endangered species, while motorways make access to villages easier and the affluence of villagers renders them prime targets.

This is an alarming view of the countryside, and undoubtedly it contains a few distilled grains of truth. But this description of the situation – crime up, community trust low, police withdrawn, villains coming out from the towns – raises more questions than it answers. Has anything really changed in the countryside? Do we not merely have a romanticized view of rural life and an exaggerated idea of urban crime? What, exactly, is a community and why is it such a different animal in urban and rural areas? How does it set about keeping the peace among its own members, and how can it deal with deviance by strangers? How has it come about that the 'village bobby' is so much valued if he – or in some areas now, she – has signally failed in the fight against crime? And why does the idea of the village bobby hold such a powerful sway on the imagination that introducing something like him ('home beat officers', 'community constables', etc.) to urban areas has become the fashion? In considering such questions, we begin to find that the answers are not at all obvious. Indeed, while it is by no means clear that villages are the 'soft underbelly of society', rural crime and more generally the relationship between formal and informal systems of social control are the soft underbelly of criminology. Very little is known about them. Moreover, to set off in search of some answers requires not only the conceptual baggage of criminology, but also, as we shall see, some ideas more familiar to rural sociologists and anthropologists.

Community and social control

First, the idea of community is notorious for its vagueness. Willmott (1987) points to three broad and overlapping meanings of the term without exhausting its potential. He refers to, first, territorial communities defined by geography; second, interest communities, examples of which might be black, Jewish, or gay communities; and third, attachment communities in which a sense of belonging to relationships or places is the defining characteristic. Such communities may of course overlap. But there are further meanings. What sense of community, for example, is invoked when we talk of community radio or community policing? There is, in the former, often some residual sense of local participation. In the latter, it is easy to take the cynical view and echo Raymond Williams's comment that community is sometimes no more than a 'warmly persuasive' word intended to encourage public support for a policy that is primarily intended to benefit policy-makers, in this case the police (Williams 1976). If we acknowledge that at the very beginning of a study of communities there is a problem of definition, life becomes very complicated when we progress from there to discuss questions of 'community trust'.

Yet communities are not entirely unknown quantities. The 1960s and 1970s saw a great increase in the number and scope of area studies, many of which had interesting and illuminating things to say about a wide range of community issues, such as the idea of 'belonging' to a place, the focal roles of institutions such as schools, and the arrangements for family and community care (see, for example, Cohen 1982; Strathern 1981). Many of these studies, done in rural areas, considered some aspects of social control – usually at the level of dispute settlements over property and the like. Bailey (1971) is, however, one example of a more detailed and thoroughgoing set of studies which concentrate more specifically on the practicalities of how social order is achieved in small rural areas – how rules of social interaction (politeness, status, and the like) are used in ways that lead to the creation of conformity and the management of deviant acts of all kinds. It is clear that in many areas, and in a routine and officially unnoticed way, people seek to observe, interpret, and influence the acts of others in ways that will, they hope, result in what they conceive of as an orderly social environment. Urban areas, too, have received such attention – Young and Willmott's (1962) study of Bethnal Green is probably the best-known example of such work, and Abrams' work in Leeds, Durham, and Cambridge among other places (reported in Bulmer 1986) one of the most recent. A few urban studies have concentrated more particularly on problems which have historically been held to have metropolitan characteristics. Gill (1977) studied a small area of Crossley, arguing that the patterns of offending and offenders in the area were related to housing policies and unemployment; Power (1982) discusses the concerns of council estate residents over matters as diverse as the poor quality of house maintenance and the fear of crime.

Community, crimes, and policing

Despite the interest in communities within sociology and anthropology, comparatively little work has been done at a similar level within the subject area of criminology. Criminologists have by and large gone to urban areas with high crime rates, more easily to find the phenomenon that interests them (a notable exception is Clinard 1978). This focus on crime has obscured one possible view of the subject, namely that what gets called crime is often an extension of certain 'problems' or 'incidents' that afflict people in particular areas. Such a view is not absent from criminology. A central tenet of labelling theory (Becker 1966) is that what comes to be called a crime is not intrinsically a qualitatively different act to 'non-crime' but merely an act which, at this time, and for particular reasons, is responded to in terms of policing and the criminal justice system. Studies of policing from Banton (1964) and Bittner (1967) onwards have commented that police are frequently called to events that some regard as 'rubbish' or 'not real police work'. Many of these 'rubbish' problems – domestic arguments might be the best example – have a complex history of who said what to whom, and when, that makes the police reluctant to intervene.

But though these views are present, they have not been dominant in the literature. The major hypothesis concerning informal social control, and it often seems implicit rather than explicit and is both contentious and untested, is that official crime rates may be higher where the possibilities for such informal order-maintenance are more limited, as for example in urban areas with a high population turnover and greater anonymity. Whether this implicit assumption is fair is as little known as the inner workings of the process of informal social control.

Some interesting gaps?

Research on crime and policing has some interesting gaps. In general, we know a certain amount about how policing appears to be done in urban areas but very little about rural policing. This is a bizarre situation, because the post-Scarman philosophy of urban policing draws heavily on ideas of community policing, which are based at least in part on notions of what the archetypal 'village bobby' does – or did, before concern about effectiveness and efficiency led to his withdrawal in many parts of the country. We know little, however, about what village bobbies actually do; how they do it; and what its effect on 'the community' might be. Cain's (1973) study is still the definitive work in this field. Her conclusions are, broadly speaking, that rural police officers operate in an environment in which they are very far from faceless and what they do matters. They must, unlike their urban counterparts, spend much of their time interacting with informal social control processes. This was characterized by the officers as 'having a cup of tea with Mrs X'.

There is a second gap in research. In such rural communities and possibly in urban ones as well, it seems likely that some kind of informal 'social contract' exists between the police and the public, making policing more like a 'partnership' than something imposed by the police. There is, however, scant evidence on this point. Cain's discussion of the rural bobby 'having a cup of tea' only extends as far as the police obtaining information, and is silent on the issue of 'local negotiations'. Talk at the policy level about partnership in policing has become commonplace, yet too little is known about what such partnerships actually comprise, if and where they exist. The 1984 Police and Criminal Evidence Act required police forces to engage in consultative exercises with communities, and while much is now known about *those* consultative processes (Morgan and Maggs 1985; Morgan 1987a), almost nothing is known about the more informal and day-to-day consultations in which officers on the beat must engage in order to carry out their work. In short, the rhetorical idea of the public and the police forming a partnership against crime may have become a formalized construct with very little to do with the reality of policing on the ground, where a real partnership would have very different, if unknown, dimensions.

Equally, a historical view of urban and rural crime shows some very strange features which ought to make us think twice about our assumptions. Rural areas are by no means the idylls that they are made out to be. In general, rural crime rates are about one-quarter the national average, though they are probably increasing faster than urban crime rates. This may be due to increased population mobility, the growth of new estates, high levels of rural poverty, or the lack of police resources in such areas. But rural poverty, in particular, has a long and grim history (Newby 1979), and it has been suggested (Hobsbawm and Rudé 1973) that, historically, riot has been the traditional and normal – rather than exceptional – form of rural protest. Low rural crime rates in this century are an interesting phenomenon, especially if they are viewed as the achievement of a community rather than as a series of decisions by offenders.

Urban areas have also had far too many assumptions made about them. They are not the opposite of rural areas – dens of vice and anonymous concrete jungles. It is now well known (see, for example, Baldwin and Bottoms 1976) that urban areas have widely varying victimization and offender rates, and there is often little evidence to indicate why the rates should vary as they do. Too little attention has been paid to such phenomena in the past, since the inner cities have acted as a magnet for research and policy initiatives (but see Bottoms, Mawby, and Walker 1987). But if the aim is to achieve a better-ordered community, it will repay us well to look at places less in the limelight. To put it crudely, if one wants to reduce crime, it is probably a useful exercise to go to places which do not have high crime rates and to find out what they are doing to achieve this.

A fourth gap is, ironically, the result of the very great advances made in recent years in the direction of victim surveys. The *British Crime Survey* (Hough and Mayhew 1983, 1985; Chambers and Tombs 1984), together with a large number of local surveys (for example, Butler and Tharme 1982; Kinsey 1984; Jones, Maclean, and Young 1986), have generated a great deal of information on the prevalence of, and views about, crime. However, the large-scale nature of such enterprises offers snapshots of crime at particular places and times, rather than lending itself to the analysis and interpretation of processes of social control which generate those victimizations. We now have a mass of information on individual experiences and views, but this has simply exposed our lack of knowledge about how, in any given social setting, such events are coped with and given meaning.

Fifthly and finally, recent interest in the 'fear of crime' has both generated some knowledge of the phenomenon and also exposed our ignorance about it. Commentators have provided a detailed picture of urban fear of crime, using measures such as the proportion of individuals feeling 'unsafe' or 'very unsafe' walking the streets after dark, and linking this to variables such as age, sex, income, and experiences of victimization (see, for example, Hough and Mayhew 1983, 1985; Skogan and Maxfield 1981). But very many corners of these 'fears' remain unexplored. We do not know, for example, whether vague fears of darkness (often of 'something awful but unpredictable' happening in the dark) have been sharpened by, say, media coverage, into a more specific fear of being attacked. Large-scale surveys such as the *British Crime Survey* leave us with the suggestion that fear of crime is related to individuals' opinions about the amount of crime in general and in their area in particular, the extent to which they see crime in general as a problem, and the tantalizing possibility that fear of crime may even be generated by avoidance behaviours rather than vice versa. Yet it is in the nature of such surveys that they cannot tell us about the rational or irrational processes by which fear of crime is produced and responded to. Further, one failing in the work done to date is that it too often uses 'fear' as a blanket term, while common sense would suggest that a range of descriptions – concern, worry, anxiety – might also be appropriate. It may be that 'fear of crime' has become, in a way, 'criminological property'; an abstract concept, rather distanced from what the woman in the street means when she says she is 'worried' or 'concerned' about victimization. The need for qualitative, rather than quantitative, assessments of the fear of crime is plain.

A need for research

This lengthy introduction leads us to the concerns of the following chapters. First, there is a need for simple descriptive work which outlines what informal action might be taken and is taken, by whom, and to what effect, in both rural and urban areas, concerning events or incidents which would broadly be described as the sort of problems in which the formal social-control mechanism of the police might also, at some point, become involved.

This entails a reversal of the usual criminological perspective. Most often, criminologists study the criminal and his or her offence (for example Bennett and Wright 1984), or the processes within the police by which an offence is recorded and dealt with (or not, as the case may be – for example, McCabe and Sutcliffe 1978). Our own study begins with the supposition that some means for the maintenance of social order and the repair of damage to it exist. Our approach tries to answer questions such as: what mechanisms exist? when do they fail to maintain order? at what point is such failure communicated to the police? and what is then done in order to see that the police do what the victim, the victim's friends and family, and/or the 'community' want? None of this is straightforward. The words 'social order' imply the existence of a consensus about what good social order is, together with action being taken in concert to create it. As we shall show, there is little consensus about order within different areas, just as there is little agreement about what constitutes deviance and little spontaneous unanimity about how to deal with it. One advantage of our approach, however, is that it does not see catching and punishing deviants and offenders as the only, or necessarily the main, task of social order. Preventing further damage, repairing that already done, caring for victims, helping the offender to rejoin the community, reassuring people about the future, and repairing the integrity of the community are also the aims of social enterprise and likely requirements for the construction and maintenance of 'ordered' communities.

Why is this microscopic inspection of social life necessary? Cannot we all continue to live our lives in blissful ignorance of these processes of social interaction? We suspect not. We argue that the actions and, more particularly, the effectiveness of major public institutions such as the police depend crucially upon these processes of informal social control.

It is now seen as axiomatic that the police cannot effectively maintain order or deal with crime unless they also have the consent of the community being policed. The demands made upon the police by the public form the largest single 'input' to which the police react. Police work is largely generated by the decision-making of individuals, affected by the communities in which they live. These decisions are not clear-cut. It is not obvious that criminal incidents or matters regarding disorder should be reported to the police. Indeed, Arthurs (1975) has argued that too great a reliance on outside agencies such as the police may be damaging to communities. They should be able to tolerate and deal with troublesome behaviour within their own networks, for the consequence of not doing so is the fragmentation of the community.

While a certain amount is known about why particular kinds of events get reported while others do not, there is little knowledge of what people expect the police to do with the matter beyond somehow 'sorting it out'. There is some evidence, however, that once a matter is reported to the police it becomes what Christie (1977) has called 'police property', and that the individuals making a report have little say in how the matter is resolved. And there is more evidence that this tendency to 'take charge' of matters is deeply resented by at least some victims (Shapland, Willmore, and Duff 1985). Whether to call the police might be, under these circumstances, a difficult decision. The link between the informal and the formal social-control processes becomes very problematic.

What the police do is in practice not just shaped by the formal demands of the law – or even by their political mandate and place amongst the institutions of the state – but also by the views of those that are policed and by the resulting pressures on individual officers from inside and outside the force. Their overall mandate is broad and diffuse, but as Reiner (1985: 4) points out: 'Since policing is centrally concerned with the resolution of conflicts using the coercive powers of criminal law, ultimately resting on the capacity to use force, there is in most police actions someone who is being policed *against*.'

Writers such as Brogden (1982, 1987) argue that their primary task has never been to deal with crime as such, but to maintain public order and, where necessary, to suppress protest against state interests. In most police actions, then, it can be the community that is being policed against. In either view – and in all those between – the essential point is again that the police mandate is by no means identical with that desired by 'ordinary people', even if (in Reiner's version) not many people are policed against and most people, most of the time, acquiesce in being policed. A range of studies has developed the concept of police occupational cultures to a considerable level of sophistication. Yet work still remains to be done on the issues of why the police – who have a broad range of discretion – handle matters in the way they do; of whether the pressures of the job and the world-view they create militate against the very idea of policing with, rather than against, a community; and of whether the tools of arrest, cautioning, and prosecution are not too blunt to be effective in keeping the peace.

Trying to describe the work of the police is, of course, trying to hit a moving target. New developments in policing policy emerge every few months if not every few weeks. Weatheritt (1986), for example, discusses five recent experiments with area beat officers and six crime prevention initiatives. The police force in our study had, prior to our fieldwork, undertaken extensive surveys on public attitudes to policing, as well as introducing an area beat officer scheme and a version of 'policing by objectives' (Butler 1984) intended to make the work of the force more effective by, among other things, identifying local problems and concentrating police attention on possible solutions. None the less, it is anything but clear that such experiments have had any positive results on official crime rates (victim-based crime rates are often not used in project evaluation) or public attitudes. For example, of the five area officer experiments discussed by Weatheritt (1986), one showed increases in crime levels and a widespread belief on the part of the officers that the public were getting a worse service from the police; one showed no effect from the change in policing; one collected too little material for an evaluation to be properly conducted; and two were evaluated in ways that did not address the significance of other changes taking place in the forces.

Quite apart from the problems encountered by the police in acquiring effective evaluative techniques, we also question the wisdom of many of the apparently good ideas that have been introduced into policing in the last few years. It seems to us that the kinds of programmes introduced have too often been based on police definitions of the situation. The public may simply see them as irrelevant to what they see as the 'real' problem. It is even conceivable that in some cases, police-proposed initiatives make the situation worse by their unintended consequences. They may, for example, nullify or destroy already existing informal means of coping with crime. A hypothetical example may make this clearer. Imagine that a village has no neighbourhood watch scheme, but does contain a number of people who in general keep an eye out for strangers, for local youths who seem to be in places where they have no obvious reason to be, and the like. Such watchers are also likely to constitute a gossip network. Now imagine that a neighbourhood watch scheme is set up. Those who previously watched may join the scheme – but there is no guarantee that they will then become more effective watchers, or pass on more information to the police. Others may join the scheme not because they have a habit of watching, but because they want to be seen to be doing something about crime. But if, in an average street, there are, say, two burglaries a year, they will get bored waiting for the action. And some of those who previously watched may give up doing so on the grounds that someone else is now doing it. It is conceivable that, at the end of the day, neighbourhood watch schemes in some areas may result in less rather than more effective surveillance of a neighbourhood by local people. The same might be said of crime prevention programmes. There is, for example, little point in persuading people to fit new locks on their doors if they are in the habit of leaving back doors unlocked, even though the new locks may make them feel more secure. Moreover, if people have been leaving their back doors unlocked for twenty years, the chances of persuading them to change this habit is remote. Another solution must be found.

The way forward in policing and crime prevention is not, therefore, to think of 'self-evidently good ideas' and then apply them. It is crucial from the policy point of view to understand what informal activities are already taking place and to take care not to damage them – because they will almost certainly not be easily replaceable. A more detailed understanding must be built up of people's ideas about deviance and crime, of what informal order-maintenance activities do go on, and of how they are affected by (and whether they affect) the way in which the police do their job on the ground.

Our programme

Any study faces a number of dilemmas. Is it better to study a small number of areas in depth or a large number in less detail? Should one formulate hypotheses and test them, or go relatively innocent to the field and see what turns up? Our methodology is discussed in some detail in the Appendix. Essentially, we felt that we were trying to create a first draft of a map for an uncharted area. We did not have any hypotheses in advance of our fieldwork and consequently could not test them by survey methods. We did not know what the physical limits of a community or a neighbourhood might be, and had little idea of what would be the major concerns of 'real people'.

We chose our research locations – two groups of villages and four city census enumeration districts – on the grounds that they offered a diversity of social environments which none the less looked, prima facie, as though they might be considered neighbourhoods or communities by the people living and working in them (a description of the areas is given in Chapter 2). We spent our time there observing what went on, talking to people, and ultimately using semi-structured interviews with residents and business people. Through these interviews, we were able to build up pictures of the kinds of problems that troubled people in the areas; of what people thought, and what they thought they knew about informal and formal social control in their area; of what was done, to whom and by whom, in the way of problematic behaviours and social control; and of the relation between the formal and informal sides of the process. These interviews also enabled us to create an index of incidents which had occurred in the area, and a rough and ready method of finding out who knew what about those incidents. In addition, we interviewed police officers working in those areas and analysed the 'message pads' – records of telephone calls to police stations – and crime files. Finally, in an effort to obtain some hard data on the extent to which people did what they said they did (in terms of, for example, not going out at night) and to provide some measure of how much opportunity existed for the neighbourhood to be watched over by people as they went about their ordinary business, we undertook a programme of formal observation periods. We logged, for different times of day and night, how much movement there was in and around particular small areas and attempted to analyse the significance of that movement in terms of its potential for the first stage of informal social control – namely, keeping track of what and who was about on the streets.

The remainder of this book is set out as follows. The next chapter describes the areas in which our fieldwork was conducted and discusses residents' and business people's views of their areas. Chapters 3 and 4 deal with the police crime reports and message pads, and with the data gathered from interviews on the kinds of problems perceived by people to occur in their area. Chapters 5, 6, and 7 push forward into less charted territory. They discuss the process of informal social control, starting with the question of who notices what; proceeding to the issue of who intervenes in events in order to exercise social control, and what they do; and ending with a new perspective on the fear of crime, the factors which influence it, its relation to crime prevention behaviour, and some new proposals on how to reduce the fear of crime. Chapters 8 and 9 discuss the police from two perspectives. Chapter 8 looks at what the public want of the police and their assessment of what they get. It argues that the public have very definite expectations of what functions the police should fulfil which are simply not being met. Chapter 9 considers the views of the police themselves on their work and argues that there are aspects of police organization and occupational culture which limit the provision of the services the public want. Ways around such problems are discussed. In the final chapter, we explore the potential for a partnership between public and police. We discuss the limits of informal and formal social control and the intrinsic problem of diversity of perceptions of social order and of the mechanisms for its achievement.

2
Areas and neighbourhoods

When criminologists have studied particular areas or communities, their major preoccupation has been to describe those facets of the areas which they think have some pertinence to their theories of crime. From Shaw and McKay (1942) to Baldwin and Bottoms (1976), broad quantifiable features of cities, such as population changes, social class, and housing tenure, have been used in conjunction with crime statistics to identify areas containing features which appear to cause, encourage, facilitate, or simply be associated with crime. However, if one starts from the proposition that the type of neighbourhood makes a difference to the level of crime, or to people's feelings about it, or to the informal action they may take to prevent it, there are many other less tangible factors which one would need to take into account – such as the cohesiveness and friendliness of the neighbourhood. The study of such factors has been much more carefully pursued outside criminology; discussions of the nature of neighbourliness, for example, are more common in areas such as the sociology of families and communities (see, for example, Bulmer 1986).

If these less tangible factors are to be taken seriously as issues which may influence the pattern of crime and its meaning to those in neighbourhoods, they must be carefully documented. This chapter describes the two village areas and four urban areas in which we worked, people's ideas about their area, and their contacts within it. The data presented here will be used in subsequent chapters to argue that such ideas and social networks affect neighbourhood views about problems and crime.

The villages

Both groups of villages we studied lay in the south of a Midlands county, in a district containing seventy-seven hamlets and villages together with two small towns. The 1981 Census put the total district population at 33,951, and those of the towns at 4,915 and 6,621.

Southton was a large village – over 1,800 residents – containing a mix of housing types and people. Its population structure, and that of the other research areas, are shown in Table 2.1. The village centre, clustered around a green and the church, comprised old private housing. Around this core were a large 1930s council estate, some modern council

Table 2.1 *Selected characteristics of the study areas*

| | Urban areas | | | | Rural areas | |
	1	2	3	4	Northam	Southton
Individuals						
Total population	354	279	557	504	1,596	1,817
Percentage turnover per annum	17	15	14	7	10	11
Percentage aged under 16	19	22	25	19	24	23
Percentage aged 65+	17	15	13	24	10	15
Percentage born in Caribbean	3	5	7	0	0	0
Percentage born in Asia	9	8	6	0	0	0
Percentage males unemployed[1]	24	20	19	3	5	6
Households						
Total number of households	142	107	195	201	540	672
Percentage council rented	1	2	2	0	16	42
Percentage private rented	22	19	9	5	5	6
Percentage bedsits	4	1	0	0	*	*

Source: *Census Small Area Statistics*, 1981.

Notes
1. Calculated as: (number of 'unemployed' x 100)/(number of 'economically active' + number of 'unemployed').
*Figures not available.

Note
In this table *and in all other tables* in this book percentages are rounded to the nearest whole number. Percentage totals may therefore not add up to 100. Subtotals have been calculated from original data and are rounded in the same way and may therefore also differ from the sum of their constituent items.

flats, two new private estates, and an old people's home. There were four pubs, several shops, a post office, and two chapels, but no chemist or permanent doctor. Several mobile facilities visited regularly, including clinics, a library, several mobile shops, and a fish and chip van. Public transport was relatively good, with both a bus service and a train station. Comparatively few people worked in the village – many were employed in the two nearby towns (both with industrial estates) and a few professionals commuted to London.

A police constable lived in the village police house. He worked on the beat which included Southton along with several other villages. An adjacent beat also had a local policeman at the time of the fieldwork, and their shifts were arranged so that each would 'cover' for the other's periods off-duty. In effect, whichever officer was on duty would have two beats to look after.

While we refer to Northam (population about 1,600) as a village, this is partly a matter of convenience. The 'village' included eight place names, each historically a separate hamlet, though relatively tightly bound together and falling within two parishes. Four of the hamlets had, with the building of new housing, become an almost continuous set of residential property. A busy trunk road separated some of the hamlets from this 'village core'. Again, there was a mix of housing and work places of different types, the latter orientated towards the urban area of our study, rather than the towns near Southton. Northam contained a number of churches and chapels, two village halls (one recently built and requiring extensive local fund-raising), a primary school, two general stores, several pubs, a large number of farms, and some small businesses. For anything other than groceries, however, one would have to go to a nearby town or our urban area. There was no resident policeman; infrequent panda car patrols were made from a village about five miles away, from either of two adjacent beats, from the nearest town, or even on occasion from the main police station for the area, some nine miles away.

The layout of both groups of villages had one important consequence. Lower population densities in rural areas than in urban are not the result of more space between houses. Population densities are calculated using enumeration districts which, in rural areas, often contain significant tranches of open land. The houses in both Northam and Southton were tightly huddled together, giving a density within the village boundaries comparable with urban area 4 and, in certain streets, with urban areas 1 and 2. While detached and semi-detached houses, cottages, and bungalows were in evidence, much of the accommodation comprised small terraced housing with party walls no more soundproof than in the city. Few houses had garages; on-street (and on-pavement) parking was common. The potential for 'problems' of all kinds, from noisy neighbours to parked cars and criminal damage, was no less here than in the urban areas.

Though we have no statistics on household income for the areas, we used a fourfold categorization of our interviewees' property and housing as an approximate measure of their standard of living. This comprised: first, houses with antiques and similar valuables; second, those with many consumer goods, such as videos; third, those with average furnishings, a TV, washing machine, and so on; and, last, those which had few consumer goods and were in a state of slight disrepair or dilapidated decoration. Northam and Southton both contained a wider spread of levels of affluence than we found in the urban area. There was a degree of apparent poverty – nine houses (twelve individuals in the samples) seemed to exist on the lowest of our four levels – while no less than one in five contained antiques, valuable plate and the like, and almost half contained items such as videos and expensive furniture. In terms of rich pickings for burglars, the villages clearly offered more potential than the urban areas.

The urban areas

We looked at four small urban areas in a Midlands city with a population of about 170,000. The four areas straddled two police beats near the centre of the city; areas 1 and 2 were comparatively close together on beat 1, while areas 3 and 4 were at opposite ends of the adjacent beat 2.

Area 1, triangular in shape, was bounded by a park on one side. It comprised only six streets with a residential population of about 350. Built towards the end of the last century, the housing stock was composed almost entirely of two-bedroom terraced houses opening directly on to the streets. Small workshops and industrial premises were either tucked into yards attached to the ends of terraces or had colonized former houses. The population turnover was relatively high – 17 per cent of individuals moved in or out of the area each year – and about one in four of the men classed as 'economically active' was not in employment. A substantial minority of people of Asian and West Indian descent lived in the area – more than are shown in Table 2.1, which only lists the proportion of those born outside the UK.

Area 2 was bounded on one side by a busy main road and bisected by another. Many of the houses, almost all two-bedroom terraces, faced directly on to the traffic flow with no front gardens. Workshops, factories, or warehouses could be found in almost every street, and shops (with some empty shop premises) lined one of the main roads. About 13 per cent of the population of almost 300 were born in Asia or the Caribbean; the population turnover was again quite high at 15 per cent per year, and the unemployment rate was around 20 per cent for males.

The houses in area 3, like areas 1 and 2, dated from the end of the last century, though the streets were laid in a rough grid. One side of the area was bounded by a main road and shopping parade. The houses were three-bedroom terraces with small front gardens. While there was some light industry, it largely occupied street-corner sites, as did the political club on the edge of the area. Of the population of about 550, about 13 per cent were Asian- or Caribbean-born. The population turnover and unemployment rate were broadly similar to area 2, at 14 per cent and 19 per cent per year respectively.

Area 4, only a short distance from area 3, looked very different. One street of very large detached or semi-detached houses stood at the edge of the area, while all the other housing comprised semi-detached, three-to four-bedroomed properties. Rear access roads or alleyways provided access to garages; there was correspondingly less on-street parking than in the other areas. A small parade of shops included three (a furniture shop, a tool hire centre, and a dress shop) which attracted city-wide custom. There were no pubs. The population of about 500 was relatively static (with a turnover of 7 per cent per year) and some residents had lived there since the houses were first built in the 1930s. There were almost no non-British-born residents and unemployment was only 2.5 per cent, but there was a larger than normal proportion of elderly people, a quarter of the population being 65 or over, compared with 12 to 16 per cent in the other three areas.

By the fourfold categorization of living standards we used in the villages, area 1 households were evenly split between the categories. In area 2, the third ('average') category was most common and no households fell into the topmost bracket. The standard of living in area 3, on our measure, was also average – only two households appeared to be 'poor' by our scale, only three better than average, and there were none in the topmost bracket. However, a degree of wealth and, indeed, an apparently affluent general lifestyle were to be found in area 4.

The two police beats into which our four areas fell each had three officers specifically allocated to them. They patrolled on foot between roughly 8 a.m. and 2 a.m., though the nearness of the main police station to beat 1 meant that police cars also used the main roads near areas 1 and 2 at frequent intervals. Beat 1 had a residential population of 4,715, and included, in addition to the kinds of housing and industry we have described, several night-clubs and large pubs (and their car parks) and a multi-storey car park. Areas 3 and 4, a little further from the city centre, were on beat 2. This beat (population 9,487) was more residential, though some large industrial units, clubs, pubs, and hostel-type accommodation were also present. Clearly, the extent of leisure facilities, car parks, and industrial premises has some bearing on the nature of neighbourhood problems, crime, and calls on the police – all subjects discussed in later chapters.

The limits of neighbourhoods

Were our areas in fact considered as neighbourhoods by those who lived there? We asked interviewees to define the area they thought of as 'their neighbourhood'. In urban area 1, half our interviewees agreed on the boundaries of their neighbourhood, all to within a hundred yards or so of each other. In urban area 2, half defined 'their area' in terms of one of the two main roads, or the parade of shops on one of them: a difference in orientation, but not in the geographical area being described. Urban area 4, comprising one section of an estate built around forty years ago, also provided a strong sense of identity and a consensus of opinion on the boundaries of the area.

Yet a substantial minority of the residents in urban areas 1, 2, and 3 did not see themselves as 'belonging' to the neighbourhood they had defined. Half the respondents in each of these areas felt they belonged to the city as a whole, or saw themselves as part of a racial rather than a geographic community, or did not feel they belonged anywhere. This pattern reflects, on a small scale, the social composition of the areas. All three areas contained residents of Asian and West Indian descent, but the area was not central to the community of either. The Asian community, for example, was spread widely over the town and saw itself as differentiated rather than homogenous: there were Sikhs, Muslims, and Hindus and, equally, Pakistanis, Bangladeshis, and Indians. While particular groupings were concentrated in certain parts of the city, organizations based on and serving them relied on a city-wide and sometimes region-wide membership.

The villages displayed a different pattern of 'belonging' and a different way of thinking about it. In Southton, the neighbourhood was defined quite simply as the village and no individual felt that he or she did not belong. But at the same time the council estate, each of the private estates, the old village centre, and one cul-de-sac were all held to have their own distinctive character. Each of these, however, formed only a small part of their residents' perceptions of their neighbourhood. Northam, being a collection of hamlets, showed a different pattern. Half the interviewees nominated their particular hamlet as their own neighbourhood, whereas, for the remainder, the local parish boundaries were also the neighbourhood boundaries. Only three individuals said that they felt no sense of belonging, while no more than a small handful of village residents saw themselves as belonging principally to a wider, but not geographically based, community.

Though town dwellers felt that they 'belonged' to a very different extent to village dwellers, the spatial area described by those who did see themselves as 'belonging' was extremely small – often no larger than two or three hundred metres across at its widest point. Even in area 4, where there were detached houses and extensive gardens, the scale was only slightly larger. Such a finding has clear implications for the pursuit of 'neighbourhood'-based policies, such as 'neighbourhood watch'.

Life and change in the areas

Our interviews and observations provide a considerable basis for asserting that the social organization, social life, and simply the 'experience of living here' differed substantially between our research neighbourhoods.

WHO KNOWS WHOM?

A sense of the continuity of everyday life and confidence in its persistence are derived from the mundane factors of who knows whom and who speaks to whom, and the knowledge that the same faces will be around from one day to the next.

In the urban areas as a whole, over half the residents thought they knew (in the limited sense of knowing where they lived) fewer than a quarter of those who lived, worked, or were usually around in their neighbourhood. In area 1, in fact, the majority of people thought they knew 10 per cent or fewer of those in their neighbourhood (see Table 2.2). Only 5 per cent said that they would know more than three-quarters of the people in their area. Indeed, given the claimed anonymity of cities and the relatively fast population turnover, it is surprising that even as many as 5 per cent would know so many people in their area, especially since about half those who knew this proportion had moved into their area within the previous four years. Equally surprisingly, even though the urban areas had a core of long-standing residents, these rarely knew many people and appeared to play little part in their neighbourhoods.

In Southton, the figure for 'who knows whom' was not dissimilar to that in the urban areas, though the size of the population against which the claims were made was larger by a factor of about three, and had recently been swollen by the influx of newcomers to the village. In Northam, however, a more typically 'village' pattern appeared to exist. Relatively few people thought that they knew less than a quarter, while over 40 per cent said that they would know or recognize three-quarters or more. A similar 'urban plus Southton' versus 'Northam' split can be seen in the answers to a second question which asked for interviewees' estimates of the proportion of all the people passing by their house whom they would be likely to recognize (Table 2.3).

The proportion of people in the area whom one knows can, however, be misleading as a general figure. Older residents may not, for example, recognize teenagers (and may be more fearful of youths for this reason). Equally, knowing whether cars belong to residents or not may make the difference between 'Mr X's car' which is tolerated and 'that bloody driver who parks outside my house'. Figures for knowing adults, teenagers, and the ownership of cars are, therefore, separated out in Table 2.3. Around half the people we interviewed in the urban areas and two-thirds of those in Southton said that they would recognize 'no' or 'very few' teenagers, while three-quarters of the Northam sample said they would recognize 'most' or 'almost all' the teenagers there. This may be because some of the Northam teenagers very obviously formed a gang and were about on the streets. Cars, like teenagers, were also relatively anonymous features of the environment everywhere except in Northam,

Table 2.2   *Who knows whom? Residents' perceptions of the proportion of other people in their neighbourhood whom they know*

| Proportion claimed to be known[1] (cumulative percentages) | Percentage of residents making claim | | | | | |
| | Urban areas | | | | Rural areas | |
	1	2	3	4	Northam	Southton
Over 90 per cent	0	10	2	6	27	0
Over 75 per cent	0	13	2	9	41	4
Over 50 per cent	6	33	26	23	54	15
Over 25 per cent	24	43	55	40	84	38
10 per cent or less	61	33	27	47	14	35

Note
1. 'Knowing' in this table is defined as 'knowing whereabouts in the neighbourhood the person lives'.

Table 2.3   *Assessments of the proportion of adults, teenagers, and cars that people would recognize as coming from their area*

| Proportion claimed recognized | Subject | Percentage making claim | | | | | |
| | | Urban areas | | | | Rural areas | |
		1	2	3	4	Northam	Southton
none	adults	12	3	0	3	0	7
	teenagers	30	17	24	8	0	18
	cars	32	25	20	12	4	55
very few	adults	27	28	15	28	11	35
	teenagers	15	30	15	19	12	46
	cars	16	32	30	27	13	31
quite a lot	adults	21	24	46	28	8	40
	teenagers	21	33	12	25	13	20
	cars	26	21	25	27	19	9
most	adults	30	35	29	28	28	15
	teenagers	23	13	27	28	26	14
	cars	19	11	20	27	12	3
almost all	adults	9	10	10	14	54	4
	teenagers	6	7	22	19	49	2
	cars	7	7	5	6	52	2

where over half our interviewees said they would recognize (that is, know who would usually drive) 'almost all' the cars driving or parking in the village.

NEIGHBOURHOOD AS COMMUNITY?

The people we interviewed tried to convey to us what they felt to be distinctively communal about their own neighbourhood. In fact, we found the difference between rural and urban areas to be matters of degree, rather than marks of a rural/urban divide. There was considerable similarity between the social processes in the rural and urban areas. Again, for some factors, such as the extent of social networks, Southton seemed more similar to the urban area than to Northam.

Community implies a sense of knowing people and being known – and also of knowing what's going on. This was an implicit theme running through everyday activities; it also surfaced during particular celebrations, or at times of crisis:

'Everybody seems to want to be very independent and no one seems to notice anything, but the factory across the road does take in parcels for me. When we had the Jubilee celebrations it was neighbourly. Neighbourliness is there, lying doggo.' (urban area 1)

These aspects of knowledge seemed more prevalent in the villages:

'The older villagers help each other – they went to the village school and they know each other. Otherwise people don't want to pry or be busybodies. If someone's broken a leg a certain type would want to go and help – a lot, most, would ignore it.' (Northam)

'People round here don't live in each other's houses but when something happens you can always rely on someone to help – for example, when I had my car accident.' (Northam)

'Knowing what's going on' also means 'noticing things' and talking about them. Such gossip has several functions. It can pass on news of those needing help; it can be an indirect way of making a complaint; or, simply, it can provide entertainment. These aspects were carefully separated by residents: 'Gossip is rife, particularly round the council estate. This end of the village we keep ourselves to ourselves' (Southton). 'The rumours are fantastic – people do notice things, but you have to sort out the truth' (Northam).

Gossip networks had certain focal points and followed particular pathways through the neighbourhood: 'The street is neighbourly but not curious neighbourly. In the old part of the village people do know what's going on. There are one or two I can rely on to give me the latest gossip about everyone' (Northam). But passing on gossip, particularly in the villages, could have its dangers: 'In a village you never know who you're talking to. You speak to one person about another and find the one's sister is married to the other's brother' (Southton).

Under these circumstances, where there was relatively little anonymity and a degree of interrelationship and other ties within the community, responsibility needed to be exercised in passing on gossip – because responsibility could certainly be attributed. Of course, people also met regularly at local shops or social clubs in urban areas. However, it is likely that the more attenuated social networks in the urban neighbourhoods led to a more patchy and less knowledgeable coverage.

But if more closely knit communities were, on the one hand, about conveying identity, helping others, and healthy gossip and scandal, they were, on the other, also about lack of escape, division, and exclusion:

'Being in this street makes you one of a certain group; professionals who can afford their own houses. Not that I'm professional, I've just put most of my income into the house. But when I joined the sports club I took a lot of stick about it and I just wasn't interested in pursuing it after a while.' (Southton)

'There is a division between the newer private houses and the council estate. When I went to the toddlers' group I was asked if I was from the 'right end of the village', and I notice the houseowners at one school gate and the council estate at the other, picking up their kids.'   (Southton)

While local divisions and disagreements seemed to be equally prevalent in the villages and the urban areas, the nature of the issues varied. In villages, there were issues affecting the whole area, such as whether a farmer should sell land for building or not, as well as matters such as dumping rubbish outside others' homes, uncontrolled children, and so on. Many people would know the principal parties in the disputes. In the urban area, disputes tended only to affect a few neighbouring houses or businesses (ten at the most). In this, they paralleled the spread of acquaintanceship and recognition.

Recognition of differences, and occasional arguments, were also conducted through village organizations in the rural areas. One Southton person who sat on several committees suggested: 'It's a split village along any lines you care to name – Labour/Conservative, private/council housing, church congregations and the rest. I guarantee it would be split even over whether we should use steel or copper screws.'

The role of such bodies, split or not, was not obviously apparent to us in the urban areas. This is not to say that they did not exist. But our urban fieldwork did not seem to bring us into close contact with social-club committees and borough councils. No one in the urban areas thought it was important that we should interview those who sat on those bodies. Compared to parish councils and the clientele of village pubs, they were in any event not so locally based and were not so close to the day-to-day life of residents and businesses. Village-hall committees and the like were much more closely watched and their activities commented upon. We were constantly being advised to talk to 'Mrs A' or 'Mr B' in order to find out about things that had happened in the village.

Finally, one aspect of life in our urban areas deserves comment, though it is perhaps a small-scale reflection of a problem more often discussed in the context of inner cities. Urban areas 1, 2, and 3 all contained a proportion of people of Asian or West Indian descent, and attitudes towards them were varied. Some people acknowledged that racism existed and was problematic, while a strain of prejudice was apparent in other comments made to us: 'There is racial prejudice but not to me – people are very civil' (urban area 3). 'There's a lot of feelings about Indians here, especially about shopkeepers. That's bad' (urban area 2). 'It used to be one of the nicest areas in the city, not rich but comfortable. You can't walk down the street now without meeting Pakistanis, Indians, Chinese, and Czechs' (urban area 3). 'The area's gone down because of the Pakis and their screaming kids – they interfere with cars and they're up to all sorts. They don't speak English when you tell them off' (urban area 2).

That such prejudice existed, though only from a minority of our interviewees, should be cause for concern. Though our subsample of interviewees of Asian or West Indian origin was very small (only twenty-five people), a majority of them had lived in the areas for over ten years and almost half had lived there for more than twenty. It appears that prejudice of this nature is an entrenched aspect of urban life, not only in inner cities, but in cities such as the one we studied. And, in common with studies of inner-city crime, we shall have cause to return to this problem.

THE ROLE OF ORGANIZATIONS

People do not only meet on the street or in each other's houses. They come into contact at meetings of clubs, societies, and councils, at sports matches, and in the more informal atmosphere of social institutions such as bars and pubs.

The majority of those we interviewed belonged to one or more organizations of some kind (Table 2.4). The kinds of organizations cited, however, differed between the urban areas and villages. Around 14 per cent of the Northam sample and 12 per cent of those in Southton were members of parish councils, village-hall committees, and the like; only three individuals in the whole urban sample were members of analogous urban bodies. About 20 per cent of the village samples, and 30 per cent of the urban, belonged to various kinds of social clubs. In the villages, these tended to be bridge clubs, drama societies, evening classes, and the

Table 2.4 *Numbers of interviewees having membership of organizations, by kind of organization*

| Type of organization | Percentage having membership | | |
	Urban area	Northam	Southton
Church or chapel	19	38	19
Social club	29	20	19
Women's Institute or similar	0	15	5
Parish council, hall committee, local council	2	14	13
Sports association	7	7	3
School association	3	11	3
Youth club	5	5	8
Trade association	5	0	0
No membership of any organization	43	29	48

like, while for the urban population they were more commonly pool halls, darts clubs, or working men's clubs.

Membership of an organization did not always imply that one would know a larger proportion of those in the neighbourhood. In the urban area there was a slight tendency in this direction; 24 per cent of members of organizations, as opposed to 18 per cent of non-members, said they knew more than half the people in their neighbourhood. In the villages, however, it was those who did not belong to organizations who were more likely to know more people; 38 per cent of Northam and only 13 per cent of Southton organization members claimed to know half or more of the people in their neighbourhood, while 45 per cent and 51 per cent respectively of the 'non-joiners' knew as many people.

This may be explained by two factors. First, the social clubs in the urban areas were often in practice a superior kind of pub. Many of those in urban areas 1, 2, and 3 had joined working men's clubs, where socializing, drinking, and entertainment took place in comfortable surroundings and among a known clientele. The rural organizations were drinking clubs only secondarily, if at all, while the village pubs fulfilled the role of the urban clubs. One Southton resident pointed out:

> 'I'm in the pub culture. If you're not in that you're isolated unless you have kids. My wife knows the mothers and toddlers group. And you needn't be concerned about acceptance, because there's lots of new people in the village.'

Secondly, the village organizations were treated with some cynicism by many longer-standing residents. They were seen as places in which newcomers sought out their stereotyped conception of the good life; the more 'committee-minded' among them could deliberate wisely, and the others could socialize. This may be an exaggerated view, and certainly a contrary feeling, stressing the need for social bodies, existed among some of their members:

'There are a few that don't want to join in. The council estates don't, but they were born here. We have to go out and mix because we have no family here, we have to find our own entertainment. They can go and visit their relatives.'

(Northam)

Indeed, in contrast to Strathern (1981), we found that newcomers were welcomed by many older residents as providing the drive to start and help in running many of the village institutions.

BUSINESSES IN THE NEIGHBOURHOODS

Small businesses in residential areas have been claimed as a sign of constant regeneration (Raban 1974) and a cohesive force for the neighbourhood (Jacobs 1965). Corner shops and small workshops have been described as informal meeting places, unobtrusive observers of street life, and caretakers for nearby residents (holding keys, passing on messages, and taking in parcels). Jacobs suggests that they 'police' their streets in so far as they notice what is going on, take note of strangers, and scold children who are 'messing about'. Yet they are often currently criticized as noisy, messy places which disturb the peace by taking deliveries and operating machinery at odd hours, and which should be zoned and relegated to estates.

There is evidence in our study for both views. Like residents, business people varied greatly in the number of passersby they would recognize and thus in their potential effectiveness as watchers within the community. This is hardly surprising – factories with few outside windows and few local employees would be less effective than corner shops and pubs. In the urban area, many business people said they only knew very few adults, teenagers, or cars passing by. However, over 30 per cent – mainly shopkeepers, car spares traders, and wholesalers – said that they knew 'most' or 'almost all' resident adults. These businesses either had a local clientele or, in the case of the wholesalers, had staff on the pavement, loading lorries, for much of the day. In Northam, business people were even more likely to claim to recognize passersby than were individual residents, and were particularly likely to recognize cars.

There was also evidence that many businesses were mindful of their role in the community and took a certain degree of care to maintain it. One person, the new owner of a car spares business, said:

'We inherited a lot of bad feeling from the previous owner, because they stayed open till late, revved engines, and dripped oil all over the place. I try to be more careful and we've got to the stage where I do plumbing for the people opposite and the man down the road keeps an eye on my lorry.'

(urban area 1)

We shall discuss the role that businesses played in the crime prevention activities of the neighbourhoods in Chapter 5.

SOCIAL CHANGE

We were only able to take a snapshot of our rural and urban areas over a short period of time – a year at the most. But a crucial aspect of areas and a major factor in people's beliefs about them is that neighbourhoods are not static places, but change with wider social factors – often rapidly. People usually say, not that their area is friendly or cold, but that it is more friendly than X or less friendly than it was. We shall, therefore, end this description of our study areas with a discussion of how they were changing as we left them.

Unfortunately, of course, the impact of change on a neighbourhood is hard to assess, not least because areas which change most quickly tend to be those in which residents are most mobile and least able to make comparisons with the area's past. We asked interviewees whether they themselves had noticed any changes in their area over the time that they had been living there; not surprisingly, the answers correlated strongly with the length of residence. The longest-standing residents more often thought that the area had changed, usually for the worse. As one elderly householder observed (in area 4):

'From the viewpoint of age one tends to think neighbourhoods go down because the kinds of people that move in are different. You and the neighbourhood grow old together. This area hasn't gone down to a drastic extent – slightly further in [to the city centre] it's a bit shabby but much nearer into town a lot of the old terraced houses are now being cared for.'

Most people in every area thought that there had been change, but the type of change varied. In urban area 1 and in Northam, it was most commonly seen in terms of the numbers and types of newcomers to the area. Area 1 was seen as undergoing the most rapid transformation. One business man summed up his view:

'It was an area going downhill with one-parent families, low earners, and unemployed – an area like this, very cheap, attracted such people. Development has brought it up but it really needs to be developed quick. The whole area needs to be reshaped before things like prostitution set in. The people here are not native residents, they came in when the properties were already dilapidated, so it would be easy to disperse them and that would solve the problem and you could get a mixed community. As it is, it's "half deprived".'

(urban area 1)

Other residents also confirmed that it was a mixed and rapidly developing area, containing moderately affluent newcomers who saw the area as 'going up' and, at the same time, containing some of the urban 'hardcore poor': 'Speaking as a typical middle-class snob, there are a lot of so-called undesirables. I had to use the public phone box and I couldn't bear the stink – it was part vandalized and used as a toilet.' 'It's changed for the better – new houses and the school. It looks cleaner, for a while the houses were boarded up as people moved out but not now.'

In Northam, the nature of the change was different, though still cast in terms of the character of the newcomers:

'People have changed lately – they're not village people, it really isn't as nice. They're friendly enough but they think they can come in and run the place – they're townies. The old ones that have been here donkey's years, they're OK. The newcomers, they don't think of the villagers' views and their feelings. It's the old-type villagers who will help you. The new ones – their ways aren't village ways.'

In urban area 2 and in Southton, the change was thought of more in terms of building (or demolition) and modernization, even though this clearly also implied a change in the population. One shopkeeper from urban area 2 said:

'There used to be a definable community bounded by three roads. About five years ago the flats opposite [just outside the area] were built. Prior to that the other side of the road was shops and it was a major shopping area. It used to be more friendly.'

In Southton, the change most often cited was the erection of the new estates. Perhaps the typification of the relationship between villagers and newcomers in both areas, was, ironically, that some long-standing residents were moving into new, centrally heated and well-insulated homes on the estates, and selling their more characterful but draughty houses to the new urban refugees.

3
What the police know about: crime and calls for police services

What did our areas look like in terms of the 'official' police records: crimes reported to the police and recorded by them (crime reports) and the records of occurrences reported to the police by telephone (message pads)? The stereotype of crime in rural areas has largely been inspired by country-house detective stories and films and by social historians of the last century. It portrays rural crime as very rare and largely composed of vagrancy, poaching of rabbits or salmon, cattle rustling, and petty thieving, with a few daring and ambitious country-house burglaries and robberies, plus some interesting murders thrown in for good measure. The criminals, in this version, are either poor farm workers or glamorous outsiders from London. Some urban police officers seem to characterize the workload of their country cousins in the same manner. We suspected that this picture was certainly an exaggeration and, very probably, a complete travesty, even given the limited sample of crimes contained in official sources (for discussions of the biases of official crime figures, see Bottomley and Pease 1986; Hough and Mayhew 1983; Bottomley and Coleman 1981).

However, we were not just interested in the legal categorizations or the absolute numbers of different kinds of crime committed. We thought it was also important to know what kinds of victims were involved, where crimes were committed, and whether those offenders that were caught were local. We therefore analysed our sample of crime reports according to the type of victim, place of occurrence, and numbers, age, and place of residence of any detected offenders.

Recorded crime: overall levels

The crime reports used comprised those for the whole year from 1 September 1981 for the two police beats that contained all four of our urban interview areas (1,384 reports) and the villages of the district council area containing our two rural interview areas (leaving out the two small towns – a total of 1,200 reports). Police message pads were drawn from the identical areas. The police data areas are, therefore, much larger than the small areas in which we concentrated the interviews, but in fact form the hinterland from which people's ideas about criminal occurrences were usually drawn. Further details of the samples and methods are given in the Appendix.

Table 3.1 *Levels of crime in the rural and urban areas (rates per 100,000 population)*

	Rural area	Urban area Beat 1	Beat 2	National average[1]
All notifiable offences	2,227	15,758	6,282	5,661
Violence against the person	80	912	242	203
Sexual offences	18	106	32	39
Burglary	613	3,711	1,992	1,465
Robbery	6	106	53	41
Theft and handling	1,255	8,674	3,247	3,248
Fraud and forgery	80	640	169	216
Criminal damage (over £20)	168	1,463	548	440
Others	9	21	0	8

Note
1. Source: *Criminal Statistics* (1982).

The first task is to estimate the overall amount of crime occurring in the urban and rural areas. One comparative measure is the rate per 100,000 population, though this must be treated with a certain amount of caution. The resident population given in Census data does not include those who work or visit places of entertainment or shops in an area. The crime rate for some city areas with large numbers of shops, pubs, theatres, night-clubs, etc. can appear spectacularly high, because the denominator in the calculation does not reflect the number of people using the shops or leisure facilities and being victimized there. This factor affected both our urban beats, but not the villages comprising our rural area. The crime rates are shown in Table 3.1, which also gives the national average for that year.

As would be expected, the crime rates for the villages were substantially below the national average. (Those for the small towns in the district council area were higher, but still below the national average.) The urban beats both gave figures higher than the national average, the poorer area (urban beat 1) having a crime rate some three times higher, in part attributable to its shops, factories, places of entertainment, etc. The difference between adjacent beats was very striking, a factor which confirms the results of the Sheffield study that adjacent urban areas can show far greater variation than is present normally between town and village (Baldwin and Bottoms 1976). Cities and towns are very heterogeneous places, a fact that is often masked by average statistics taken over a wide area (subdivisions or electoral constituencies). Our two urban beats both contained shops, housing, and factories, were both close to the city centre, and both contained relatively similar kinds of housing. Yet the crime rate varied substantially.

Table 3.2 *Proportions of crime (percentages)*

	Rural area	Urban area Beat 1	Beat 2	National average[1]
Violence against the person	4	6	4	4
Sexual offences	1	0	1	1
Burglary: domestic	11	12	16	13
other	17	12	15	13
total	28	24	32	26
Robbery	0	1	1	1
Theft: from motor vehicle	20	15	10	14
of motor vehicle (incl. taking and driving away)	5	14	11	12
of pedal cycle	1	4	7	4
shoplifting	1	3	3	8
handling	0	1	1	1
other theft	29	18	20	18
total	56	55	52	57
Fraud and forgery	4	4	3	4
Criminal damage: arson	1	1	1	1
other	6	9	8	7
total	8	9	9	8
Others	0	0	0	0

Note
1. Source: *Criminal Statistics* (1982).

The second point to note from Table 3.1 is the improbably low level of crime in the rural area. There were seventy-seven villages and hamlets in the area, which implies that the average village would have had only six incidents of theft and handling and one of criminal damage over £20 in a year. Either these villages were exceptionally well-ordered places in which crime and disorder never reared their heads (or vandals took care to smash only very small panes of glass), or a greater amount of offending went unreported than in the towns. Hough and Mayhew (1985) suggest that, nationally, a fifth of vandalism is reported. Even this multiplier seems to produce astonishingly low figures for crime in our rural areas. The presumption must be that though there may be less offending, there is likely also to be less reporting than in towns.

The differences between rural and urban areas (and those between beats)

Table 3.3 *Victims and targets for property crime (percentages)*

	Rural area	Urban area Beat 1	Beat 2
Victims			
Council or public utility			
(gas, electricity, etc.)	10	6	2
Company	23	20	17
Individual acting in business capacity			
(publican, shopkeeper, etc.)	12	9	7
Private individual	54	65	73
Target			
Cash	10	14	14
Petrol/gas bottle/vehicle excise licence	9	2	2
Cheque cards/credit cards	1	3	3
Food/cigarettes	4	7	10
Tools/tyres	8	4	5
Livestock/crops	4	0	0
Car/car parts/car radio/(m)cycles	20	29	27
Antiques/jewellery	5	2	3
Other industrial goods	13	15	10
Other personal goods	19	17	17
Nothing taken	7	7	9

were not due to any bulge in any particular form of crime in any area. Table 3.2 shows that the proportions of different kinds of crime according to legal categories were very similar everywhere. Rural crime was not different in kind from urban crime – only in prevalence. The slight difference in types of theft/burglary in Table 3.2 could well have been the result of the activities of one or two individuals who were caught (for example, the theft and subsequent use of ten cheque cards by two individuals would cause the differences in fraud and forgery). There are a number of facets of property crime, not easily visible from the tables, which also tend to break down the urban stereotype of crime. Breaking into meters, for example, was proportionately as popular in the rural areas as in the urban. Auto crime was indeed a slightly greater problem in the town, but only because whole cars, rather than parts, were stolen and because cars were a more likely target for vandalism in the town.

Property crime: victims and targets

We were able to distinguish four types of victims: public utilities and the councils; companies; individuals acting in a business capacity (publicans, shopkeepers, etc.); and private individuals (see Table 3.3). For property crime, victims in the urban area were predominantly private individuals. Half the property crime in the villages, however, was directed against companies, the council, utilities, shops, pubs, or small businesses. There are several possible explanations. One is sheer density. The town contained more houses per hectare, but may actually overall have contained fewer council or public-utility roadside works (with their attendant gas bottles, compressors, tools, and so forth) and less street 'furniture' (the technical term for road signs, street lights, benches, litter bins, etc.) for the equivalent population. Another explanation may be that businesses in urban areas took greater care over crime prevention, locking up or taking away all removable things not actually in use. Businesses in rural areas may have been easier, more isolated targets (though given the likely extent of non-reporting in the country, the business victimization rate there must have been very high).

There has been a tendency in western criminological research to dismiss victimization of businesses, mainly on the basis of the idea – common also as a technique of neutralization for offenders (Sykes and Matza 1957) – that crime against businesses is somehow less serious than crime against individuals. This is a fallacy. The legal loser in a business is indeed a company, but the effects of the offence, other than the financial ones, will fall on individuals: they must account for the disappearance of property, report it to the company and possibly the police, arrange for replacement, and generally cope with the situation. They are likely to suffer emotional effects, particularly if they have been personally confronted by the offender. Indeed, it has been shown that the victims of violent crime in places of work suffer more serious and persistent effects than most other personal victims (Shapland, Willmore, and Duff 1985). The extent of the victimization of businesses also points up their role as providers of opportunities for crime. There were far fewer businesses than households in all areas, so the proportionate victimization rate for businesses was very high indeed. Given the importance of businesses in relation to crime, we shall attempt throughout this book to indicate their reactions to crime and disorder and the differences between them and householders, though the number of businesses in our small interview areas was relatively low in absolute terms, and so our findings can only be regarded as tentative.

Table 3.3 also shows the types of property that were the targets of property crime in both rural and urban areas. Easily used and easily resold property (cash, petrol, gas bottles, food, cigarettes) was a popular target everywhere. Theft of food in the town included shoplifting and not paying for restaurant meals. Its greater prevalence was a function of the greater numbers of shops, takeaways, etc. Tools, tyres, and vehicle parts were relatively more popular in the villages (whole cars might be stripped on some main roads); this reflects what we perceived as a greater propensity to DIY in villages.

The burden of auto crime (theft of or from cars) fell largely on private individuals in both urban and rural areas, rather than on businesses. Businesses mostly suffered theft of or damage to stock (industrial goods, food, cigarettes, tools, and loose tyres). The value of goods taken was normally low, as has been shown again and again in the national *Criminal Statistics*. About half the offences resulted in the loss of £50 or less in both rural and urban areas. Valuable property crime was rare: only about 13 per cent was worth over £500 in the villages and 7 per cent in the urban area. Theft of motor cars represented 35 per cent of property crime worth over £500 in the villages and 60 per cent in the town.

Police officers, particularly the CID, tend to have a notion of 'good-class crime' – crime which involves the theft of valuable property and which is presumed to be the work of 'professionals' or 'good-class villains'. Greater effort is often expended to try to solve this crime. A similar concentration of attention can be seen in the annual reports of chief constables (Shapland and Hobbs 1988). There is no accepted definition of 'good-class crime', but it seemed to us that it would be likely to include theft or burglary of property worth over £500, or of antiques and jewellery. Using this definition, we found that there was proportionately more of this type of crime in the rural area than in the urban. Crimes in the town were more numerous, but also of lower value (and less interesting to the CID). Equally, the CID in rural areas had as much 'important' work to do, in CID terms, as did the CID in our urban area.

Where crime occurs

Crime reports contain information not only on victims and targets, but also on where crime occurs. This in turn allows us to construct the opportunities for crime in rural and urban areas and, thereby, the problems that residents and business people might suffer. Table 3.4 shows the places in which offences were recorded as having happened.

At the most basic level, the distribution of crime reflected the different kinds of physical space, the types of premises, and the architecture of the areas. So, for example, it would be expected that only a small proportion of urban crime would take place on open land; that big leisure events in the country taking place over several days would account for a substantial proportion of rural crime (our rural area seemed to contain the leisure places for the whole region); and that places with more shops would have more shoplifting.

What was more unexpected, at least from stereotypes of rural and urban crime, was the prevalence of rural as well as urban crime committed in commercial premises and on roads or public land, and its relative scarcity in or around dwellings. The influence of businesses in respect of criminal opportunities was not just confined to the crimes of which they

Table 3.4 *Where offences occurred*

	Rural area %	Urban area Beat 1 %	Beat 2 %
Dwelling	15	19	24
Outhouse or garden of dwelling	9	2	14
Commercial factory/garage	10	7	6
Commercial service premises (hotel, pub, café, shop, etc.)	15	23	16
Offices or school	6	4	4
Building site	2	1	0
Farmland or country land (including parks)	10	2	1
Road or public land	23	42[1]	34[1]
Big leisure centre	11	—	—

Note
1. Of which car parks accounted for 13 per cent in beat 1 and 0 per cent in beat 2.

were victims; private individuals were also often victimized in commercial or public places. The largest category of commercial premises affected were service premises (hotels, pubs, cafés, shops, etc.). Decreasing the number of property crimes through opportunity reduction seems not just to be a matter of targeting the behaviour of private individuals in their own private space, but also their behaviour in public or in commercial premises, and of improving crime prevention strategies of commercial premises.

One element that has been prominent in discussions of opportunities for property crime is design. The influence of design (see Poyner 1983) was apparent in several types of settings. The variation between the two urban beats in the 'outhouse or garden' category may be largely explained in terms of the general lack of garages and outhouses in urban beat 1 (terraced housing with doors opening straight on to the street) and their relative prevalence in urban beat 2. Beat 2 also contained many back alleys ('jitties'), used by law-abiding citizens to gain access to their garages and by offenders to gain access to other people's garages.

Auto crime is a large segment of property crime and its influence is seen in the proportion of crime that took place on the road/public spaces. In urban beat 1, two or three medium-sized car parks accounted for a staggering 13 per cent of recorded offences. Design was again a factor. The car parks were either unsupervised multi-storey ones or were

Table 3.5 *Detection rates ('no crimes' omitted)*

	Percentages
Villages	
All offences	33
Property crime	28
Burglary	24
Urban area – beat 1	
All offences	31
Property crime	25
Burglary	22
Urban area – beat 2	
All offences	28
Property crime	25
Burglary	22
National average[1]	
All offences	38
Burglary	30
Theft and handling	38
Criminal damage	27

Note
1. Source: *Criminal Statistics.*

surrounded by the blank back walls of factories and shops, so that it was impossible to see what activity was occurring in them.

The final point which can be culled from Table 3.4 is not immediately obvious – because it is a lack of crime in a place where crime would be expected. A large area of grassland in the middle of urban beat 1 had acquired a reputation as a crime-ridden and fearsome place, to be visited at one's peril at any time of day, but definitely to be shunned at night. (The police had even taken to driving, rather than walking, along the well-lit paths at night – and some officers locked the patrol car doors before starting to drive across.) In Table 3.4, it has been coded as 'farmland or country land' – and quite clearly there was extremely little crime of any sort there. Either residents did indeed avoid the area and so were not victimized there, or the reputation of the area was undeserved, at least in 1981–2. We shall return to this in Chapter 7.

Who commits crime?

Police data can, obviously, only tell us about offenders caught by the police. Hence, as usual, the detection rates in our urban and rural areas only provide information about a small minority of offenders (see Table 3.5).

Table 3.6 *Distances from offenders' homes to places where offences were committed*

Rural area	%	Urban area	Beat 1 %	Beat 2 %
Same village	38	Same beat	32	35
		1–2 km	40	44
1–5 km	16	3–5 km	19	12
6–10 km	17	6–10 km	4	5
11–15 km	5	11–15 km	4	2
16–20 km	9	16–20 km	0	1
21–30 km	4	21–30 km	1	0
Further away	11	Further away	0	0

Though detected offenders were a minority, they were not an unimportant minority. It was these detected offenders who informed police views of patterns of offending in each area and, consequently, media reporting. In so far as residents and business people read the local papers and victims were told by the police about 'their' offenders, these views also influenced public opinions. Feedback from the police was not wonderful at that time (see Chapter 8), but media reporting of *local* events certainly influenced concern about crime in the area (Chapter 7).

The proportions of juvenile and adult (over 21) detected offenders were relatively similar in all areas – with about one half being adult. This is a similar proportion to that in the *Criminal Statistics*. The majority of detected offenders (in the urban beats, about four-fifths) also appeared to be working on their own, rather than as part of a group or team.

Table 3.6 shows the distance between the place where detected offenders lived and where they committed the offences. It is clear that the majority of offenders lived fairly close – with a substantial minority living in the same village or the same beat (an area usually less than one kilometre square). Despite some police stereotypes to the contrary, village crime was not committed wholly by outsiders. This pattern held over all types of crime, with burglaries in villages being committed by the local adult or juvenile burglars (surprisingly prevalent – see Chapter 6). The figures for the urban area are broadly similar to those reported by Baldwin and Bottoms (1976) and Davidson (1984), and again show extreme localization. The moral may of course be that the 'successful' criminals live some way away from the scene of their crimes, but, as we shall see in Chapter 6, residents were often aware that offenders came from the next street, rather than from across the town. If this pattern holds for other cities and towns as well, it has considerable implications for crime prevention strategies. Preventing offending means preventing or deterring local offenders – and a strategy which involves thinking of offenders as outsiders or constructing a fortress round a neighbourhood is not going to be effective.

Calls on police services

Public contact with the police is, of course, not restricted to reporting crimes. The public also telephone the police, come into police stations, and hail officers on patrol for a wide range of other matters, ranging from traffic accidents and civil emergencies to lost property and found dogs. These contacts essentially concern problems which members of the public feel they cannot deal with on their own, or which they feel the police should know about. They are also, potentially, sources of information for the police on the problems in particular areas and the priorities of residents. However, as we shall see in Chapter 9, it is only recently that police forces have realized the potential value of these contacts as information, though the force in which the fieldwork for this study was done was one of the pioneers in this field and, by the end of the study, was beginning to provide beat officers with breakdowns of demands from the public in their areas.

As with all organizational data, however, the interpretation of police records of telephone calls and visits to the police station from the public is not unproblematic. These message pads, though an extraordinarily rich source of data on public need for the police and police response, are neither verbatim records of what the public demand, nor do they contain a log of every telephone call. The ways in which the meaning of such calls is changed as the problem passes from the caller, through the officer (controller) receiving the call, to the officers attending are now documented as occurring in a very similar fashion in different forces in England and also in America (for example, Shapland and Hobbs 1987; Morgan 1987c; Slovak 1986).

We discuss some of the problems of interpretation of message pad data in the Appendix and the topic is explored in greater depth, including comparison with matters received by the police from the public but not recorded on message pads, in Shapland and Hobbs (1987). Essentially, it seems possible to conclude that:

1. message pads are likely not to contain calls which do not, in the view of the controller taking the call, require police attendance;
2. the way in which the matter is referred to in the written record is an amalgam of the way it is presented by the public (often as a relatively confused narrative, susceptible of several interpretations) and the controller's view of the possibilities for police action. These

possibilities will reflect the ways in which policing is carried out in the subdivision and the resources available to the controller at the moment the call is received (see Manning 1980);

3. none the less, most of the calls requesting police attendance or some police service are recorded and it is relatively easy to differentiate between those reporting crimes that have occurred in the past, those describing trouble or disturbances currently happening, those concerning traffic conditions, and so forth. The classification of message pads used in Table 3.7 was developed by the researchers, but it is essentially an elaboration of the codes being developed by the police themselves during the course of our fieldwork.

Table 3.7 shows the number and type of messages recorded by the police in the rural and urban areas. Figures for the urban area are given both for urban beats 1 and 2 and for the rest of the subdivision – though the latter are based on a smaller sample of days.

In comparing rural and urban areas, two aspects stand out. The first is the greater number of calls in the urban area, both numerically and per head of population. People seemed to call on the police more often in the town – there were 9,069 calls per 100,000 population there, as opposed to 2,715 in the rural area (though of course this measure will again be affected by the greater transient population using the facilities in the town). However, the kinds of things they were calling about appeared to be proportionately very similar in both.

It is very difficult in practice to classify calls into 'crime', 'services', etc. The problem is that 'crime', at the level of telephone calls to the police, is a very fuzzy concept. Reports of property crime having occurred are relatively easy to classify as 'crime' – and public and police views of whether a crime had occurred in our study seemed to be very similar, as was reflected in the high proportion of such calls that formed the subject of crime reports. However, reports of disturbances, suspicious incidents, and burglar alarms are far less easy to place unequivocally in a category of 'crime'. Instances of possible public disorder are particularly difficult, as the person reporting will almost certainly only gain a partial view of what is usually a chaotic situation moving from one place to another and involving different numbers of people (see Johnstone and Shapland 1987). It was extremely difficult to draw the line between our category of potential crime and that of social disorder which was likely not to involve crime.

Jones, Maclean, and Young (1986) have argued that many analyses of message pads have minimized the importance of 'crime' as a problem affecting the public and have consequently inferred that the service role is the one that occupies most police time. We would suggest that the attempt to divide calls upon police services into such broad categories

Table 3.7 *Types of messages received by the police*

	Rural area		Urban area			
			Beats 1 & 2		Rest of subdivision[1]	
	no.	%	no.	%	no.	%
Potential crime						
Property crime occurred	126	13.7	257	20.0	263	24.5
Activated burglar alarm	43	4.7	97	7.5	89	8.3
Disturbance occurring (fight, assault, noise)	44	4.8	129	10.0	111	10.3
Suspicious incident	62	6.7	103	8.0	88	8.2
Potential future breach of the peace	32	3.5	45	3.5	45	4.2
Absconder	47	5.1	2	0.2	6	0.6
Assault/other non-property offence occurred	35	3.8	47	3.6	45	4.2
Bomb/explosive	4	0.4	6	0.5	7	0.7
Total	393	42.6	686	53.3	654	60.8
Social disorder						
Loose animals	27	2.9	6	0.5	8	0.7
Environmental nuisance (noise, litter, gypsies)	64	6.9	71	5.5	67	6.2
Missing person	13	1.4	20	1.6	26	2.4
Matrimonial dispute	3	0.3	8	0.6	3	0.3
Disturbed person	13	1.4	38	3.0	20	1.9
Abandoned cars	29	3.1	59	4.6	48	4.5
Major emergency (gas leak, train crash)	2	0.2	0	0	1	0.1
Fire brigade calls	23	2.5	33	2.6	28	2.6
Sudden death	8	0.9	4	0.3	3	0.3
Illness — gain entry to house	10	1.1	3	0.2	3	0.3
Total	192	20.8	242	18.8	207	19.3
Roads						
Traffic accident	97	10.5	48	3.7	45	4.2
Bad weather/traffic conditions	46	5.0	8	0.6	19	1.8
Road crossing patrols	1	0.1	2	0.2	2	0.2
Total	144	15.6	58	4.5	66	6.1

| | Rural area | | Urban area | | | |
| | | | Beats 1 & 2 | | Rest of subdivision[1] | |
	no.	%	no.	%	no.	%
Personal services						
Messages to be passed on (ordinary)	13	1.4	22	1.7	9	0.8
Messages to be passed on (death)	8	0.9	9	0.7	5	0.5
Lost animals and property	4	0.4	0	0	2	0.2
Locked out of house/car	4	0.4	4	0.3	5	0.5
Keep eye on property while away	20	2.2	21	1.6	33	3.1
Found property	9	1.0	7	0.5	16	1.5
Injury occurred	3	0.3	5	0.4	8	0.7
Request for crime prevention advice	1	0.1	3	0.2	0	0
Flood	0	0	2	0.2	3	0.3
Deposition of money at station to rescue stranded person	0	0	6	0.5	1	0.1
Total	62	6.7	79	6.1	82	7.6
Police-based						
Information from public about previous offence	23	2.5	41	3.2	15	1.4
Information from public about future offence	0	0	10	0.8	2	0.2
Public making appointments	6	0.7	11	0.9	0	0
Complaints against police	3	0.3	7	0.5	1	0.1
Internal police calls (requests for visits, reporting sick, etc.)	90	9.8	133	10.3	36	3.3
Total	122	13.2	202	15.7	54	5.0
Not specified	8	0.9	21	1.6	12	1.1
Total	922		1,288		1,075	

Note
1. Based on 23 days' data (all other columns based on 72 days).

as 'crime', 'services', etc., with their apparently pejorative overtones, is an enterprise doomed to failure and misunderstanding. At the time of calling the police, the public may, on occasion, be clear as to exactly what they are reporting and whether they see it as 'crime' or not (though see Chapter 6 on the difficulties of intervention). Once the police have visited the scene and spoken to the complainant, they too may have made up their minds about the nature of the incident. During the brief period of conversation on the telephone between the two, confusion is rife. The police are really only interested in getting the name and address right, and in ascertaining how urgent the call is. Controllers will normally wish to leave decisions on the type of incident to the officer attending (Shapland and Hobbs 1987). And it is the police who control calls (or at least attempt to do so). Discussion of police and public priorities is much more profitably conducted in retrospect – with the problems of prediction of these kinds of incidents then being taken into account when deciding upon operational responses to calls. And that strategy would tend to argue for a personal response by the police to most calls that seem urgent since, as Ekblom and Heal (1982) have shown, their telephonic content is a bad guide to their seriousness.

Categorization becomes, moreover, almost immaterial when one considers that 'crime' is itself a social construction, built up in discussions and negotiations between police officers and members of the public involved as victims, witnesses, and offenders. The usefulness of employing the notion of 'crime' (and the consequent baggage of crime reports, crime files, prosecutions, etc.) is apparent to all parties in the case of property crime which has obviously occurred. 'Crime' may not be at all a useful or pertinent idea in the case of minor assaults, rowdiness, disturbances created by mentally disturbed persons, and the like, when both public and police really want the immediate problem to calm down or stop and the cause of the disturbance to go away, instead of being prolonged through official recording and investigation (Shapland and Hobbs 1987; see also Chapter 8).

As we shall discuss further in Chapters 8 and 9, a more useful notion in describing the wish of the public to bring in the police may be that of using the powers of the police to employ 'coercive force', where necessary. This idea, originally proposed by Bittner (1967), runs across the categories of 'potential crime', 'social disorder', and 'roads'.

In so far as there were differences between the villages and the town, they could be characterized as an increased emphasis on potential criminal matters in the urban area and an increased emphasis on traffic problems in the rural. The greater emphasis on crime, both property and violent, is reflected in the greater number of crime reports from the urban area (Table 3.1), though of course the proportionate use of crime reports between property and violent crime is not affected. Traffic matters in the rural areas were not just accidents. There was substantial reporting of bad road conditions, to warn the police themselves and so that they could warn others. This is likely to be a consequence of the greater road mileage and importance of the state of the roads to country dwellers (and an appreciation of the fact that the police were thinly spread and were unlikely to come across any problem themselves). Services and facilities were well spaced out in the country; many people had to travel many miles every day; and one blocked or flooded road might entail detours of many miles. Other, more minor, differences between rural and urban areas also reflected environmental features. The rural area contained greater proportions of loose animals (especially sheep, some of which seemed able to escape through any fence or hedgerow). There were also two homes for delinquent and disturbed teenagers, some of whom absconded relatively frequently.

The police response to calls from the public

When people called the police, how did they respond? We can use the message pad data to find out whether the police provided the services the public seemed to require and whether the police agreed with the public in their diagnosis of the problem.

Where, for example, the public were reporting that a 'property crime occurred' (Table 3.7) did the police respond? Did they record the event as a crime? Or did they see it as a mistake on the part of the public? In fact, for that category, not only did the police respond to the call in the vast majority of cases (89 per cent in the rural area and 96 per cent in the urban area), but complainants almost all turned out to be correct in their deduction that a property crime had indeed occurred. A majority of such calls resulted in property crimes definitely being recorded by the police (67 per cent in the rural area and 56 per cent in the urban area). If we add those which, since they apparently involved damage costing less than £20, did not fall within the Home Office definitions for indictable offences, and those being investigated further by the CID, it turns out that only a very small percentage of calls in either area proved definitely not to refer to crimes (6 per cent in the rural area, 8 per cent in the urban area). An equally small percentage (7 per cent of calls in the rural area and 8 per cent in the urban area) concerned cases in which the police did not proceed further (because advice was given or the complainant did not wish to press charges). As far as property crime is concerned, therefore, public and police perceptions of what the category should contain seemed to be very similar. The public were being very accurate in reporting not only incidents which turned out to be crimes, but also incidents in which the police wished to proceed further.

The data also show that the extent of police non-recording of this, fairly ooviously crime-related, category was minimal. The non-recording of reported crime enumerated in the *British Crime Survey* (Hough and

Mayhew 1983, 1985) may perhaps be more likely to take place in the categories of 'suspicious incidents' and 'disturbances'.

Those reporting suspicious incidents and disturbances were requesting emergency action from the police – to come now to deal with the problem and to make it disappear. Almost all these calls did result in a visit by a police officer, but, unfortunately, the message pads did not include any mention of the time at which the visit was made and so we do not know how rapid the response was.

Another major characteristic of calls about disturbances was the potential criminal content of the incident: disturbances, if still occurring when the police arrive, may often lead to criminal charges such as behaviour likely to cause a breach of the peace. They may even produce more serious results such as assault, criminal damage, or other property offences. Yet the majority led to no such action. In the villages, only 9 per cent led to a crime being recorded or an arrest being made. In 39 per cent, the situation was 'all regular' by the time the police arrived (often from a considerable distance). In the majority of cases, however, 'advice was given' (52 per cent). In the urban area, similarly, only 12 per cent led to a recorded crime or an arrest, 23 per cent were 'all regular', the complainant declined to proceed in 2 per cent, and in 62 per cent advice was given or the offending persons (youths, drunks) were moved on. Unlike reports of property crime, disturbances seemed not to result in any use of the formal powers of the police, except in rare circumstances. The aim of the police appeared to be to quieten down the situation and send everyone away – to stop the incident and solve the problem, rather than to invoke legal processes.

Another category of calls on the police is that of 'environmental nuisances'. This is the category into which most of the problems defined as major by residents in both villages and towns would fall – the ragbag collection of nuisances caused by children, youths, motor cyclists, drunks, tramps, gypsies, and other 'undesirables'; noise from parties, vehicles, and industry; dumped rubbish; parked vehicles causing an obstruction, blocking the light, or just in the caller's 'own' space; disputes with neighbours; and low-flying aircraft (see Chapter 4). Even the vast majority of these prompted a visit by the police, both in the rural and in the urban areas (though it was this category which, of all those discussed so far, was most likely to be overlooked if police resources were stretched).

The action the police can take following such calls is limited. If crimes have been committed or traffic regulations broken, then the criminal process can be invoked. This, however, occurred in only four cases, all urban. The use of the criminal law did not seem to be seen as appropriate by the police. Sometimes the police could take other forms of direct action themselves (such as removing offending vehicles if they were causing an obstruction); this happened in 15 per cent of urban calls and 6 per cent of rural calls. Sometimes they could use their powers of persuasion and their authority to persuade others to take action (such as council officials or one of the parties in the dispute) – remedies that shaded off into simply giving advice or calming down a situation (37 per cent of urban calls and 59 per cent of rural calls). Only very rarely indeed would it be recorded that the police had taken no action (5 per cent of urban calls and 6 per cent of rural calls). Some police officers may feel that such duties are not part of the police role, but in both the rural and the urban areas it seemed that the controllers and the supervisors would still dispatch officers who would attempt to find some resolution of the problem.

These incidents exemplify the range of police response to calls from the public. The police seemed almost always to respond to a call by sending an officer, but were only likely to classify an incident as a crime and start considering the prosecution process if a crime had obviously been committed or property was involved. Otherwise they would 'sort out' the problem in some other way which, however, was unlikely to involve the active participation of the complainant. Calling the police did not necessarily promote prosecution, but it did result in the police taking action by themselves.

The usefulness of crime reports and message pads

The crime reports and message pads described above are the major source of written information possessed by the police about particular areas. They are a record of the problems, including crime, brought to the police by the public. The public had regarded these particular problems as important enough for them to want to inform the police about them. Crime reports and message pads also contain a summary of police actions, including the decision to term a problem a crime and deal with it as such.

They therefore have two uses as far as this study is concerned. Their potential usefulness to the police can be identically expressed. The first use is as an information bank about problems in an area and their possible correlates; the second is as a source for computing police resource allocation and the setting of priorities. In our opinion, the double usefulness of the data to the police is currently limited by the design of the forms and the ways in which they are analysed. The major source of analysis of crime reports is the *Criminal Statistics* and the identical analyses done in each police force. There, the categories of analysis relate almost exclusively to legal offences, with minimal information being given about type of victim, place of offence, and so forth. However, all the necessary information is on the crime report form which could easily be redesigned to enable such codes to be entered. We hope that this chapter has shown how useful this would be and how the information points up crime patterns and environmental effects (for example, the extraordinary concentration of crime in a few car parks in urban beat 1). Other local surveys of crime have used similar measures of the patterning of offending (for example, Baldwin and Bottoms 1976); Davidson 1984; and Brantingham and Brantingham 1984) and all have found them useful. We hope that the computerization of crime reports and message pads now being undertaken in several forces will not only allow more effective spatial representation of problems, but also more effective representation of the nature of the problems themselves.

Both the crime reports and the message pads indicate that the stereotype of rural crime presented at the beginning of this chapter has little foundation in reality, at least for the countryside in the middle of England. The types of problems and crimes affecting residents and business people seemed to be similar in towns and villages. And, indeed, the extent of variation between adjacent beats in the town was greater than that between villages and towns. These similarities are, in fact, unsurprising. The reality is that villages contain industrial units and factories, leisure facilities, pubs, and shops; and that rural houses, like urban ones, contain cash and personal effects which are tempting to offenders. The difference between urban and rural crime, as far as can be seen from police data, is the volume of crime and problems – the density of disliked happenings, as it were – rather than any qualitative difference in the nature of these problems.

A correlate of the quantity of crime, particularly of property crime, that occurs in urban areas is that those investigating it are likely to be swamped with offences involving property of a low to middle range of value which are discovered some time after the offence and which are committed primarily against private individuals. In the country, the lower volume, the relatively greater victimization of the commercial sector, and the significant number of high-value 'good class' crimes are likely to give heart to CID officers investigating them. Urban CID officers are faced with offences important to the victims concerned, but which do not correlate with 'good' work and which do not offer great opportunities for detection: a much less satisfying and more bureaucratic job – as it is now constituted. In addition, many offenders appear to be very local, as far as can be ascertained from those detected. The possibilities for detection of local offenders must rely on local knowledge. These facts all have implications for the organization and practice of detection, which we shall take up again in Chapter 9.

The apparent localization of offending, as we discussed earlier, also has implications for the prevention of crime and for the normal policing of areas – as do the localization and frequency of the non-crime problems shown in the message pads. As we discussed on pp. 34–35, tactics which rely on offenders being kept out of residential areas are likely to be ineffective, since the offenders will come from inside the 'fenced-off' area. Such tactics will be counterproductive and cause splits within communities. Tactics which aim to cope with offenders living next to victims are only now being discussed (see Osborn 1987). So far, these 'community safety' solutions – programmes where the neighbourhood, the local authorities, and the police collaborate in tackling both environmental design and management, and more 'social' programmes giving people more to do and to be involved in – have only been advocated for inner-city or 'problem' estates. The localization of offending indicated in this study would suggest that they are also applicable in other settings with lower crime rates.

However, advocating solutions at this stage is definitely premature. We have seen that the police data tend to indicate a pattern of localization. Our data allow us to explore this question in far more detail – to discover what people actually see as a problem, whether crime falls into that category, what tasks the police are being asked to undertake, what is being kept within the area, and what kinds of action people are taking themselves. These are the subjects of the next few chapters.

4
The nature of problems

Crime is not, of course, the only problem which worries people, upsets communities, lowers the quality of life, or results in calls to the police. A National Consumer Council (1982) survey identified, along with vandalism and crime, excessive rates, traffic volume and noise, dirty and badly maintained streets, bad street lighting, public transport fares, and difficulties with neighbours as serious problems adversely affecting large segments of both urban and rural populations. Many situations and incidents from this catalogue – though probably not complaints about rates or bus fares – find their way to the police (Ekblom and Heal 1982). In general, studies of policing indicate that such calls are often disparaged as 'not real police work'. The NCC survey also mentions, interestingly enough, widespread dissatisfaction with the assistance offered by the police in non-crime matters.

Yet such problems cannot be discounted as 'not real police work', primarily because the public seem to think that it is precisely the police who should deal with them. Moreover, they may bear a significant relationship to patterns of crime. Wilson and Kelling (1982) argue that signs of 'disorder' in a neighbourhood, from broken windows to drunks, tend to attract further disorderly activity. They argue for increased police input to such problems as a way of preventing crimes. NACRO (National Association for the Care and Resettlement of Offenders) now mounts council estate improvement projects aiming at better facilities, housing management, and maintenance, and quick repair of vandalized street furniture, on the grounds that residents identified problems in these areas as encouraging further and more serious disorder (see, for example, the Pepys and the Finch House estates project reports (NACRO 1982a, 1982b)). Power's (1982) account of the Department of the Environment's Priority Estates Projects on three estates (two council, one part-private and part-council) argues a similar case. She recommends localized estate management and the involvement of community groups in management as a strategy for improvement.

However, the link between crime and other problems may not be so direct. Skogan (1987) shows, using neighbourhood data, that disorder and crime in his American communities are so highly interrelated that it is difficult to work out whether one causes the other, or whether both have similar other causes. Certainly, disorder was more prevalent in poorer, less stable, minority neighbourhoods (as was crime). It also seemed to coexist with poorer community life – less informal co-operation to prevent crime, less frequent social interaction, a greater desire to move. But disorder was linked strongly to economic factors, especially unemployment, poverty, and the presence of illegal industries (such as drugs); and also to social factors, such as housing. These wider factors may well also be primary causes. They must not, however, be associated solely with urban areas. Bradley (1983) reports that in the rural areas he studied, 8 to 10 per cent of families were living on less than supplementary benefit levels. Recently, however, rural deprivation in Britain has not been associated with serious public disorder and crime in the same way as the endemic urban deprivation has – perhaps poverty and deprivation in the countryside are less concentrated and their victims more isolated.

Conditions in particular areas can be the result of local or central policy decisions (Skogan 1987; Bottoms and Wiles 1986). Gill's (1977) study of 'Luke Street' Crossley (a council housing area) argues that the area's rough reputation and the large proportion of offenders living there were the consequence of a sudden influx of new families in the 1950s, with overcrowding and a disproportionately large adolescent population (among whom there was a high level of unemployment) by the early 1970s. While Gill does not discuss the point, he opens up the possibility that some problems are cyclical in nature. For example, while newcomers to an area may see vandalism as a serious problem, long-standing residents might remember the influx of new couples fifteen years ago, and say that 'their kids are at the difficult age now; they'll settle down in a year or so and the problem will be solved.'

On another tack, some anthropological studies discuss problems of various kinds in the context of the social control of undesirable behaviour and the regulation of relationships. Bailey (1971) found that in a rural community in the Valloire 'undesirable' behaviours and lifestyles encompassed conspicuous consumption and inappropriate familiarity, as well as rudeness, fighting, and vandalism. Informal sanctions, including gossip and poison-pen letters, were deployed to control such deviance. Forsythe (1982b) in Orkney, and Strathern (1981, 1982) in Cambridgeshire, both address the problem of the socialization of newcomers into tightly knit communities. Again, locals sought to prevent what they saw as the potential destruction of their community by deploying a range of informal sticks and carrots.

One point to carry forward in our own discussion, therefore, is that many problems may actually be rooted in competing versions of what the 'community' should be. This may clearly be the case in motorway and development plans or closures of schools, post offices, and other 'focal institutions' (for examples, see Forsythe 1982a; Quayle 1983; Wild 1983). But it may also apply in neighbour disputes, for example. One example from our own research concerned villagers who saw on-street parking as a necessity, given the lack of garage space in the area, and others who saw it as an eyesore on an otherwise picturesque village green and wanted it banned.

Problems in our rural and urban areas

Our own data, while based on small geographical areas, are quite detailed. We asked residents and business people a general question about any problems that affected them, and then asked whether a range of specific problems affected them or occurred in their neighbourhood. Since the interviews threw up specific instances of problem events, we were able to chart who was directly affected by, and who knew about, particular incidents. Finally, the extent of certain problems is empirically verifiable. We used direct observation methods to assess the actual extent of some claimed problems, such as volume of traffic.

PEOPLE'S FIRST THOUGHTS ABOUT PROBLEMS

In every area, we discovered – as others have done – that the kinds of problems mentioned ranged from vandalism to a lack of local shops, from planning policy to fear of burglary to annoyance with particular aspects of policing. We coded up to four problems for each interviewee, creating a 'master list' of thirty-four kinds of problems.

We found, and our findings buttress others' experience (National Consumer Council 1982; Butler and Tharme 1982), that a comparatively small list of problems accounted for the majority of all problems mentioned and that the list was very similar in all areas, both rural and urban. Butler and Tharme, for example, in their survey of the Chelmsley Wood Subdivision of the West Midlands Police, found vandalism, burglary, and litter figured in various permutations as the major problems cited. Our own 'league table', set out in Table 4.1, shows damage to be the most commonly mentioned item in all three areas, while three other problem types were common to all areas – parked cars (other people's cars outside one's own house, parking on pavements and grassed areas, obstruction by lorries); noise (diverse sources including low-flying military planes, farm machinery, traffic, lorries, night-clubs); and teenagers (hanging about, looking as if they were up to something, and sometimes acting rudely). Yet while this 'league table' shows consensus on the prevalence of some problems, it also shows that crime (specifically, worry about crime, usually burglary) was important enough to mention only in the urban area.

Our direct observations of the study areas made it clear that some problems were more or less continuous and others more sporadic. The

Table 4.1 *Most commonly cited problems*

Urban		Northam		Southton	
1=	damage	1	damage	1	damage
	parked cars	2	teenagers	2	teenagers
3	crime	3	noise	3=	parked cars
4	noise	4=	parked cars		planning
5	teenagers		children on cycles	5	litter
6	neighbours	6	suspicious people	6	noise

streets with high volumes of traffic were indeed the ones in which residents complained that traffic was a problem. However, people complaining about youths or drunks were presumably noticing occasional incidents, since neither groups of youths nor drunks were often to be seen by us.

In every area, 75 to 80 per cent of people cited one or more problems, yet no particular type of problem was mentioned by a large proportion of our samples. In the urban area, damage and parked cars (the most common problems) were each mentioned by only twenty-five individuals – 18 per cent of the total urban sample – while problem neighbours, the sixth category, were nominated by 10 per cent. One reading of this is that people feel particularly put upon only by specific things that happen in their immediate neighbourhood and which affect them personally. We can give some examples of the situation in our four urban locations which illustrate this extreme localization of problems. In urban area 1, damage was mentioned by residents from one street only; in the other three areas those mentioning it were more widespread, though in each area there was at least one street unaffected and in urban area 4 there were four. In urban area 3, teenagers hanging about were mentioned on one street only. And urban area 1 contained a car spares shop which (despite the owner's attempts to solve the problems – see Chapter 3) annoyed everyone we interviewed who lived within 50 metres of it but no one else (though others in the neighbourhood knew about the problem). The issue was that customers' cars and the firm's own vehicles blocked parking spaces, while some customers fitted large items, such as gearboxes, on the street. Again, parking was a problem in only one street of urban area 2, where parking spaces were taken up by local employees and delivery vans in the day, club-goers at night, and shoppers on Saturdays.

Many problems were thus extremely localized, though seen as problematic by most in their immediate vicinity. The only qualification to this is that some forms of noise were particularly liable to affect whole neighbourhoods, rather than parts of streets.

VIEWS ON SPECIFIC PROBLEMS

We also asked people to comment on a list of specific problems, culled from the results of previous surveys. They were asked whether each listed item was a major or a minor problem, or existed but did not amount to a problem, or did not exist (see Table 4.2). The list comprised: children or youths damaging things; teenagers hanging around; strangers (volume of strangers, crowds, door-to-door salesmen); parked cars or other vehicles; abandoned cars; traffic; noise; drunks; pubs and clubs; dogs (strays, barking, dangerous dogs, fouling of pavements, etc.); loose animals (the kind of animal was not defined, resulting in references to cats, sheep, cows, ferrets, and various exotic creatures).

We also divided each area up into streets and analysed the problems experienced and their perceived severity. Within a street, if a certain set of things had occurred, then most people who were around would tend to cite it as a problem. The personal and social characteristics of residents and business people did not seem to affect whether they saw it as a problem. The only variable with explanatory power appeared to be place of residence. However, people differed as to a problem's seriousness – as to what constituted a 'major' problem. That seemed to depend not only on personal attitudes, but also on whether the culprits were known. A known group of youths or gang was definitely thought to be less problematic than one only seen from afar, of unknown provenance.

Some items in the taxonomy are worth examining in greater detail.

PUBS, CLUBS, AND DRUNKS

Despite Wilson and Kelling's (1982) focus on drunks as signs of disorder, they were viewed by the vast majority of our respondents as colourful but harmless features of their neighbourhood. One view, that of a person in urban area 4, was typical of both urban and rural residents' perceptions: 'Once a week the drunks go past, on Saturdays, singing. But they're an amusement really, not a problem.'

Drunks, pubs, and clubs all clustered mainly in urban areas 1 and 2, both of which bordered on an area where drunks and tramps tended to gather and to stay overnight. Though residents were wary of plans to open day centres and overnight shelters in the area, they found it easy to avoid drunks on the street and few considered that they gave the area a bad reputation (though people from other parts did consider it so). Noise (music, slamming car doors, drunken laughter) and debris from night-clubs and pubs with music were much more harshly regarded.

Table 4.2 Individuals affected by problems, and individuals considering them to be major problems, by area

| | Urban areas | | | | | | | | Rural areas | | | |
| | 1 | | 2 | | 3 | | 4 | | Northam | | Southton | |
Problem	affected %	major %	affected %	major %	affected %	major %	affected %	major %	affected %	major %	affected %	major %
Vandalism	61	24	28	10	37	10	54	17	55	30	40	8
Teenagers	42	18	14	=	20	=	50	6	35	22	32	8
Gang	18	0	=		=		6		48		25	
Problem youths	6		23		15		11		=		32	
Noise	41	22	47	23	59	13	45	14	27	12	20	2
Pubs/clubs	46	15	19	13	18	18	0	0	7	0	13	=
Drunks	40	13	27	7	=	0	0	0	0	0	=	0
Strangers	19	0	21	=	14	0	9	6	5	3	4	0
Parked cars	32	7	55	28	78	51	69	36	46	21	42	12
Abandoned cars	28	=	8	0	18	0	=	0	13	3	=	=
Traffic	25	6	61	25	27	14	58	22	28	14	21	2
Stray dogs	0	0	0	0	=	0	14	0	17	4	8	=
Barking dogs	7	0	=	0	0	0	=	6	5	5	=	0
Dangerous dogs	0	0	0	0	0	0	0	0	11	3	0	0
Fouling dogs	22	=	0	0	23	11	26	14	28	16	20	2
Loose animals	0	0	=	0	8	=	0	0	6	0	0	0
Number in sample	33		30		41		37		94		87	

Note

The column headed 'affected' comprises the percentage of those saying the problem was either 'major' or 'minor' in that area. The column headed 'major' only includes people who said it was a 'major' problem. 'Gangs' and 'problem youths' did not appear in our list of specific problems and so no description of the extent of the problem is available. Where only one individual in a sample stated that there was a problem, this is shown by '='.

VANDALISM

Damage thought to be caused by vandals was seen as a major problem by a substantial proportion of villagers and by residents of two urban areas (1 and 4). Much of the actual damage was of a relatively minor nature: 'There are stupid things that happen. We've had two aerials snapped off our car outside here in the last few weeks. My husband has fitted one now that he can bring in with him at night' (Southton).

Damage was usually ascribed to local children or youths – often to a specific group of youths who had become very visible (or even notorious) within that area. Though damage to private property was cited in support of people's perceptions of it as a problem, most of the incidents that seemed to influence views about vandalism involved damage to public or semi-public property (street furniture, playing fields, community centres, graffiti in obvious places). The evaluation of vandalism showed no consensus (see Chapter 6), with many seeing it as a passing phase (though a reprehensible one) which the offenders would soon grow out of. Views as to whether it was a major problem or not were linked both to its prevalence and to perceptions of its seriousness.

TEENAGERS AND YOUTHS

Damage was only one of the problems associated with youths. We also asked about teenagers hanging around, larking about, and generally being a nuisance. Much of the problem was said to lie not in what they did but in their attitude: 'I don't feel there's any more vandalism than when I was young – but the *language* is more violent and upsetting' (Southton).

They were said to hang around – though not necessarily to be a nuisance – in all areas. It was only in Northam that as many as 22 per cent of interviewees said that they caused a major problem – more, in fact, than in urban area 1 (18 per cent). Those for whom they were a major problem lived near a particular bus shelter, recreation ground, or street corner where the youths gathered. The problem was, therefore, again extremely localized.

Some of the village residents had a certain amount of sympathy for the teenagers, and suggested that there was a degree of intolerance over quite minor incidents:

'I would tolerate high spirits in youngsters but I don't think other people will. Town-mindedness isn't the youngsters' fault – they hang around because they don't have things to do. They used to be able to haymake, but today farms are dangerous places and the machinery is so heavy. There aren't any land jobs or somewhere to go.' (Northam)

This theme was echoed elsewhere. In Southton, villagers repeatedly mentioned a lack of clubs and organized activities for youths:

'There's not a lot for teenagers. Boys from the older families go rabbitting and that, it keeps some of them occupied. In the village there's only the Boys and Girls Brigades, and the leisure centre in town. My son isn't a "joiner", but he knows the village cricket team. Other than that there's just the pubs, or going into town.'

Some people suggested that such facilities as did exist were controlled by adults or required the youths to 'join'. They therefore attracted teenagers up to the age of perhaps 14 or 15, but then a vacuum occurred. One person, now in his twenties, remembered:

'Growing up in a village is just boring. Between when I left the Boys Brigade and when I got a car there was nothing to do. I used to hang around with the others on the wall of the pub and on the rec – they're the only places you can hang around, here.'   (Southton)

Others felt that the village was probably anyway too small to cater for the youths, which led one to conclude: 'The dreadful thing is the bus service. Youngsters can't get out to the town. We have given lots of lifts, and never had any trouble. One even tried to give us a pound for the petrol' (Southton).

However, it is far from clear that better transport would improve the situation, since the facilities in the nearby town were not a great improvement over those in the villages.

GANGS

Gangs did not figure in our list of problem topics but were mentioned by interviewees when we asked for their views of problems. The term 'gang' has been used for groups of youths whose behaviour is comparatively organized, some having, for example, a name, roles such as leader and lieutenant, and a degree of planning associated with crimes and fights (Thrasher 1963). Such gangs are qualitatively different to groups just hanging around on the street. People in both rural and urban areas talked about 'gangs', but were referring to groups of youths with local reputations for being obstreperous and for committing (usually minor) crime. These 'gangs' had no collective name, no leader as such, and individual members might act independently of the others.

Just under half the Northam sample and around a quarter of those from the other areas thought that their area had a 'problem gang'. But many more people, both in Northam and in other areas (for example, Southton and urban area 2), described the same boys as problematic individuals rather than a gang.

The number and size of gangs varied. Southton had only one gang as such – half a dozen boys aged about 15. In Northam, there were two or three gangs of different age-groups, from 11–12 to 15–16, only one of which was thought to pose serious problems. Because Northam was geographically fragmented, the gangs by and large stayed within their own parts of the area.

In urban area 4, one resident described the situation thus:

'There's a couple of gangs. One is 13- to 14-year-olds. The problems start when they go from lower to middle school. The vandalism is centred on the church. The other gang is 15 to 18 – it's ex-members of the [church] youth club who have outgrown it, the area doesn't cater for them. So there's friction between them and the 13-year-olds. The older ones are quite organized. For example, last Saturday I saw one loitering in the church, he was looking at the collection box.'

These gangs were said not to come from the immediate neighbourhood – the youth club mentioned catered for a much wider area. Residents did not know them, but accused them of, among other things, scrumping, spraying graffiti, and attempting to set fire to garages. Some claimed that one group was organized by adults and had broken in to several garages taking tools and had taken food from freezers. The situation in the other three urban areas was more fluid. Several teenage groups were noted in all these areas, but were typically quite small. Some were said to have committed burglaries and thefts, but others mostly just hung around, albeit that this also meant playing on factory roofs and firing airguns at tins lodged in trees.

A large proportion of village residents recognized their local gang members when they saw them. In Northam, many knew the identity of at least some of the members. While those we interviewed who knew the Southton gang agreed that they were 'aggravating little sods', as one person put it, those who knew them as individuals often got on with them at a fairly superficial level (and this was also true in Northam):

'I know the rough element, the children who vandalize things, but I've always found them perfectly OK. But then I treat them as adults and they treat me with respect when we meet.'   (Southton)

'They have little mopeds and bikes and stand around the street opposite the school. It makes people think why are they doing that. They are rather mischievous but you can walk quite peaceably up the road past them. But I know them and they know me so maybe it's that.'   (Northam)

But many people in both villages identified one group who gave the appearance of being completely unaware of the gangs' activities – the parents of gang members:

'The point is a large percentage of people can name the children but all the parents refuse to believe their children are doing it – it's very annoying, the school had done what they can, bringing it to people's attention – they don't know what to do.'   (Northam)

Moral judgements about 'what ought to be done' with the gangs differed according to how well the respondent knew the gang members – and, therefore, between rural and urban areas. Where the individuals were known (in the villages), it was often said that they needed 'help' rather than punishment. This point of view was, surprisingly, also held by many other youths in the gang's age range, almost all of whom were dismissive of them, did not mix with them, and to some extent excluded them from the general run of social activities. But the expectation in all areas was that, in a few years, the gang would 'grow up' and the problem would stop. This view of the cyclical nature of gangs, common to both the villages and the urban areas, was particularly espoused by older residents who remembered previous cycles:

> 'There used to be a problem of damage in years gone by – one generation of kids ten years ago. They're all married now. They broke aerials and wing mirrors, broke garden walls down and fought. They would go via here to the clubs – they lived on the nearby estate.'   (urban area 4)

> 'It comes in waves – it's been going on for two years. I don't remember it before, but the older locals say there was trouble with another group of lads and then they grew up. It goes on everywhere – next year it'll be somewhere else.'   (Northam)

The spasmodic nature of gangs is very important for any understanding of the nature of problems. Gangs can only form where there are sufficient young people in the appropriate age-group. Thus, if young parents colonize a particular housing estate, area of town, or village, their children will grow up together and form a bulge of a particular age-group. When they have grown past the 'gang' age, many problems may disappear for ten or twenty years. When they return, produced by a new generation of gangs, older residents will remember the last 'spasm' and put the present one in context. But if communication between age-groups is lacking, or there is a high population turnover, this calming effect may not be present.

Businesses and problems

We interviewed sixty-nine business people – forty from the urban areas and twenty-nine from the rural – and some interesting points emerged (see Table 4.3). First, as we have seen, problems experienced by residents tended to be extremely localized. This was no less true for businesses. For example, many businesses were concerned about the possibility – or likelihood – of their windows being smashed, and the large replacement costs. But this happened regularly only on a particular parade of shops in urban area 2.

Secondly, business people differed from residents in terms of the kinds

Table 4.3 *Comparison of businesses and residents affected by selected problems or regarding them as major*

| | Urban | | | | Rural | | | |
| | Businesses | | Residents | | Businesses | | Residents | |
Problem	affected %	major %	affected %	major %	affected %	major %	affected %	major %
Vandalism	54	21	41	13	48	35	48	32
Teenagers	28	10	33	9	54	17	32	14
Gang	8		7		57		33	
Problem youths	18		12		=		20	
Noise	30	8	55	21	35	13	22	6
Strangers	28	=	15	2	14	10	3	=
Parked cars	62	21	60	37	56	24	42	15
Abandoned cars	18	0	12	1	=	0	7	2
Traffic	32	6	56	20	58	=	20	8
Number in sample	40		101		29		152	

Note
The column headed 'affected' comprises the percentages of those saying the problem was either 'major' or 'minor' in tht area. The column headed 'major' only includes people who said it was a 'major' problem. 'Gangs' and 'problem youths' did not appear in our list of specific problems and so no description of the extent of the problem is available. Where only one individual in a sample stated that there was a problem this is shown by ' = '.

of problems that they experienced. They were slightly more likely to
consider that they had a 'vandalism problem'; less likely to experience
a problem with parked or abandoned cars; and, in the rural areas, more
likely to claim that there was a problem gang.

The problems of business people and residents may differ for several
reasons, not least of which is that many urban business people thought
that they themselves caused residents' problems: 'I don't like the double-
parking delivery boy. I don't want to cause nuisances' (urban area 1).
'We have a tannoy system and compressors on the front and deliveries.
We cause noise. But we don't get complaints. It's strange' (urban area
2).

But other factors may also contribute, such as some business people's
greater surveillance of their neighbourhood (Chapter 5), and business
people's hard-headed calculation of whether a particular problem was
bad for business, or increased costs. It did seem that business people
evaluated problems using such 'rational' criteria. For example, while not
being able to park near the business might be annoying, it would not be
a problem. If delivery lorries could not unload, or if employees did not
like working late because they were afraid to walk the 200 metres back
to their cars in the dark, then there was a clear problem. This latter example was in fact a significant factor for several businesses. We shall
explore this 'rational' orientation further when considering business
people's attitudes to crime prevention and victimization in Chapter 8.

Incidents

One item on our questionnaire asked for specific instances of problems,
and the answers provide an intriguing glimpse of what kinds of things
were known about neighbourhood goings-on, and about how people
heard about them.

Comparisons of numbers of incidents must be made with caution. Just
as official statistics do not enumerate all crime, our figures do not record
everything that might reasonably be called an 'incident'. And just as
recorded crime figures are collected within the Home Office 'counting
rules', so commonsense 'counting rules' seemed to be applied by our
interviewees. For example, an incident might comprise one burglary, or
ten committed on the same street over a very short space of time. Ten
burglaries would only become ten incidents if they were committed on
the same night by different people, or if perhaps two or three days
elapsed between them. Equally, different incidents appeared to have
different life-spans. We asked about events in the year prior to the interview, but were told about some (usually particularly serious) happenings
which were still part of neighbourhood gossip up to two years after they
had occurred. Finally, a small handful of incidents were not mentioned

Table 4.4 Frequency of incidents

	Number of interviews	Population	Number of incidents	Incidents per head of population	Incidents per head of sample interviewed	Number of incidents outside area
Urban area 1	33	354	110	0.31	3.3	3
Urban area 2	30	279	111	0.40	3.7	3
Urban area 3	41	557	98	0.18	2.4	8
Urban area 4	37	504	111	0.22	3.0	14
Northam	94	1,596	226	0.14	2.4	15
Southton	87	1,817	104	0.06	1.2	8

by some interviewees for the very good reason that they happened during the interview period but after the person was interviewed.

None the less, a rough analysis of the figures is possible (see Table 4.4). The number of incidents mentioned by our samples can be indexed by the numbers of interviewees in each area, or alternatively, by the population of the area (on the assumption that we collected a roughly consistent proportion of incidents in each case). In both cases, urban areas 1 and 2 showed the highest proportion of incidents per person. Urban areas 3 and 4, together with Northam, fell into a middle range and Southton came last.

WHAT HAPPENED?

Our coding frame ended up with no less than seventy-eight distinct categories of incident. Many concerned bizarre or rare occurrences. We found only one example of abusive behaviour that could definitely be attributed to racial motives; one case each of sudden death and suicide (which we coded together); and four murders committed near one area in the previous three years, all nationally reported and one sparking off a nation-wide manhunt. Despite these more sensational happenings, most of the incidents were quite low-key.

As with the distribution of problems, no one type of incident predominated (see Table 4.5). Damage, theft, and burglary, together with a limited collection of nuisance types, accounted for around three-quarters of all the incidents reported, but each of these categories combines a variety of acts. At a more fine-grained level, the most common single category we used – damage to cars, motor cycles, or bicycles – accounted for only 8 per cent of the total, while the total of all the categories involving damage still comprised only a quarter of all incidents. Parked cars, which caused significant problems in some neighbourhoods, only accounted for 2 per cent of the incidents. The quarter of incidents which do not appear in Table 4.5 can only be described as 'miscellaneous'. They include the spectacular cases mentioned earlier, plus peeping Toms, unattended burglar alarms, suspicious packages, smoke from bonfires, and fumes from burning industrial waste.

There are probably several reasons why the incidents, compared to the problems, concerned apparently criminal acts. Crimes are likely to register as discrete events. They can thus be retailed as stories with a beginning and a middle (though maybe not an end) and may spice up general small talk within the area – the philosophy being the same as that which leads local newspapers to extensive crime coverage (Smith 1984). Long-term states of affairs such as noisy neighbours or badly parked cars are not so newsworthy for casual conversations – or indeed for academic

Table 4.5 *Types of incidents mentioned*

| Type of incident | Urban areas | | | | Rural areas | |
	1 %	2 %	3 %	4 %	Northam %	Southton %
Youths	=	8	4	5	11	4
Noise	6	4	7	5	=	7
Fights	7	3	4	5	2	6
Suspicious people	4	7	5	=	8	8
Damage	27	33	25	29	23	25
Theft	16	11	11	19	18	16
Burglary	27	21	8	16	8	11
Total	86	86	64	79	69	77
Subtotal damage, theft + burglary	70	65	44	65	49	52
Total number of incidents	110	111	98	111	226	104

Note
Where only one person mentioned the problem it is shown as '='.

papers. However, while many incidents might fairly be thought to involve crimes, a large proportion of respondents did not see all the damage incidents, for example, as criminal (see Chapter 6).

Finally, many of the things we were told about, and damage in particular, were attributed to youths. Beyond this, teenagers and youths hanging about appeared in themselves to constitute an incident in some people's eyes. Incidents of this nature accounted for 9 per cent of cases, while reports of youths messing about, climbing on roofs, trespassing in building sites, swearing, shouting abuse at passersby, revving motor bike or scooter engines, and performing wheelies, collectively accounted for a similar percentage.

OPPORTUNITY STRUCTURES?

Table 4.5 shows the proportions of different kinds of incidents quoted in the various areas. The principal variation between the areas is that over 60 per cent of incidents in urban areas 1, 2, and 4 involved damage, theft, or burglary, while in urban area 3 and the rural areas the proportion was less than half. This variation tallies with the greater level of reported crime in the urban areas. We saw in Chapter 3 that differential 'opportunity structures' appeared to exist for recorded crime across different areas. Our log of incidents enables us to show this in greater detail.

Damage is a good example. In urban area 1, it was mainly vandalism to cars, but in area 2, shop windows were the major target. Area 1 had widespread street parking, while most shops in area 2 fronted a main road which was a major route home for late-night revellers coming from city-centre night-clubs. In the villages, public property was the most concentrated target – and again the site for youths hanging around and people attending functions. Damage in Southton was concentrated around the village hall and the railway station, and in Northam around the village hall and church.

WHO KNEW?

Common sense – and the stereotypes of rural and urban areas – would suggest that in anonymous urban areas, news of local incidents would travel slowly or not at all, while cosy villages would have a well-developed grapevine. Measuring the spread of knowledge is difficult. In the four urban areas, only twenty out of some 430 incidents were known about by five or more individuals coming from two or more households (i.e. by 12 to 15 per cent of those we interviewed). News of incidents apparently did not travel in urban areas. But the rural figures were very similar. The same criteria would require incidents to be known by at least fourteen individuals (to make up the same percentages). Northam had eleven such incidents of a possible 226, and Southton only three out of 104. In every case, then, only between 2 and 7 per cent of incidents enjoyed more than minimal circulation.

However, to apply the same standards in both urban and rural areas, given the larger geographical size of the rural areas, may not be a sufficiently sensitive measure to capture any spread of knowledge. If we apply the same *absolute* standard – five or more individuals from two or more households – then 20 per cent of the Northam incidents and 22 per cent of those in Southton count as 'on the grapevine'. Another indication that the villages did indeed have a stronger grapevine is that a greater percentage of incidents mentioned to us in the villages were 'heard about' by, rather than directly involving, the interviewees (see Table 4.6). So, despite a comparatively small number of people in all areas knowing about any one incident, there is some evidence for a slightly stronger gossip network in the villages, at least in the sense that a larger proportion of interviewees knew of other people's experiences.

Other factors may also, of course, have affected whether people knew of an incident. Again, it seems common sense to assume that some incidents – such as vandalism – are 'public property' because they are openly visible, while others, such as thefts, are 'private property',

Table 4.6 *Incidents directly experienced and incidents heard about*

	Number of incidents directly affecting or directly mentioned to interviewee or household	Percentage directly affecting interviewee or their household	Percentage of incidents heard about at second hand from others
Urban area 1	102	74	27
Urban area 2	101	79	21
Urban area 3	78	79	21
Urban area 4	85	76	24
Northam	113	70	30
Southton	51	65	35

Note
The table excludes incidents from the incident log which neither affected interviewees directly, nor were subsequently mentioned to them by others directly
affected (i.e. events reported in the media, etc.).

depending on the victim to spread the word. This is, however, only
roughly true. The 'well-known incidents' (whichever of our unexacting
definitions is used) included:

1. vandalism (tyres slashed on many cars in one street in a single night,
    several shop windows smashed at one time, paint sprayed on the
    windows of a betting shop (all urban area); council grit bins upended
    and contents spilled (Northam); railway station timetable board
    broken down (Southton));
2. burglary (ten burglaries in one street in a single night (urban area);
    a burglary (actually two years previously) in which a house was
    completely emptied (Southton));
3. robbery (armed robbery of an Asian corner shop (urban area));
4. nuisances (children on cycles performing stunts in a road to make
    traffic stop (Northam); all-night parties in one house (urban area);
    youths gathering regularly on a recreation ground, shouting, revving
    motor bikes, and drinking (Southton)).

Of this selection, only the burglaries and the armed robbery would have
left no publicly visible trace. The key factor in the dissemination of
knowledge about the burglaries was their audacity (clearing the house
completely in one case, covering so many houses close together in the
other).

Obviously, some incidents left traces which ensured that they would
become widely known – broken windows or graffiti, for example. This

was remarked upon by one interviewee: 'We see the after-effects of things, not the things themselves. It promotes cynicism about what's happening. You don't feel you're in a position to correct it' (urban area 4).

But if such traces were quickly cleared up, events did not necessarily become common knowledge: in Northam, particularly, damage to public property was often repaired the same day by nearby residents, and knowledge about the incident would be less widespread (see Chapter 6). Equally, as one resident of area 4 remarked: 'Graffiti is something we've lived with long enough to not notice it.'

By contrast, things mentioned by only one or two people often involved private property, property hidden from casual observers (such as Southton church), or events which would only be known about by the victim unless he or she chose to broadcast them. Businesses, in particular, did not seem to publicize their misfortunes. Illustrations of such 'private' incidents are:

1. vandalism (aerial damaged on firm's van, chrome strip taken from car, children knocking coping stones from a garden wall (urban areas); fire started in a post-box, stones thrown at church window (Southton));
2. burglary (burglary of a house, burglary of a warehouse (urban areas); burglary of a pub (Northam));
3. theft (theft of electrical equipment from a business (urban area), theft of tools from a farm, theft of pedals from a bicycle (Northam)).

Stories without proper endings

If people had not been involved directly in an incident, they usually only knew the simple fact of its having occurred. A typical 'story' of an incident was: 'The chap over the road saw a youth late at night jumping on his car – he caused no end of damage' (urban area 4). The details of the damage, the youth's identity, and the actions of the chap over the road were never discovered. It was only where people were directly involved (neighbour disputes and the like), or where the incident later acquired special significance, that a fuller version of the incident was known. An example of the latter is:

> 'A lady down the street saw two youngsters at 4 a.m. with a safe in a shopping trolley. She noticed it because of the noise of the trolley. When I went to work the next morning [in an adjacent street] it turned out to be my boss's. It had £15 in it. I called the police – she never called the police, which was dreadful. When the police came, I directed them to her.'   (urban area 2)

This fuller story still lacks an ending (did the police call on the lady? were the youths found?). But the stories that lacked endings often shared one common factor; they ground to a halt at 'then the police came and I didn't hear anything after that'.

The lack of endings to the stories is an important clue to people's lack of knowledge about the criminal justice system. Why was this happening? One factor is the lack of information possessed by those directly involved such as victims. The inability of victims to discover what the police did in their case is now well-documented (for example, Maguire 1982; Shapland, Willmore, and Duff 1985). The police themselves did not broadcast their own knowledge, partly because they were rarely around in the areas to chat to people (see Chapter 9), partly because releasing information to those not involved in incidents was not considered good practice by them. In general, police policies all too rarely make clear commitments to the provision of detailed feedback to the public about neighbourhood problems and police responses.

Informal action, by contrast, was often better known and more frequently talked about, especially if it was taken collectively (for example several people blocking in a car causing an obstruction, or a small group of men 'having a word' to move on noisy youths). Equally, in the villages, decisions of parish councils and public pronouncements by people such as vicars went on the grapevine. Parish and other newsletters occasionally carried details of problems and remedies.

It was, however, the police who were the major non-providers of information. Their stance had several important consequences. One was that the complainant, witness, or whoever – in a figurative sense, the person 'owning' the incident – saw a call to the police as washing his or her own hands of the matter. Such people saw the 'professionals' as wishing to attempt to resolve problems without any further public assistance, and as tending to exclude other parties, including victims, from participation in remedial action. They had come to feel that it was almost improper to ask about police actions. This was not something people *wished* would happen; indeed, the sense of lack of control was frustrating and people felt keenly that their exclusion did not contribute to lasting solutions. If this problem of information is addressed – and it will require a significant shift in police practices on the ground – attitudes to the police may change radically. The need for such change is discussed in Chapters 9 and 10.

Lastly, a cautionary note. If knowledge of incidents was sketchy, people padded them out with speculation. This was often, of course, not a difficult exercise. When bags of glue were found in alleyways in urban area 4 and in Southton, people deduced that someone had been sniffing glue in the neighbourhood. But speculation can be wrong as often as it is right. In Southton, the railway notice-board had been broken by local youths twice during the fieldwork period. But when workmen accidentally shattered the notice-board's glass front while trying to screw it into place, the story circulated immediately that the youths had smashed it again. Many deductions rely on stereotypes and reputations, and this is but one of several clear cases of mistaken accusations we encountered.

Summary and discussion

Four broad conclusions follow from the material presented here. First, the kinds of problems which confronted individuals in day-to-day life were broadly similar wherever they lived. Nor were problems *experienced* as less severe in rural as compared with urban neighbourhoods. A larger proportion of people in Northam than in urban area 1 considered that they faced a serious problem with vandalism.

Second, damage, teenagers hanging around, and, in the urban areas, crime were all salient problems for large numbers of people. Yet previous approaches to 'disorder', such as that of Wilson and Kelling (1982), have a limited applicability in our study areas at least. While people were uneasy about – for example – youths on street corners, the 'street-corner youth count' was very low. Other 'disorderly' people, such as drunks, did not seem to bother most of our interviewees (though they may have been more peaceable drunks than those studied by Kelling in Newark, NJ). The 'problems' people experienced were actually very varied, ranging from parked cars to low-flying aircraft.

Third, while many people may be affected by one type of problem, it may not be the same problem. Problems were very localized in time and space. Their foci were small areas such as specific street corners, parades of shops, bus shelters, back alleys, or noisy households. They were often limited to early mornings, late evenings, or school holidays. Moreover, there was a remarkable unanimity about the perceived existence of particular problems. Place of residence rather than age, sex, or social class was the determinant of whether or not a problem was perceived. It wasn't who you were but where you lived that determined what you would cite as a problem. Residents and business people, however, differed in the criteria they used in assessing whether a state of affairs constituted a problem – the latter using a hard-headed profit-and-loss approach.

Fourth, the rate of specific incidents experienced or known about by local residents was highest near the city centre. But if some incidents acquired notoriety (and the best-known incident we collected was told to us by around 40 per cent of the interviewees in the area) the majority, in rural as well as urban areas, were virtually the 'private property' of a small handful of people. The best-known events were those which left publicly visible traces (minor damage to cars excepted, perhaps because people do not spend much time carefully studying the paintwork on other people's vehicles). And even where an incident was 'on the grapevine', the knowledge of what had happened was often fragmentary and the role played by the police usually entirely unknown. These findings give grounds for pessimism about 'solving' or 'managing' problems. The extreme localization and diversity of problems imply a need for local and diverse approaches which are hard to generate centrally or encourage locally. Knowledge of problems is fragmentary. They are often experienced as problems-for-the-man-down-the-road rather than problems-for-the-community. There may be little consensus about the seriousness of the problem and hence what would constitute a solution.

Take, for example, the problem of how to stop a certain group of youths who regularly meet on a particular street corner. But of course the youths live in the area too. The street corner is a public space and they are (usually) not committing any clearly criminal act. The police can move them on, but this would be open to interpretation as harassment; they can probably arrest them for some offence (using the Public Order Act, 1986?), but this would benefit no one while alienating the youths, their parents, and in all likelihood the person who called the police in the first place. We shall return to the inappropriateness of the formal powers of the police and other bodies, such as parish councils, in Chapters 9 and 10.

Problems of disorder may be ones which neither the informal nor the formal control mechanisms of society can address in any more than makeshift ways – often ways that address symptoms and not causes, that divide rather than heal neighbourhoods, that make one wish, after the event, that one hadn't done *that* to solve the problem. But in order to get a clearer idea of the options available we now need to look more closely at the nuts and bolts of these makeshift structures of social control.

5

The beginnings of control: watching and noticing

Informal social control is a very daunting term, but it describes a very common process, one which we all take part in every day. It comprises all the processes we use to shape the people around us into our particular culture or ways of behaving. Some of these are quite subtle and wide-ranging, such as the example set by those who are respected, or the values promoted through the media, or the ways in which power and resources are distributed (see Cohen 1985). They affect the whole realm of social order – from styles of dress to patterns of social behaviour and the way we drive. Here, however, we are concerned with problems of crime and disorder, and we shall focus on the most obvious form of active informal social control in respect of these problems: dealing with perceived deviations from acceptable patterns of behaviour in the areas where we live or work.

This process of informal social control has to start with someone seeing something, classifying it as problematic in some way, and noting that something must be done about it – even if only bearing it in mind in case it happens again. If no one sees anything, there can be no social control. Watching is the first requisite, but watching is not sufficient. People must also notice the event and define it as being an example of disorder. And then they must decide what to do about it and what to say about it to whom. These are social decisions and they will be affected by social factors: others' perceptions of one's actions and how important those others are; how serious the event appears to be; what resources are available. We shall be treating the process of decision-making as largely sequential: watching, noticing, and defining, making decisions as to action, taking action. It must be sequential, in the sense that if the first parts of the chain of events do not happen, the later ones cannot occur either. However, later decisions or information can call earlier defini-tions of the situation into question. Realizing that the nearest source of help is a long way away can cause the redefinition of an incident as 'problematic' or 'suspicious' rather than 'definitely criminal'. Manning (1983) has shown that decisionmaking by professionals in the criminal justice system is tied to situations and affected by perceptions of what will happen in later parts of the process. Decisionmaking by ordinary people in the course of their daily lives is just the same.

In this chapter, we shall concentrate on the processes of watching and noticing: who watches, what they pick out as unusual, what they define as suspicious, what ideas they have about what is disorderly. In the next, we shall look at what action they take, what it is designed to achieve, and the likelihood of its success.

Previous work on watching and noticing

There is very little empirical work on which to build a theory of watching and noticing. Most studies have looked at either bystander intervention or the response to obvious criminal events. The bystander studies have used very public places and offenders unknown to the watchers (for example, van Dijk, Roell, and Steinmetz 1982 and Steinmetz 1984 on bicycle theft; and Steinmetz 1983 on assaults in youth clubs). The early American work tended to use laboratory studies and must be viewed with caution. Victimization studies have had to utilize retrospective analysis of decisions taken about incidents defined in the context of the interview as obviously likely to be criminal and have concentrated on the point of view of the victim rather than of the witnesses (though see Steinmetz 1984; Kinsey 1985). They have all found a large amount of non-reporting to the police, the major reason offered for this being that the offence was 'trivial' (see Skogan 1984 and Block 1984 for a review of such studies; and Hough and Mayhew 1983 and 1985 for the British findings). Rarely has any greater detail been elicited. As Greenberg and Ruback (1984) comment:

> We have reached a critical stage in such research. While there is an abundance of evidence documenting the reluctance of various categories of victims to notify the authorities, there is a noticeable paucity of theoretical frameworks for making sense of these findings.

However, there have been several evaluations of the methodological pitfalls of research into intervention. The most comprehensive, by van Dijk, Roell, and Steinmetz (1982a), involved the comparison of an experiment staged in the street on the theft of a bicycle with both self-report questions and hypothetical questions about an identical incident. They found that respondents gave a far larger proportion of responses involving positive action (such as actually confronting the thief or calling the police) when answering the hypothetical questions than they did when asked for self-reports of their own experiences over the last two years. The results of the staged experiment were similar to those from the self-report. It seems that measuring intervention by means of hypothetical questions alone is extremely misleading, but self-report gives as good results as staged experiments. But the mounting of experiments is ethically problematic (bystanders become distressed), as well as being expensive in time and police manpower (police officers were detailed to stand near the 'theft' so as to be available for reports of it). Nor can such techniques explore incidents taking place on private property.

We have, therefore, concentrated on self-reports of watching, notic-ing, and intervention in this study. We asked respondents whether they had seen anything suspicious or stopped children doing anything. Their reactions to incidents they had become involved in over the last year were also monitored (using our questions about problems in the area, and also the direct victimization and witnessing self-report questions). The answers to these questions were backed up by data collected in other ways. Some incidents occurred during our periods of observation. The message pads gave a picture of the kinds of incidents and people that were reported to the police as suspicious. Three hypothetical questions included in our interview schedule (on strangers seen walking round the back of a house opposite or sitting in a car outside, on someone seen tampering with a car, and on someone seen damaging a telephone kiosk) tapped attitudes on watching as well as on informal action.

Watching: nosiness or neighbourliness?

The prevalent idea about villages is that they are close-knit, friendly places, where everyone knows everyone else's business (Merry 1984), though this may be a mixed blessing, as is shown by the example of those that flee to the towns for anonymity (Forsythe 1982b). Conversely, towns are thought to be soulless, concrete jungles, where no one cares and all sorts of misdeeds can flourish unseen or overlooked by the residents. The net curtain-flapping suburbs presumably come midway in this mythological spectrum of social control.

Of course, the amount of watching that goes on in a place is not only affected by people's propensities to watch. It is also affected by their ability to watch, according to their lifestyle and the amount of time they spend in that place (see Steinmetz 1984); by whether watching is seen as a socially desirable thing to do (neighbourliness or nosiness?); and by whether the design of housing and businesses allows people to see anything (are kitchens at the back or the front, for example?).

If the myth is correct, we would expect villagers to be more prone to watch their neighbours' activities and to regard watching as much more socially desirable. People in Northam seemed to fit this pattern. As is shown in Table 5.1, two-thirds of respondents said that they themselves would notice most things that happened near their house and believed that their neighbours would do so as well:

'Yes, they notice – absolutely – they monitor you. They know at what time of night you go out. I love it, it's not really nosy, it's caring about what's going on. I've always been like that myself. I like watching people. I'll grow up to be one of them.'

Table 5.1 *Patterns of watching*

	Urban area %	Northam %	Southton %
I myself notice most things	35	66	31
I myself notice some things	22	6	44
I notice few things because of environmental design factors	8	11	9
I notice few things because of lack of interest	12	6	4
I notice nothing, but others do	21	11	13
No one notices much	2	0	0

'A part of human nature is being nosy. In a community like this it's inevitable.'

Some of the younger people stressed the disadvantages:

'I think there's very little escape here – if it's not one it's the other. I know exactly what's going on here. Look at X opposite the pub – she knows without even being nosy. I think in a village it's inescapable.'

'Sometimes, if you get strangers coming into the pub, the locals will view them with suspicion and sort of freeze them out.'

Only a few people on the new estates and those living in isolated houses away from the village said that they did not watch out themselves.

Northam, then, conformed to the image of the village. But in Southton fewer people were keen on watching (or admitting that they watched). And, more importantly, the urban area produced figures very similar to those of Southton. In the urban area 57 per cent of people said that they themselves would notice some or most things, with another 21 per cent saying that they themselves wouldn't necessarily, but certainly others in the street would. Only 2 per cent of people in the urban area felt that no one noticed much at all. The image of an anonymous city where each household is isolated from its neighbours, and where no one notices or helps, was very far from the view of residents and businesses in the urban area. People might themselves be working elsewhere most of the day, or be unable to see very much, but they were usually sure that even if they themselves were not able to watch, others in the street could and did:

'We do listen out and look out at night. We notice noises, but the old boy next door notices everything.'

'We watch next door because they're out to work. We have their key. We watch the young couple that have just moved in and become friendly. We're a couple of old watchdogs.'

'I think some are quite aware. I feel safer in this place here from a security angle than on the industrial estate. . . . I myself am very aware of noise outside. I just go and walk out to the front and I know the sound of some of the delivery lorries, so even if I'm in the back I notice and in the front I can see out into the street.'   (wholesaler)

Nor was watching seen as nosiness – as unjustified activity. In both rural and urban areas, watching was defined as a 'good thing' (85 per cent of people in the urban area, 68 per cent in Southton, and 70 per cent in Northam). People stressed either the neighbourly aspects of watching – looking after neighbours' houses and making sure the elderly were all right (urban residents, Southton) or the crime prevention benefits (urban businesses, Northam).

In all areas, therefore, people approved of watching and thought that at least some of the residents and business people were actively engaged in it. Who were these watchers?

Who were the watchers?

The people cited as watchers by their neighbours and who themselves agreed to the description fell into two main groups: the elderly and business people. Older people were more likely to be at home during the day and saw watching as a service they could perform for their neighbours – sometimes in return for the shopping and odd jobs their neighbours did for them. However, their watching was done from front windows or the doorway (in good weather), and was necessarily confined in its physical scope.

The owners, managers, and employees of some kinds of businesses were also very important watchers – both in the town and in the villages. These were almost all businesses in the service sector, but were not confined to the small shopkeepers made famous by Jane Jacobs (1965). They included garages, farmers, pubs, second-hand motor spares places, shops, and delivery men (milkmen, postmen). Even in the busiest parts of the town, shopkeepers said that they recognized many people waiting in the bus queues as regulars and knew several hundred people by sight. People in manufacturing industry were not against watching, but there tended to be a conflict between it and 'getting on with the job', particularly since most machinery was situated so that the worker could not see out of the factory. Where the design allowed it, however, watching was encouraged, as long as not too much time was given to it (for example, in a specialist engineering factory and in a wholesaler of decorating materials – both in the urban area).

The observational part of the study reinforced these findings from the interviews. A considerable proportion of workers in the service sector were constantly monitoring what was going on outside their businesses.

Publicans, betting-shop proprietors, and shopkeepers would look up as people passed by outside or if they heard an unusual noise (in the villages and quieter parts of the towns, many knew the noises made by the regular vehicles). The process was almost unconscious.

The most graphic illustration of who the watchers were occurred in Northam. During an observation period, a massive timber lorry succeeded with great difficulty in negotiating the very narrow streets and disappeared out of view. A few minutes later a rough-looking man appeared, walking up the street, looking around him, and clutching a piece of paper. In quick succession, the garage owner and the publican came out on to the street, looked at him, and crossed over to talk to each other, obviously discussing him. He finally approached a woman who had come out to put something in her dustbin and they talked for a minute or so. He was, of course, the lorry driver, looking for directions and exasperated by the lack of street signs (removed by the local gang of youths). Later, the researcher learned that the old lady who lived opposite the pub had also been watching the man through her window, but of course this was invisible to someone in the street. By that evening, the identity of the man and his destination were known to the publican and to many others in the village.

Business people and some residents also 'adopted' small areas of public space around their premises. They took care of the street outside, even in the urban areas, one person even going so far as to sweep up dog mess and litter. Residents mowed grass verges and disposed of rubbish, loudly disparaging the dumping of metal objects. They became annoyed if others parked cars on 'their' verge.

Larger public spaces such as parks, however, were so big that no individual felt that they could get to grips with them. They were beyond the territorial capacity of individuals, and, since this aspect of informal social control was essentially individual and solitary, it was rare that any joint or community enterprise developed without a spur from an official body. Individuals were concerned about them, but did not 'adopt' them. Only in villages were there organizations which had responsibility for large public spaces (the playing fields association, etc.).

The observations also produce figures of who was out and about in the town and villages and so had the opportunity to observe public spaces (in addition to the residents and business people who could watch the area immediately around their premises). The first point that stood out was that people's activity was clustered round certain foci – shops, post offices, post-boxes (but not telephone boxes), mobile vans, garages, other on-street businesses, pubs (in licensing hours), and schools (at the beginning and end of the school day). If a street had none of these, it had a dead feel. Objectively, as well, the number of people and vehicles using it was very much smaller. These foci were not just centres of activity – they were also centres of communication. Around 20 to 30 per cent of people going in or out of such a place would stop and talk to each other, both in the villages and in the urban area.

The observations also allowed us to specify the kinds of people that were out and about with sufficient frequency to be able to notice anything going on. Car and van drivers were not very helpful in this respect, because they tended to pass through too rapidly. People who were most likely to be out in the street, travelling relatively slowly, were (in approximate order of frequency, greatest first):

Urban area: delivery men, bicyclists, dog walkers, pram pushers, people with young children.
Villages: dog walkers, pram pushers, tractor drivers, people with young children, bicyclists, delivery men.

The dog walkers were more likely to be out in the evening, business people and those with babies or young children in the daytime.

The influence of design on watching has been well cited and chewed over in the literature (Newman 1972; Poyner 1983; Clarke and Mayhew 1980; Mawby 1984). The effect of physical space and sightlines are obviously important in permitting watching, should people care to practise it. There has, however, been only minimal concentration on the watchers themselves. The elderly have often been assumed to be watchers, and our study confirms this. Less attention has been paid to the very important role of businesses. We found business people were not only watchers, but in some cases provided a focus for others to visit, watch what was going on, and communicate their concerns and their observations. A totally residential street did not have this possibility. Current planning fashions are for the segregation of many types of business, including some of those we have identified as neighbourhood foci. We would argue that this is likely to be a regressive policy, in that segregated business areas will not provide opportunities for observation and communication. The discussion about the influence of design on crime needs to take into account not only the siting of houses, but the routes taken by people and the businesses they need.

What did people notice?

The next question, having isolated who is likely to be watching, is to ask what people notice. Obviously, people take an interest in all sorts of things concerning the area in which they live or work: their neighbours' visitors, the clothes they wear, their cars (particularly their new cars), the doings of their children, DIY activities, and so on. We are interested, however, in instances of problems, disorder, or crime – that is, in instances which seem to be suspicious.

The word 'suspicious' seems to have connotations of strangeness and uncommonness, but suspicious happenings or people need be neither. The activities of a gang of youths are none the less suspicious if they occur every day. It does, however, have some moral connotation. Suspicious incidents or people are those which do not fit into the watcher's view of how life should be lived in that area. Definitions of what is suspicious are likely, therefore, to vary between places and between cultures.

Our data provide a number of ways in which we can try to isolate what people mean when they say that something is suspicious. One is the responses people gave to our interview question as to whether they had ever seen anything suspicious in their area. These responses can be compared to those given in answer to the question as to whether they had ever stopped children or young people doing anything. We also have message pad data showing events reported to the police as being suspicious happenings or involving suspicious people.

NOTICING SUSPICIOUS INCIDENTS OR PEOPLE

A substantial proportion of people in both urban and rural areas said that they had seen something or someone suspicious at some time in their area or had stopped a child or young person doing something (see Table 5.2). Some areas showed a proportion comparable to the 70 per cent of residents of an American city who said that they had seen a suspicious incident in the last year (Mangione and Noble 1975). The differences between the areas may reflect both differences in watching behaviour and differences in the occurrence of incidents regarded as suspicious. For

Table 5.2 *Likelihood of having seen a suspicious incident or having stopped a child or young person*

	Suspicious incident %	Child or young person stopped %
Urban area		
Area 1	34	21
Area 2	62	21
Area 3	26	27
Area 4	57	31
Villages		
Northam	60	72
Southton	54	53

example business people were far more likely to report that they had seen a suspicious incident (or stopped a child or young person doing something) than private individuals – and the relative density of businesses varied greatly between our small areas.

The incidents mentioned to us included some in which people's behaviour gave rise to suspicion (60 per cent); those in which people's appearance (for example, tramps) looked suspicious (30 per cent); and those in which suspicions were raised because of noises or things out of place, with no obvious human agent around (10 per cent). All the cases of suspicious behaviour or things seemed to relate to suspected criminal behaviour, and it was relatively easy to specify what the watcher thought the person was up to. For example, a person seen climbing into a house, a person seen sitting waiting in a car, or adult men or youths hanging around were definitely being suspected as potential burglars ('they were obviously casing the house'). The behaviours and people observed, and the likely offence people linked them with, are shown in Table 5.3.

By far the most frequent suspected offence was burglary. This accounted for 55 per cent of the reports in the urban area, 61 per cent in Northam, and 64 per cent in Southton. In urban areas, reports focused on immediate and obvious signs of potential burglary – people climbing into houses, etc. – while, in the villages, it was enough to hang around, especially if you were a strange adult man, to be suspected of being a burglar. One of the researchers was approached by the subpostmaster of one of the villages with just this suspicion whilst conducting an observation session early on in the fieldwork! Again, the focus in rural areas was on adult men, rather than the equal emphasis given to men and to youths in urban areas.

Incidents or people suspected of damage or theft were much rarer, as were those provoking concern about assault or sexual assault (including peeping Toms, prevalent at the time of the fieldwork in each area – see Table 5.4).

People suspicious because of their appearance alone seemed mainly to be travelling salesmen, who were thought a great nuisance in all areas, particularly by older people. Gypsies and tramps, however, as we saw in the last chapter, were not considered worrying, problematic, or fearsome – people watched them, but didn't worry about them: 'We do have tramps but not so much lately. We had one which slept in church and left a lot of mess. I had one come in Saturday evening and he wanted a cup of tea and off he went.'

This categorization of tramps poses some problems for the British Crime Survey, which currently classifies them as incivilities (Hope and Hough 1986). In urban areas, tramps and gypsies did not exist, their place in the suspicious, but not really worrying, league being taken by drunks and mentally disturbed people from community homes.

Table 5.3 *Types of suspicious incidents and suspicious characters*

	Potential offence	Numbers of incidents		
		Urban area	Northam	Southton
Suspicious behaviour				
Person climbing into house	Burglary	7	2	1
Person sitting waiting in car	Burglary	2	13	5
Adult men/man hanging around	Burglary	5	6	7
Youth/youths hanging around	Burglary	6	0	0
Speeding car	Burglary	1	0	0
Men interfering with car	Theft of/from car	1	0	0
Fight	Assault	2	0	0
Potential child-molesting	Assault	0	2	0
People carrying TVs, etc.	Theft/receiving	2	0	0
People selling things cheap	Theft/receiving	2	0	0
Shoplifting	Theft/receiving	2	0	0
Opening cashbox	Theft/receiving	1	0	0
Theft of milk from doorstep	Theft/receiving	1	0	0
Theft from a building site	Theft/receiving	0	0	3
Kids vandalizing cars	Damage	2	0	0
Kids damaging property	Damage	1	0	1
Ill person damaging property	Damage	1	0	0
Fire	Damage	1	0	0
Suspicious people				
Travelling salesman	Burglary/fraud	3	5	3
Lone walkers at night	Burglary	0	1	0
Peeping Tom	Assault	0	6	2
Diddicois/gypsies	?	0	5	0
Tramps	?	0	6	0
Disturbed/drunk	?	4	0	2
Homosexual	?	1	0	0
Prostitutes	?	1	0	0
Suspicious things				
Noises, lights, & movement	Burglary	2	1	0
Debris from use/occupation/break-in	Burglary	4	2	0
Abandoned car	Theft of car	3	0	1

Table 5.4 *People's experiences of suspicious incidents or characters, by potential offence*

	Urban area %	Northam %	Southton %
Burglary	55	61	64
Theft of or from cars	7	0	4
Assaults/threats (including sexual assaults)	4	16	8
Other theft/receiving	15	0	12
Criminal damage	9	0	4
'Funny people'	11	22	8

POLICE MESSAGE PAD REPORTS OF SUSPICIOUS INCIDENTS OR PEOPLE

Our other source of data is the police records of those incidents reported to them by the public as suspicious in some way. This is obviously a more select group, since these incidents were sufficiently concerning for a member of the public to report them to the police and for the police to record them as a 'message'. The categorization as suspicious may also owe something to police perceptions, since officers do not write down verbatim the words of the caller, but paraphrase them according to their views and their perceptions of the action likely to be needed. We isolated from the message pad data incidents seen as suspicious, people reported as causing a disturbance or likely to cause one and reports of disturbed people. We then classified these calls according to the kinds of offences the callers thought were most likely to be about to occur (Table 5.5). Only ten calls from the urban area and eight from the villages could not easily be classified into likely crimes.

The results were almost identical to those for the interview data regarding self-reported experiences. The most frequent suspicious event concerned burglary. Calls about burglary far outweighed its actual occurrence. The suspected culprits were all men, usually adult men but occasionally youths. In the rural area, even a strange man sitting in a car outside a house with a 'For sale' sign on it might be reported to the police. In the urban area, youths were more often thought to be potential burglars and descriptions centred on behaviour thought to be practised by burglars. Urban dwellers seemed to need to be more certain that a crime was being committed before picking up the phone. The premises thought to be targets for burglary were as often industrial or commercial as domestic. Individuals seemed to see themselves as guardians of the factory next door as much as of the house on the other side. Another worry was travelling salesmen, who were often thought to be conmen.

Table 5.5 *Offences suspected by people calling the police (message pad data)*

| | Urban area | | Villages | |
| | Calls | Recorded crime | Calls | Recorded crime |
	%	%	%	%
Burglary	51	26	74	28
Theft of or from cars	15	25	9	25
Fraud (conmen)	6	4	6	4
Assaults/threats (including sexual assault)	7	6	4	5
Other theft/receiving	9	28	2	31
Criminal damage	6	9	2	8
Absconders	0	0	4	0
Drugs	4	0	0	0
Robbery	2	1	0	0

Yet other types of crime, which were as visible as, and certainly more prevalent than, burglary and fraud, did not seem to rouse suspicions (for example, damage or theft from or of cars).

In contrast, those thought to be causing a disturbance were largely youths in all types of area. Youths or youthful motor cyclists 'causing trouble' provoked the largest single category of reports from the villages (30 per cent). Again, people in the town seemed to need to be more certain of the kind of event taking place before calling the police. All the message pads from the town concerned trouble actually occurring, whereas some of the messages from the villages related to trouble likely to occur or brewing up.

Disturbed people, with whom the caller did not know how to deal – the confused elderly, drunks, the mentally disordered, or young children – were found in both rural and urban areas, but the frequency per head of population was much higher in the latter than in the former (a ratio of seven to one).

STOPPING CHILDREN AND YOUNG PEOPLE

The prime suspicious person appeared to be the adult male. The same conduct from children or young people did not seem to be seen as suspicious. But was it seen as reprehensible? Would anyone have taken any action about it? We also asked our respondents in the interviews about any incident in which they had stopped a child or young person doing something (see Table 5.2).

Again, there was a rural/urban difference, with a majority of village

dwellers and a significantly smaller percentage of town dwellers reporting such an incident. The range of activities mentioned in both areas
was much wider than the lexicon of suspicious incidents. The potential
offence which respondents had in mind when stopping children or
young people was not burglary, but vandalism (42 per cent). Assaults,
threats, and theft/receiving were also significant. There was also a
significant number of nuisances, most of which were not criminal at all,
such as ringing doorbells and running away, throwing things around,
or making a noise.

As Baumgartner comments from her study of an American suburb,
young people are often thought of as 'unruly youths', likely to be about
to engage in vandalism and other uncomfortable acts of high
spirits:

> though, in many cases . . . it is not at all clear to an observer that the
> problem in question was created by human forces at all, as opposed to those
> of wind and weather or sheer deterioration with age . . . to a large extent
> young people in this suburban town have come to occupy a role filled
> elsewhere by djinns, leprechauns and sprites.
>
> (Baumgartner 1981: 198)

Stereotypes of suspicion

People clearly had quite definite ideas about what they saw as
suspicious and what they would report to the police. They had
stereotypes of problematic situations – stereotypes which included ideas
about what behaviour was suspicious and about what kinds of people
were likely to be the culprits for different kinds of misdemeanour.
These can be summed up as follows:

1. Suspicious happenings usually involved people doing something,
   rather than inanimate objects in odd places. Abandoned cars were
   often noticed, and indeed roused suspicions, but they did not
   produce the same emotional charge and concern as people.
2. Men, particularly adult, unknown men were often thought to be 'up
   to something'. Women were almost ignored (as one of the researchers found). Youths and children were often suspected of being up
   to no good, particularly if they had a reputation in the area as
   troublemakers, but they were seen as just that – causing trouble,
   or disturbances – rather than as suspicious. In the villages, youths
   were regarded almost entirely as lesser troublemakers (likely to
   answer back, be rude, cause some damage). In the town, youths
   were more likely to be seen as suspicious (capable of burglary, as
   well as damage). However, the youth as thief or burglar would tend
   only to be reported to the police as suspicious if it was clear to the

watcher that an offence was likely to be committed imminently.
3. Rarely did people seem suspicious because of their appearance alone. The problem and the offender were inseparable in the stereotype. A similar phenomenon was found by Lejeune and Alex (1973): people did not necessarily believe they were being victimized if the offender looked different from their expectations.
4. Suspicious incidents all involved conduct which in some way was seen to be deviant or was disapproved of. Unusual but approved behaviour was of course noticed, but was seen as eccentricity, not as worthy of suspicion.

Judgements about suspiciousness were, then, moral judgements about tolerance, seriousness, and the limits of criminality, in which ideas about offences, offenders, victims, and situations were all rolled up into one package. If one element was missing – the likely offender was a woman, say – then the idea that an incident was suspicious might fall.

It may be argued that the definition is circular: suspicious events may be being defined by the fact that some action was taken by the watcher, such as reporting to the police, and that it was the fact of taking that action that subsequently led people to define the incident as suspicious. Why should we invoke some more abstract moral notion? One answer stems from the comparison between people's views of what was suspicious and the kinds of situations which led them to stop children or young people doing things. The incidents described in the question about stopping children certainly caused action, but they did not provoke suspicion in the watcher.

It may also be questioned why we need to postulate another set of moral judgements, when people may be using the boundaries of the criminal law as defining suspicion. Certainly, the most suspicious incident involves an imminent breach of the criminal law, but again, many breaches of the criminal law are not accompanied by suspicion (such as the activities of children). And some suspicious activities, such as groups of youths hanging around in public places, do not necessarily involve any breach of the criminal law (at least at the time of our study: the Public Order Act, 1986 has brought criminality more into line with suspicion).

Nor was suspicion in our areas just a reaction against strangers – though being unknown was one of the factors wrapped up in definitions of suspicious individuals. The xenophobia described by Baumgartner in the United States was not so pronounced in our villages or towns:

> Simply being [a stranger] in some technically public places at all can be an offense in Hampton. Quiet residential streets, and the public parks scattered among them, are used on a day-to-day basis almost exclusively by

neighbourhood people. If outsiders become visible in such locations, they are likely to arouse uneasiness or even alarm. . . . Even downtown, those who appear to be outsiders – by virtue of race or unconventionality – may deviate by their very presence.

(Baumgartner 1981: 185–6)

In Northam or Southton, being a particular type of stranger who was believed to be likely to perform harmful acts (tramps, gypsies) was itself likely to arouse suspicion. But lone children, young people, and women could loiter with relative impunity, compared to men. The interdependence of the packaging of the various elements in the stereotypes of suspicion was very strong.

The implications of the stereotypes of suspicion

If people have these clearly defined notions of what they think is a suspicious package of behaviour/people/events, then this has strong implications for what will be reported to the police and for crime detection and crime prevention. If something is thought to be suspicious, then of course it may still not be reported to the police, as we shall discuss in the next chapter. The watcher may not be sure enough about what he or she has seen; or may think the problematic consequences of reporting outweigh the benefits. But if something does not fall within the stereotypes of suspicion, there is no way it will be reported. It may not even be noticed, so that if questioned afterwards, the watcher may have no recollection of the event. The stereotypes limit the universe of events that could lead into the criminal justice system.

Burglary was the most prevalent likely offence in our reports of suspicious occurrences. The stereotype of the burglar, particularly in the rural areas, was that of an adult, unknown man or men sitting in a car outside the premises to be burgled (rather similar to the image conveyed by early crime prevention films). This combination is, however, relatively rare even in respect of offenders detected and prosecuted by the police. The *Criminal Statistics* (1985) indicate prosecuted burglars to be largely young. A significant proportion is likely to be youths from neighbouring streets (Baldwin and Bottoms 1976; Davidson 1984; see also Chapter 4). But these youths, who may well be familiar, at least by sight, to watchers, were suspected of criminal damage or rowdiness, not burglary.

The police currently rely upon members of the public for most primary detections of burglars (bringing the person to the notice of the police in the first place, as opposed to the secondary detections produced by his confession to other offences (Burrows 1986)). The purpose of the house-to-house enquiries which are supposed to be carried out after most domestic burglaries is to uncover any suspicious conduct seen by neighbours (Shapland and Hobbs 1987). Detection of burglary relies upon suspicions, and the stereotypes of burglars appear not to fit.

Equally, policies which attempt to involve the 'community' more closely in the prevention and detection of crime, such as Neighbourhood Watch (Bennett 1987) or the various versions of 'community policing' (Weatheritt 1986), also trade on people's suspicions and seek to make more use of them. If the stereotypes are incorrect, and if the packaging is so strong that each element has to be in place for the watcher to acknowledge something as suspicious, then Neighbourhood Watch, for example, will fail at that most basic hurdle.

The solutions to this dichotomy between crime and people's suspicions of crime are quite complex and we shall discuss them in more detail in Chapter 10. They need to take into account the diversity of perceptions in communities and the likely effects of adjusting stereotypes to include local people. They also require the police to collate information about offending and to be prepared to divulge it – which is often not current practice (see Morgan 1987a).

Crime is crime is crime?

People's ideas about crime are clearly central to their practices of watching, noticing, suspecting, and taking action on instances of problems and disorder. The holistic packaging of views about offenders, offences, victims, and situations that we found in the moral judgements of suspicion immediately suggests a parallel with the interactionalist ideas of Schafer (1977) and others, which emphasize the necessity to look at offender, victim, and offence together as a triadic set producing the crime. So we attempted to gain some idea of respondents' views about crime by asking people whether they employed any distinction between what is really criminal (which we shall term, as they did, 'real crime'), and what is merely reprehensible, high spirits, thoughtlessness, and so forth.

Some people spoke about shades of criminality: there was 'real crime' and what was called 'other crime'. However, even where people distinguished between 'real crime' and 'other crime', they were still keen to point out that all of these were still acts which were against the criminal law and were morally wrong and reprehensible. 'Other crimes' were not so heinous as to demand serious action (such as calling the police) or lead to real worry about the character of the neighbourhood or personal safety, but might still lead to action.

Other people saw the question of criminality in black and white – either it was criminal or it was not. They did of course make distinctions between levels of seriousness of criminal acts, but there was no 'grey area' of 'other crime'.

Table 5.6 *Beliefs about crime*

| | Urban area | | | | | Northam | Southton |
| | 1 | 2 | 3 | 4 | Total | | |
	%	%	%	%	%	%	%
There is 'real crime' and there is 'other crime'	27	40	19	35	30	79	78
Things are either criminal or not criminal at all	32	32	77	42	46	13	11
Other view	41	28	4	23	23	8	11

Clearly there was a difference between rural and urban areas (Table 5.6). Well over 70 per cent in both villages acknowledged a grey area of 'other crime', whereas only 30 per cent did so in the town. The admission of such a distinction was not correlated with age, sex, whether one was a resident or business person, social class, or experience of victimization. It was an individual difference, whose incidence was strongly affected by whether one lived in a rural or urban area and, to a lesser extent, by the type of urban area. We also suspect that believing in 'other crime' may be linked to the actions that people felt they could take in the incidents they observed. We discuss this further in the next chapter.

There were vast individual differences in the kinds of events that people placed into their categories of 'real crime' and 'other crime' and the point where they drew the line between them. This makes it extremely difficult to present the findings clearly. However, some acts seemed to be thought of as 'real crime' everywhere and by almost everyone (and were always placed into the category 'crime' by those with black and white views). These were robbery (mugging in the street and armed robbery of shops, banks, etc.); serious violence involving the use of weapons and causing injury; sexual assaults (though not other sexual offences such as under-age sex or exhibitionism); domestic burglary where entry was forced and property taken; and deliberate arson of domestic property. These same crimes appear at the top of the list of serious offences in the *British Crime Survey* (Hough 1986). There were also a few offences which never fell into the category of 'real crime', such as fights between people who knew each other, disturbing the peace, or minor theft not from a house or car. In a few cases, most notably vandalism, there was considerable dispute, both in rural and urban areas. It was regarded by some as very serious, whether it was done to private or public, non-commercial or commercial, property. Others regarded it as 'other crime', if it was done to public property, by juvenile offenders, or the damage was minor. Theft from cars, bicycle theft, taking and driving away, petrol siphoning, and theft from business premises also caused widespread disagreement.

It is clear that the distinctions being made do not automatically follow from the legal definitions of offences, which are often extremely broad, nor from a consideration of the degree of seriousness within an offence category. The holistic parcelling of offence, offender, victim, and situation which pertained in notions of suspicion also applied to ideas about crime. People were not only talking about types of offence when they talked about 'real crime' (or more serious crime, if they did not make that distinction), but also about types of offenders, types of victims, and types of situations. A change in one of these could be sufficient to make the act appear completely different in character – qualitatively different – meriting a different categorization and, as we shall see in the next chapter, a different type of response.

The packaging of crimes

We shall deal with the factors cited in respect of offenders, offences/situations, and victims separately, whilst trying to draw attention where appropriate to their combination.

CULPRITS

One of the most important factors was the age of the supposed culprit or culprits. In the urban areas, known juveniles were generally excluded from definitions of 'real criminal activity' (as were drunks), while in the villages, this privilege was extended to all local juveniles, including, in one village, the local gang. The reason for this may partly be that, in every area, at least some residents or business people knew precisely which youths were involved; and that a large number of people recognized them and knew roughly where they lived:

'It's all the same kids. I could name every one. Last night ten or fifteen of them were hanging around between here and the church.'

'It [vandalism] is worrying in a village when you're not accustomed to that level. It is a gang – bored out of their minds – you can see them wandering

Table 5.7 *Associations between 'real crime' or 'other crime' and the suspected culprits*

| | Numbers of associations made Committed by: | | | |
	Local youth	Local adults	Strangers	Total
Rural areas				
'Real crime'	0	1	10	11
'Other crime'	90	10	0	100
Total number of associations	90	11	10	111
Urban areas				
'Real crime'	21	13	30	64
'Other crime'	6	4	0	10
Total number of associations	27	17	30	74

along the road. . . . They all come from good homes – not the poorer quarters; they're not newcomers – some were born here, some have been here ten years. But we mustn't make them think they're newsworthy.'

Various reasons were given for their behaviour: boredom, excitement, challenge to adults, and so on. Whichever was held, often as a pet theory, by the resident, it was clear that the culprit was being distinguished from the stereotype of the 'real criminal' – an adult acting with premeditation (see Table 5.7).

In the urban area, local youths and teenagers were far more likely to be seen as the perpetrators of 'real crime' (Table 5.7), but here they were less likely to be known to the respondents. It is possible that this process of associating 'other crime' and local juveniles is both necessary and instrumental for villages. It can be seen as increasing cohesiveness and minimizing the damage that might be caused were villagers to have to live with the thought that they have 'real criminals' in their midst. There was some evidence that if a 'real crime' were to happen, it would be characterized as being done by outsiders and, as a corollary, that offences committed by local juveniles were being minimized to count as 'other crime'. For example, the victim of one burglary in Southton was a hospitalized old lady whose house was stripped of all its valuables during her absence. Everyone who commented upon this incident to the researchers said that it 'was done' or 'must have been done' by an outside gang, the majority plumping for a gang from London, with a few commenting unhappily that someone in the village must, either deliberately or unwittingly, have told one of its members that the house was vacant: 'It only takes a stranger to come into the pub and everyone's keen to talk to him because he's a new face. I bet a criminal would know what houses to do inside fifteen minutes.' Local burglars, it was claimed, would go to other villages to commit offences, so as not to stir up hostile feelings.

The corollary of this attitude for local offenders was that they could avoid any minor offences being thought of as really criminal *because* one was a member of that community, willy nilly. Equally, as far as the community was concerned, this attitude promoted cohesion. A small community is placed under great stress if offending is seen to be both serious and local. The only possibility is to exclude the supposed offender. Given the amount of offending that does occur in villages (and the local origin of the culprits identified by the police – see Chapter 3), the exclusion of juvenile offenders would lead to neighbourhood disintegration.

In the urban areas, however, there was not such a sense of belonging or 'community' (Chapters 2 and 7). Many of the urban sample harboured suspicions (or knew) about local criminals doing 'real crime' and operating in their neighbourhood: 'I think I know who it was who burgled us last time. You get a couple of families up the street and if there's any bother it seems to end up being them.'

However, these families might end up being scapegoated. It will be interesting to explore this question of neighbourhood solidarity, cohesiveness, and tolerance of criminality further in the context of the current replication of the Sheffield study (Bottoms and Wiles 1986), in which high criminal areas with high victimization rates were found in the original Sheffield study to be either splintering, transient places or stable, long-established areas.

This holistic packaging of ideas about criminality does, however, have disadvantages as well. From the point of view of crime prevention policies, attempts to change stereotypes to reflect more closely the actual pattern of offending in an area may also promote concern among residents about the kinds of people who live there and their own ability to take informal action. Ideas about crime are also ideas about the reputation of areas.

VICTIMS, OFFENCES, AND SITUATIONS

The kinds of victims, details of offences, and the situations in which they occurred also provided reasons why something was 'real crime' or 'other crime'. Theft and vandalism caused particular lack of agreement between respondents. But thefts of small items, shoplifting, and pilfering (by employees from employers, by children from school, and by passersby from farms) were seen in all areas as not 'really criminal'. And building sites, unlike grouse, had open season declared on them all year round. In general, theft from an individual was regarded more seriously than theft from an institution, though there was ambiguity about the status of public property – some seeing crime against public property as less serious than an equivalent act committed against a private household and others seeing it as more serious.

Victims were important not only through who they were, but also through what they had done. Property left lying around (a common occurrence in certain kinds of businesses) or belonging to certain public facilities appeared to acquire some idea of 'contributory negligence' if it was subsequently damaged or removed. As one Southton resident said:

> 'The [railway] timetable wouldn't have taken much knocking down – I know some people think they [the culprits, thought to be the local gang] used sledgehammers, but for all the special glass and vandal-proof what's-its, it's only mounted on a couple of 4-by-4s, no match for a pair of Dr Martens. It's a golden opportunity to test the laws of physics – if we lever it from the top, will it break?'

Another view: the attitude of business people

There were some indications that business people saw the question of 'real crime' or 'other crime' differently from residents in the same area, though our sample size for businesses is too small for us to assert this with confidence. Offences seemed to be 'real' or serious if they affected businesses adversely in a financial sense, but not solely because they were criminal (except for the seemingly universal top five of 'real crime': woundings, sexual assaults, burglary of a dwelling, robbery, arson).

> 'There is a gang of kids who occasionally take things when they're here and other individuals do sometimes nick things when they can't afford them. I'm not very bothered – there's nothing you can do abut it in this kind of place. We will sell things for what the buyer has on him, say £7 for something marked £10 and sting him for the extra £3 next time he buys.'   (motor spares: urban area)

> 'There are other kinds of crime apart from burglary, etc. For instance, when I give credit, some people try to extend it . . . and sometimes there's no chance of getting it back. . . . And there are other kinds of scams, like if builders put extra houses on to estates without planning permission.'   (Northam)

However, the same business people reacted in the same way as their neighbours when discussing offences committed against private property (their own or housing situated around the business).

We have outlined people's views about watching and the things they considered suspicious. The question now is whether these views only affect their watching behaviour, or whether they also carry over to the action that people take when they see a suspicious incident.

6

Intervention

Once something has been noticed, the watcher will start turning over in his or her mind what to do about it. In some situations, the action to be taken will seem quite obvious and will be put into train immediately. In other situations several possible sequels will be envisaged, with none that seems particularly likely. Deciding what to do is a process fraught with difficulty, in which the consequences of mistakes may be quite serious. Is that strange man having difficulty getting his key into the door of the house opposite a burglar? Will I be beaten up if I go over and ask him what he's doing? Is he a relative? It will be very embarrassing if I call the police in that case – and very difficult if my neighbours find out that I didn't call them if he is a burglar.

With these kinds of decisions to make, it is hardly surprising that delay in decision-making has been noted in several studies of reporting to the police (for example, Spelman and Brown 1981). Disparaging comments have often been made about such delay, but this is to ignore the essential ambiguity of many situations involving disorder, the possible lack of fit between the options the watcher thinks are available and those he or she anticipates will produce the desired result, and the need constantly to reconsider what to do as the situation changes.

Decision-making about intervention is a very complex process, one that we can only start to unwind here. Studying it is made more difficult because it appears that people do not seem to have access to their actual reasons for making decisions. If people are asked why they did something, the reasons they give will depend on the audience they are addressing and will essentially be rationalizations of what they did, as opposed to reasons why they started to do it (see Fitzmaurice and Pease 1985 for a review of this evidence).

Another possibility for studying intervention would be to make an inductive typology of people's actions from their own and others' reports of incidents that occurred just prior to and during our fieldwork, using our log of incidents from the rural and urban areas. However, the kinds of incidents that we have are extremely diverse and numerous in both situational and individual characteristics.

Our goals must necessarily be much more limited. We can use the incidents in the incident log and the answers to the hypothetical questions to indicate the range of potentially acceptable options for action (such as whether watchers in that village would ever consider calling the police in a particular situation). We can also attempt to set out the situational and individual factors which seemed to predispose watchers to take one rather than another course of action and look at the consequences which they said they had in mind. For one or two kinds of incidents, we have enough data to try and put all these factors together and construct a model of intervention. Testing the model will, however, have to await much larger-scale studies and experiments.

The range of immediate options

The first task is to set out the range of options for action that watchers were using in both rural and urban areas. We shall make a distinction between immediate action, taken by the watcher directly, and further action, which is set in train by the watcher but which involves a series of events or the co-operation of several people.

The kinds of immediate action taken can be divided, broadly, into nine options, revolving around acting oneself, finding others with whom to act, continuing to watch to see what will happen, plus, of course, the option of doing nothing (see Tables 6.1, 6.2). The most minimal response, apart from ignoring the situation, was to continue to watch and see what transpired next. Sometimes, continuing to watch required a small amount of effort, such as moving from window to window, or going outside to get a better view: 'I have been out at night or sent my husband out to investigate if our dog or next door's dog barks, but we've never seen anything' (urban area). 'I'd try and organize myself to keep an eye on them rather than go rushing to the telephone and if they went, I'd think "OK" and then afterwards I'd say somebody called on you today' (Northam).

On some occasions, watchers became marginally involved in the situation. They tried to make it clear to the suspect that he or she was being watched, by, for example, ostentatiously going into the garden to water the flowers.

Another set of responses to noticing some problem comprised involving someone else. A relatively common strategy was to tell the owner or caretaker of the property involved about the incident when they were next seen or came home: 'They might watch but they wouldn't say anything [to the suspect]. They might mention it to us when they saw us' (Southton resident).

A variant on this, commonly found in victimization studies when people are trying to decide whether to call the police, was to talk the situation over with friends or neighbours (see Shapland, Willmore, and Duff 1985):

'I'd keep an eye open – if he looked a shady character, I would do something about it but not otherwise. I'd knock on the door and see how she [the owner] was – or tell [X] what I'd seen and go and have a look at what's happening.'
(Northam)

Table 6.1 Self-reported incidents — action taken (percentages)

	Urban area		Northam		Southton	
	All incidents	Stranger	All incidents	Stranger	All incidents	Stranger
Ignore it	23	34	6	0	16	18
Go on watching if possible	0	0	0	0	0	0
Take active steps to watch	1	3	13	24	19	9
Take active steps to watch and be noticed	0	0	4	14	0	0
Challenge person alone	57	28	65	43	52	45
Find others to challenge person	2	6	0	0	0	0
Talk to others about it immediately	2	0	4	5	2	9
Tell owner or others later	1	3	1	0	0	0
Ring the police	14	25	6	14	11	18
Sample number	155	32	112	21	63	11

Table 6.2 *Hypothetical situations: action taken (percentages)* (see p.93)

	Urban area			Northam			Southton
	Stranger	*Car*	*Telephone*	*Stranger*	*Car*	*Telephone*	*Stranger*
Ignore it	18	9	22	2	4	0	17
Go on watching if possible	5	4	0	3	0	5	5
Take active steps to watch	19	8	0	39	4	5	5
Take active steps to watch and be noticed	2	5	7	3	8	3	7
Challenge person alone	14	21	33	31	60	56	21
Find others to challenge person	1	0	0	3	2	5	2
Talk to others about it immediately	5	6	11	2	4	5	9
Tell owner or others later	1	0	0	7	4	5	7
Ring the police	35	47	26	11	14	15	26
Sample number	105	78	27	65	50	39	42

One way of involving other people in solving a problem of course is to call the police.

The position of maximum involvement is for the watcher to approach the suspicious person, or in some other way take direct action. There were many quite subtle ways of eliciting whether the person was up to no good:

'If I know people are out, I wait until they [the intruders] come out and . . . [ask them what they are doing]. I usually go down to the gate if anybody pulls up.' (Northam)

'I've noticed people wandering around. Especially at the back of the church and questioned them. There was one old man who looked a bit odd, I think it was my lodger who noticed him first and said he looked a bit funny and in the end I went off and questioned him. He was just a harmless old man.' (Southton)

'In the shop, we had a spate of trousers disappearing. Black youths. They always came in when I was on my own. One day they came in and started to fiddle with the clothes. I locked the door and gave them a lecture. They ended up asking about overheads and profit margins. Not so bad after all.' (urban area business)

'We made our feelings felt [about a car parked in an inconvenient place]. A specific person was doing it and we boxed them in.' (Northam)

The range of further options for action

Other strategies involved action over a longer time-scale. Such action might include not just friends and neighbours, but also more formal bodies, such as schools and parish councils, or people with responsible positions, such as publicans, teachers, or vicars. In the villages, there appeared to be a plethora of such possibilities for further action. A first step might be just spreading knowledge of the misdeeds that had been committed amongst other villagers – either to put them on their guard, or to warn the troublemakers that they had been detected:

'I kept getting phone calls with no one at the other end, from a phone box. I quite loudly told people in the village – it stopped soon. I said it when I thought the culprits were around: "I shall ring the police."' (Northam)

On a more sophisticated scale, the village newsletter in Northam was used by the parish council and village hall committee to publicize the misdeeds and vandalism of the local group of youths, and warn them that their identity was known and any further problems would bring in the police. (In fact direct eyewitness proof that the youths had committed the vandalism was lacking, so the police were not involved.) 'Responsible' people might be asked to pass a message on to an offending party.

But direct action was also possible. A group of neighbours might decide to accost a person thought to be up to no good. We did not, however, have any incidents reported to us of actual vigilante action in the sense of physically punishing any culprit; group action was entirely verbal. In Southton, for example, several residents went out together to talk to a group of children kicking balls against a garage and making a noise. On another occasion, it was claimed that when youths had congregated in one part of the village during one summer, drinking and abusing passersby, a group of local men had gone out to confront them and succeeded in moving them on.

Occasionally, further action might be preventive, rather than deterrent or punitive. 'Target-hardening' activities were undertaken by both individuals and organizations, such as using toughened glass where windows were repeatedly broken or concreting in litter bins constantly overturned by kids. The parish councils in both villages tried this approach with limited success: the damage didn't stop completely, but the precise targets became less popular. In Northam, the council also used a more imaginative approach: 'They planted trees around the hall – around 100 – and they tried to think of how to stop the kids pulling them up. Mr M wrote a piece in the newsletter – would the kids look after them? There weren't any vandalized.' Councils also made arrangements for the children to be taught in the local schools about how wrong vandalism was and about the relationship between it and their parents' rates.

The trickle of information that came the way of teachers, councillors, and others might lead to the matter being raised at a council meeting. This occurred in both villages in relation to litter, noisy motor cycles, and vandalism to public property. The formal powers of the council were often limited, however, to putting up notices, especially since the property involved very often did not belong directly to the parish council. However, consultations on planning decisions could give an opportunity to raise problems of disorder affecting things like telephone boxes, railway timetables, or street lights. Pressure could also lead to the closure or stricter regulation of noisy discos where trouble had occurred.

School governors tried sometimes to play a similar role, but were again frustrated by their lack of powers:

'We had a governors' meeting at the school and we discussed the vandalism – I suggested the school should be fenced off because the gang can ride round and be completely unseen. The Governors said yes and we wrote to the authority. The authority wrote back in due course and said they couldn't afford to put up the fence.'   (Northam head teacher)

The options for further action described above were only available in the villages. In the urban area, such resources did not seem to be available. There appeared to be no 'responsible' people, partly because the centralization of local-authority and other agencies' services (including the use of religious team ministries) meant that such people did not live locally or were responsible for such a large area that very few residents knew them personally. Parish councils do not exist in towns, and the borough council covered a much larger area (the whole town). There was only one relevant councillor, who was occupied with problems from a much wider area and was relatively unknown to residents or business people. Group action also seemed to be much rarer and there were no residents' associations. The only further action we uncovered was in urban area 1, where several neighbours in one street co-operated in watching for and catching a peeping Tom. He was given a verbal lashing, but nothing more, and the police were not informed.

Frequency of use of options for informal action

We have two sources of data on the informal options which people used when they encountered suspicious or strange events. The first is our log of incidents that people reported to us as having happened to them in their area. This gave us a total of 155 responses to incidents in the urban area, 112 in Northam, and 63 in Southton. Table 6.1 shows the responses given by watchers to these incidents. Note that the numbers are not equivalent to those discussed in the last chapter, because the log necessarily spans a length of time greater than one year (interviews were conducted over six to nine months in each place). Some of the incidents described matched closely the type of incident used in the hypothetical question described in the next paragraph about a stranger or strangers walking round the house opposite. These have been separated from the others and appear in Table 6.1 under the heading 'Stranger'.

The second kind of data is the answers to three hypothetical questions about what people would do if they saw: (a) strangers sitting in a car or walking around the back of the house opposite ('Stranger' in Table 6.2); (b) someone tampering with a car ('Car'); or (c) someone damaging a telephone kiosk ('Telephone'). Some respondents found it very difficult to give an answer to these hypothetical questions – some said they simply didn't know (a reluctance found also by van Dijk, Roell, and Steinmetz 1982). A few were, unfortunately, not asked all three questions. Obviously, the answers must be treated with great caution (see Chapter 5). None the less, they indicate the kinds of options that people think of when confronted, even verbally, with particular situations, as opposed to those that would never cross their minds.

Self-report questions also have their problems. For example, they tend to exaggerate the incidence of people taking direct action themselves, just as hypothetical questions tend to increase the proportion doing the socially correct thing and ringing the police. Equally, self-reports contain a greater percentage of incidents in which people have been personally involved, as opposed to incidents which they turned away from and forgot about or consulted others. It is more socially desirable to take action, rather than to refrain from it (as long as one does not make unfortunate mistakes). We, therefore, present both sets of data here.

It can be seen from both tables that about half the range of nine options which we identified were commonly used (or crossed people's minds when they were presented with the hypothetical situation). The more popular options also clearly varied with the situation and according to the place the watcher lived.

One particularly important situation for possible intervention is when a stranger is seen walking round a house opposite. Even in this archetypally suspicious situation – one which as we have already seen almost screams 'burglary' at watchers – options other than calling the police were commonly thought about and employed. However, if people were allowed a second choice in the hypothetical questions, then calling the police became a majority response. It was at the back of people's minds, but they were often not prepared to go that far themselves as an immediate response. Business people, however, were far more likely than residents to say they would take direct action – either by calling the police or by challenging the person directly.

The two villages showed very different patterns of response. People in Northam seemed more prepared to rely on their own resources – either to challenge the stranger themselves or to take active steps to go on watching. Ringing the police was not rated so highly. In Southton, however, the police meant their own local police officer. More people in Southton than in Northam were prepared to involve the police (Table 6.2, compare the 'Stranger' columns), and indeed did so (Table 6.1).

For residents of higher-crime areas – urban areas – there appeared to be little middle way between reporting strangers to the police and ignoring a whole incident. They were far less prepared to take informal action. This is contrary to the hypothesis of Greenberg and Ruback (1984), who postulated that people from lower-crime areas were more likely to involve the police.

If we turn to other kinds of incidents, less redolent of burglary – a 'real crime' for many people (Chapter 5) – we find that respondents to the hypothetical questions about tampering with a car or a telephone kiosk seemed even more willing to take immediate action rather than watch. In the urban area, people would either challenge the person or ring the police. In Northam, the trend was towards direct action, with few residents and business people seriously contemplating involving the police. Compared to potential burglaries, incidents characterized as 'assaults' (fights, shooting airguns, robbery, etc.) were likely in all areas to be ignored – rather uncomfortably and often because the watcher was scared to intervene – or else the participants would be challenged directly by the watcher. Verbal abuse would be dealt with by watchers themselves, or just ignored. Theft, even theft from private property, might well be ignored – though on occasion the perpetrator might be challenged. Damage offenders would be challenged in the villages, but might be reported to the police in the urban area. Nuisance offenders (making a noise or other disturbance) would be watched to see what they got up to or perhaps challenged directly. Tramps, drunks, and the like would be watched actively and the watcher's presence made known in the villages; ignored or reported to the police in the urban area. Abandoned cars were always reported to the police, but debris left from possible attempted break-ins might easily be ignored.

We have been referring above solely to the options people used for their immediate response to incidents. However, as we noted earlier, possibilities for further action may also present themselves: bringing in responsible people or bodies to take action against the offenders and so forth. In fact, in only about one in twenty of the incidents reported to us as occurring in Northam or Southton (Table 6.1) was any such form of further action taken. However, though rare, such incidents in fact involved at one time or another a considerable proportion of the village. In both villages, further informal options were preferred, where at all possible, to involving the police: 'The police are the last resort. But if they [the gang] are getting away with it too much then they have to be called in. For petty things the police are kept out of it as long as possible' (Northam).

The role of organizations, such as schools and parish councils, in dealing with problems was both strong and – in Southton – somewhat controversial. The formal aspect of parish councils' powers was unanimously regarded as pretty useless. With regard to dogs fouling the footpaths, for example: 'The parish council does put notices up – penalty £25 – we never catch anyone' (Southton). Instead, residents and business people would tell members of the parish council, school teachers, etc. and expect them to intervene in the problem, particularly if the culprit was not known personally to the watcher (see Baumgartner 1981, for similar findings in an American suburb).

These demands for action by organizations placed these bodies in a difficult position, since their own options were limited. Letters might be written to the parents of named children, for example, or the police might be contacted about the general problem. This latter course, however, was not always in tune with the original expectations of the watcher who contacted the body.

The situation of the council was further complicated by the amount of popular support it could command. In Northam, there was considerable support (perhaps because of the large number of villagers involved in various bodies that controlled public spaces and facilities). Here, the council could act with a degree of confidence. In Southton, membership of the parish council and ancillary bodies was restricted to a relatively small slice of the village population and the council was often regarded as misguided, both in its assumption that certain acts of damage were vandalism and in its proposed remedies. For example, the measures taken by the council to stop parking on grass verges were thought by many to be more obnoxious than the parking.

District councils also played some role in the solving of problems in villages, though generally their sphere of influence was considered to lie more at the civil than the criminal end of the legal spectrum – with street lighting, smells, and planning, rather than with disturbances and vandalism.

None of this existed in the urban area. We uncovered not a single instance of a suspicious incident, crime, disturbance, or nuisance being referred to any council, responsible person, or any body other than the police. Nor did any respondent bemoan the lack of such things. It seemed as though options for further informal action in the urban area not only did not exist, but were not even considered.

Factors affecting responses to suspicious incidents

What was it that affected how people behaved when they saw a suspicious incident? Clearly, the kind of problem involved or the nature of the suspicious incident was very important. Responses to strangers walking round the back of houses were different to responses to someone tampering with cars or telephone boxes, or to drunks, or to youths making a noise. But that was not the only factor. Indeed, implicit in the situation itself is not only the bald behaviour (theft, damage, noise), but also the nature of the suspected person and the kind of property or person being offended against. Other factors include the personal characteristics of the watcher (age, sex, toughness or fragility); and the potential consequences of different courses of action, including consequences for the watcher's social relationships and place in the social life of the area. Of course, since we are considering decision-making by the watcher, these 'objective' factors, measurable by outsiders, cannot be the only ones. Decision-making about which option to adopt will also be influenced by the watcher's beliefs about whether the situation being observed is deviant rather than customary behaviour in that neighbourhood (and whether it is wrong in that watcher's moral code); how certain the watcher feels that the characteristics of the situation really are as he or she perceives them to be; how many options the watcher thinks are open and how attractive one is with respect to the other.

We shall attempt to construct a model of intervention to explore which factors seemed to be the most important in our rural and urban areas to explain which options for action were taken. We shall discuss each type of factor separately, before attempting to bring them together to consider the reasons why people would or would not call in the police. First, however, it is worth examining the previous literature to see which factors have been isolated in previous studies using self-report techniques (or hypothetical responses to believable suspicious incidents).

Previous studies on self-reported intervention

Unfortunately, there are only a few previous research studies which have used ethnographic techniques in real situations or self-reported incidents (and only one of these is British).

Ethnographic studies of intervention include that of Baumgartner (1981), who observed that residents of an American suburb tended to avoid confrontation almost entirely. They either tolerated and avoided deviant conduct or made secret complaints about it to officials. This seemed to be possible because there were so few strangers, and even fewer suspicious incidents involving strangers (though any stranger was likely to be regarded as a suspicious incident himself!). Local officials were also relatively efficient, powerful, and helpful in stopping deviant behaviour (whether or not they officially had the powers to do so).

Mawby (1984) believed that in his (1979) study of incidents in nine areas of Sheffield, bystanders were more willing to become involved when the offenders were juveniles. They seemed as likely to intervene when the targets were businesses as when they were individuals. Experimental bystander studies in America have also concluded that the social and environmental context of the incident is more closely related to the type of intervention than are the personal characteristics of the watchers.

Of the survey studies, Mangione and Noble (1975) found in an American city that the most common response to seeing suspicious strangers was to ignore them (the response of 50 to 60 per cent of residents, depending on the part of the city). Other possibilities were to call the police (18 to 35 per cent) and to check out the situation oneself (about 25 per cent).

The Dutch national victimization study for 1983 included questions on what people would have done if they had witnessed twelve different kinds of crime (Steinmetz 1984). Of the Dutch population over the age of 15, 32 per cent were estimated to have been a witness of one of these offences during 1982. Situational factors seemed to be far more important in predicting whether people would take any direct action to intervene than socio-economic or other personal factors, both in the pilot study and in the full study. The factors of knowing the victim, knowing the offender, and the offence being viewed from the watcher's home were significantly related to active intervention. Non-intervention – ignoring the situation – occurred in as many as 61 per cent of the incidents. Non-interveners either felt the watched situation to be none of their business or thought intervention would be too dangerous. It is interesting that the figures for intervention in our study are far higher both in the rural and urban areas.

Steinmetz (1983) also observed aggressive incidents in a Dutch youth club. He found that few witnesses intervened and that those that did either had some official caretaking function or were youths protecting their girlfriends. The majority of people in the club just walked round the incidents and were neither bothered nor intervened. Interveners were likely also to be victims or offenders in other incidents of the same type. The national survey also found a correlation between being a witness and being victimized. Van Dijk and Steinmetz (1983) have hypothesized that being victimized may lead people to look out more for similar kinds of situation and so be more likely to realize when they are witnesses.

Personal characteristics of watchers

Our data are necessarily scrappy, in that they comprise all the incidents that happened in a number of small areas in the course of around eighteen months. They do not include all the types of possible suspicious incidents, nor all the kinds of possible watchers. None the less, it is significant that our data follow the same pattern as those of the Dutch in finding that personal characteristics of the watchers did not seem to have any influence on which kind of informal or formal action options would be chosen. We did not investigate the personality profiles or political beliefs of watchers; but the broad socio-economic variables, such as age, sex, socio-economic status, whether individual or business, marital status, and time lived in an area, did not even approach significance in determining which of the options in Tables 6.1 and 6.2 were chosen. Some of these personal characteristics (particularly sex) have a major influence on fear of crime and beliefs about victimization (see Chapter 7). They may have some effect on informal action, but a major survey will be needed to tease out any influence, since, in respect to intervention, they seemed to be eclipsed by the situational variables of the type of conduct, victim, suspect, and acceptable responses in that area. We shall, therefore, concentrate next on setting out a model of the situational characteristics that seemed to influence intervention.

Situational characteristics of intervention: a model

The range of options for action when something suspicious is seen is very wide. In our log of incidents, almost all the options were used by someone at some time faced with a particular kind of situation. Can we now pull out of that morass of data the factors which lead people to take one course of action rather than another?

FACTORS CONCERNED WITH THE INCIDENT ITSELF

The most obvious set of factors concern what the person being observed is thought to be doing – the potential offence or the behaviour of the suspect. We have mentioned many of these in previous chapters. In Chapter 4 we explored the distinction between 'real crime' and 'other crime'. Where people made such a distinction, it served not only as a typology of offences, but also as a pointer towards action. If watchers were reasonably certain that they were witnessing a real crime or the precursor to it, positive action would be considered – ringing the police, or getting someone else to ring the police, or going out to confront the suspect. And that action would be taken, unless the watcher was either disenchanted with the police or concerned about future retaliation by the suspect. But other crime would provoke a different range of considered responses – warning off the culprit, telling the owner, informing the police later, or taking further action.

Many watched behaviours, however, are not nearly so clear-cut – people hanging around outside houses, for example. In these cases, watchers seek clues as to what they may be seeing. A prime clue was the kind of person being watched, coupled with the watcher's stereotypes of who does what. As we have seen, certain kinds of people tend to be associated with particular offences. Strange adult men were stereotyped as burglars; youths as troublemakers or vandals in rural areas and also as burglars and thieves in urban areas. The behaviour being viewed can, therefore, influence two elements of people's decisionmaking – the distinctions being made between real crime and other crime/nuisance/disorder, and the decisions about what is actually going on.

FACTORS CONCERNING THE SUSPECT

There were two major factors relating to the person being watched which affected the watcher's preferred course of action: (a) whether the person was known to the watcher, and (b) his or her age – in particular whether the person was characterized as a child, a youth, a girl, or an adult. The characterization, however, did not always tally with the actual age of the person – those between 11 and 20 years old often being given quite different labels by different watchers.

If the watched person was known, the response tended to be particularized: action would be tailored to that individual, rather than being a generic or 'tariff' response to 'children', 'youths', etc. Unless the suspect had previously inspired fear in some way, action taken against someone known personally was more likely to involve the watcher personally in some positive action, such as challenging the suspect, telling him or her off, or informing parents:

'Teenagers know me because their parents know me from the [club]. So I do intervene if I see them doing something. I can tell them to stop something and they do. I buy them drinks in the [club] and they do respect me.'

(urban area)

'It depends on who it is: if I knew them and they weren't meant to be there, I'd go round and say how are you and cause a conversation. If it was strangers, I wouldn't know if they were meant to be there, so I'd mind my own business. There'd be 359 phone calls to the police without me adding another one.'

(Northam)

Attitudes to the local gang were far more mixed – some being afraid, some treating them as large, unruly children. Responses varied accordingly.

The perceived youth of the person being watched was one of the most powerful factors affecting intervention. The increased willingness of people in the urban areas to call in the police to deal with more minor crime was due both to differences in categorization of crime and, more particularly, to different stereotypes of youths. Certain kinds of minor crime were more likely to fall into the category of 'real crime' in urban areas – and those often seen to be committing such crimes (youths) were also more likely to be suspected of doing something much more serious (with some basis in fact – see Chapter 3). In general, people were far more prepared to take direct action themselves against children than against youths, and against youths than against adults. Children would be stopped, where youths would be warned and adults watched or ignored.

Previous researchers have attributed this greater willingness to intervene directly against young people to their lesser potential to hit back physically: to their perceived lesser likelihood of immediate retaliation or of causing injury to the intervener (Greenberg and Ruback 1984; Steinmetz 1984). In our study, the likelihood of physical retaliation was one factor in people's minds in the urban area, but a far more important factor in both rural and urban areas seemed to be social retaliation – fear of embarrassment. Challenging someone or, even worse, telling someone off and then finding he or she was on legitimate business was a very worrying possibility to most of our watchers. However, young people seemed to be fair game for telling off – the more so the younger they were. It was thought that little blame would be attached by neighbours or parents to those who told children off wrongly – and, of course, the children might well not tell their parents. The older idea of communal chastisement (that each adult has a duty and a responsibility to control the children in the area) only persisted in parts of the villages, but the licence it gave to interveners remained everywhere.

FACTORS CONCERNING THE POTENTIAL VICTIM

Many of the potentially obvious distinctions between types of property as potential targets did not seem to have any influence on people's willingness to intervene or on the type of action they took. Businesses, for example, were as well protected as houses. Business people did not usually expect their (non-business) neighbours to feel responsibility, but the neighbours often did. People would ring up the owner of a shop next door to tell him that one of his windows had been left open, or report to the police any youths hanging around a factory, as much as they would with a neighbouring house or flat.

The most important variables were possession and social obligation. Possession is the most obvious – if it was your property, then it was definitely thought to be up to you to take action. No one else was expected to do anything, if they knew you knew what was going on! This was partly because social ownership of an incident would be assigned to the owner of the target property (or the victim, in an assault). It was partly a pragmatic judgement: the owner was assumed to have a much higher probability of knowing whether the behaviour really was deviant and wrong than anyone else (you're supposed to know who is allowed to use your property). Of course this did not take into account the difficulties that victims are known to have in assessing whether a crime really has been committed. Maguire (1982) and Lejeune and Alex (1973) have both shown how problematic it is for victims to realize they are victims: burglary victims, for example, tend to assume that their children have messed up the house, rather than that a burglar has been in.

If the watcher was the victim, then this assignment of social ownership and responsibility drastically cut down the options for action. The victim might go and discuss the incident with neighbours or others, but ultimately the choice was up to him or her: either to go and deal with it or to ignore it and accept that nothing would be done about it.

Possessing the target of a crime is the clearest form of ownership. However, in terms of intervention, being officially responsible for it or feeling responsible for it (because you are on the committee that runs it or it is just outside your house and in some way an extension of your territory) also amounted to a (less powerful) form of ownership. It correspondingly increased the likelihood that the watcher would take positive action. In our study, business people took on the responsibility for their premises; and members of organizations, responsibility for the territory belonging to the organization: 'If they were on the village hall field, I'd stop children or adults. If they were looking for a scrap I'd call the police – I feel responsible for it' (chairman of village hall committee).

Where membership of organizing bodies was fairly widespread – in the villages – this form of ownership involved substantial sections of the adult population. In the urban area, such organizations were town-wide, rather than localized to the residential area, and were largely hobby-based rather than facility-based. There was less ownership and less potential for intervention. Businesses that operated in the street (such as car dealers/repairers and news vendors) took responsibility for their part of the street. Householders were not really involved.

There may be scope for increasing this kind of intervention in urban areas: the movement towards tenants' groups (NACRO 1987b) and the action projects inspired by NACRO and the Priority Estates Project of the Department of the Environment are seeking to tap this mechanism in order to stabilize declining areas. Such groups seem to be moderately successful in that they are prepared to take action within bounded facilities such as community centres, but they may not care about the streets. It may be necessary to use other people such as street vendors for this. One problem, though, is that the form of direct action taken may not be to the liking of the official agencies that set up the informal groups/businesses – or indeed the residents. A major difficulty with harnessing and promoting informal social control is that, by definition, it cannot subsequently be controlled by official agencies which depend for their information and input on the informal mechanisms. Groups may become too powerful, too deviant, for the liking of some. We shall return to this problem of 'policing' informal social control in Chapter 10.

A less powerful form of responsibility than that of ownership derives from the social ties between neighbours – social obligation. In the villages and, to a lesser extent, in the urban area, watchers felt they were responsible for protecting property situated within a particular distance around their homes. It would be possible to draw a 'spatial area of social obligation' for each household, containing all the premises and ground over which they felt some responsibility. Social obligation was an amalgam of friendship and nearness. People felt responsible for their friends' houses, but they also felt responsible for their neighbours, even if they didn't know them or didn't like them. As we saw above, they even felt responsible for next-door shops, offices, and factories. These areas of social obligation were not circular – their boundaries were drawn by lines of sight and by friendship ties. There might even be several small areas for one household.

Spatial areas of social obligation must not be confused with feelings of 'community', in its cosy sense of feeling that you 'belong' to an area. 'Community' is a much used and often ill-used term (see Chapter 1). In our particular case, feelings of 'belonging' were relatively rare in the urban area (see Chapter 2), with only 41 per cent of residents saying that they felt they lived in a named and cohesive part of the town. There was also no correlation between someone feeling that they belonged in this minimal way and their propensity to watch their neighbours. One may, after all, be equally nosy about people one distrusts or hates!

We are suggesting that it is possible to draw out for each household or business four kinds of spatial areas: the radius of watching; the spatial area of problems thought to affect that particular neighbourhood; the spatial area of residents' or business people's knowledge about the occurrence of problematic instances that have happened over, say, the last year; and the spatial area of social obligation. In general, we feel that the radius of watching is the smallest. It will be confined by sight lines from rooms at the front of the house, except for businesses or residents who spend much time in the street. It is likely that the spatial area of problems is the next largest, normally confined to a street or part of a street. Knowledge of incidents is the greatest, extending over several streets. Social obligation is likely to be an irregularly shaped area, perhaps with several distinct parts. It will vary in size considerably according to membership of organizations and friendship ties, but is likely to be larger than the radius of watching. All of these areas, however, are far smaller than the named parts of cities or villages, and smaller than what are usually termed 'communities'.

The action expected of those in a position of social obligation was not as great as that expected of owners, or those in a position of real responsibility. It was to do something, rather than to do any particular thing. Carrying on watching and telling the owner about the incident later, or ringing up the owner immediately, was as much approved of as direct confrontation with the suspect. It was permissible to 'pass the buck', which definitely stopped with the owner.

Social obligation was increased if the potential victim was particularly vulnerable (an old person, for example) or if it was known that the potential victim was out or away: 'The house opposite previously had an elderly lady and the children climbed over the garden wall. I told them to go away. They talked back about that but they went' (urban area – only incident of direct intervention for female watcher). 'If I know people have gone away, I keep an eye on them without being asked to. If I saw people there and I was certain they were strangers, I would go up to them' (Northam).

Social obligation was decreased (and in some cases vanished) if the neighbour often had strangers around. The fear of embarrassment became greater than the obligation: 'One does keep an eye on things like people pulling up opposite – you do watch and see. But I wouldn't take notice of the bungalow opposite – they sell things – so there are always people round the back' (Northam).

CONSEQUENCES OF ACTION

The potential offence, the kind of person involved, and the likely victim form the raw material of the situation that the watcher is weighing up when deciding what action to take. But the decision is also crucially affected by the potential consequences of action for the watcher. And as new facts about the situation are revealed, so the consequences are constantly being re-evaluated.

Previous research has focused on the most obvious consequence – immediate retaliation by the suspect and possible danger for the watcher if he or she intervenes personally (van Dijk, Roell, and Steinmetz 1982; Steinmetz 1984). In our study, immediate retaliation was a significant factor determining inaction in the urban area:

'You hear screaming. At one time we would go out to see what the problem was. Now we stay in and leave them to it – people are now unpredictable round here. Sometimes you hear such a commotion, but we turn the lights out.'

Steinmetz (1984) has argued that a person meeting a known offender need not fear retaliation, but this of course depends on the offender's reputation. In general, though it was true that known offenders inspired less fear than strangers (see Chapter 7), adults or the local gang of youths might still be sufficiently unpleasant for people to desist, even in the villages:

'If I see three or four kids, I say "scheming little buggers, what are you scheming?" And they say "Oh Christ, it's [X] again." I say "Yes it is, I've seen you, so go home." You don't argue with them – just keep walking and talking and they'll do it. They know me. People are frightened because of the abuse they'll get – women don't want it – but they'll never use foul language on me.'   (Northam shopkeeper)

In the villages, the fear of immediate retaliation was certainly less important in promoting inaction than the fear of social embarrassment (confronting strangers wrongly) or subsequent retaliation (for example, damage to one's car) by the offenders. In the urban area, it was more seriously regarded, but generally still only in respect of drunks and people known to be abusive or violent.

These conflicts illustrate the high emotional charge that infuses decisions about intervention. As Greenberg and Ruback (1984) show, just realizing you are watching a disorderly or criminal event causes anxiety. From our study, this distress seemed not only to be a result of realizing you have the potential responsibility to do something about a serious situation, but also a result of being aware that the consequences of your actions, if mistaken, are likely also to be serious – to yourself, to your relations with your neighbours (whichever way you make your mistake), and to your relations with the police, if you've brought them out on a wild goose chase. Seen in this light, delays before notification of the police become both unsurprising and likely. Intervention is a serious social decision, placed suddenly upon people who are often surprised and shocked that they have become involved in such a situation.

PERCEPTIONS OF DEVIANCE

So far, we have been treating the nature of the situation as relatively unproblematic. However, people vary in the degree to which they class incidents as deviant for their particular place and time. People vary in their views as to the criminality of different kinds of conduct. They vary in their tolerance of disapproved-of conduct displayed by particular groups, the old being far less tolerant of the activities of the young than the young themselves, for example. And they vary in their moral tolerance of, for example, crime committed against businesses, as opposed to that committed against individuals. As has been shown in local crime surveys (for example, Jones, Maclean, and Young 1986), areas are split. People have different views. In high-crime areas, with high proportions of both victims and offenders, people may be frightened of each other. Disorder is, by its very nature, a product of conflict. We must not assume that we shall find a consensus of views in any area. Nor, as Smith (1987) has said, can we assume that such consensus can be produced either by policing or by informal social action.

CERTAINTY

Watchers may decide that they are viewing a deviant situation but they can never be sure. Is that man really a burglar? Is that screaming girl out there in the dark at the end of the street being assaulted or in high spirits? Instances of public disorder – fights, rowdiness, assaults, menacing groups – are intrinsically impossible for any one person to watch and define, as we have argued elsewhere (Johnstone and Shapland 1987). They move around, involve different people at different times, form, split, and reform again.

In the current study, we found from the police message pads that people in the urban area seemed to need to be more certain that an offence was actually taking place before they contacted the police. This seemed from the interview data to be due partly to the lower proportion of neighbours known in the urban area; partly to the greater likelihood of seemingly strange conduct with legitimate explanations; and partly to a greater unwillingness to become involved at all (stemming from fear of immediate retaliation and less knowledge of the offenders): 'There are people walking past with TVs, etc. all the time, but here people are moving in and out every five minutes, so I can usually think of reasons for suspicious things' (urban area). 'At the time you think it is out of the ordinary. But not enough to do anything. It's a public road – he has a right to be there' (urban area).

ALTERNATIVE COURSES OF ACTION

Finally, it is of course true that people rarely have only one course of action open to them. They are juggling with the possibility of several. There was always choice, and watchers were aware that there was that choice. As we saw above, the situations were stressful and the consequences serious. Yet often decision-making had to be accomplished quickly, if any action was to be taken at all.

The alternatives considered were, as we saw at the beginning of the chapter, relatively similar in rural and urban areas. However, residents in urban areas did not seem to have the possibility of engaging community groups or responsible individuals in further action. Not only did this seem to restrict the scope for informal social control in the urban area, it also put more pressure on watchers to act immediately. Having further action as an alternative implies the possibility of deferring a final decision until the matter has been talked over with others. Where it is absent, and where fewer neighbours are known (Chapter 2), support in decision-making is lessened. Differences in perceptions of deviance, certainty, etc. between watchers are likely to become more prevalent and differentiation in decision-making is likely to become more pronounced. Lack of a group context for taking decisions about problems will also tend to decrease certainty and promote inaction, given the likely negative consequences of inappropriate action. It is hardly surprising, therefore, that urban residents both used the police more, and for more trivial incidents, and, at the same time, ignored more problems, crime, and disorder.

To cope with all this uncertainty, watchers seemed to rely on stereotypes of suspicious events for their decisions on immediate action. These stereotypes were an amalgam of the most likely offender, victim, behaviour, and result in a particular situation – the 'ideal' situation, as Christie (1986) would term it. The more constant aspects of the stereotype seemed to cover the nature of the offender, the potential victim, and the offence. The preferred option for action, however, seemed to be more personal to the watcher, though almost all watchers were aware of all the options and would use each one in particular situations. In the language of Greenberg and Ruback (1984), people's repertoires of incident-related scripts for action were similar, but their favourite story differed.

Involving the police: one option for action

Bringing in the police is just one of the options open to watchers, victims, and responsible people. These have the responsibility of choosing whether to involve the police, and at what time, and in what manner. We have referred to that option several times in the development of the model; it is now time to bring those suggestions together and consider in what situations the police are likely to become involved.

The clearest situation in which the police would definitely be called was an instance of real crime. People would call the police not in order to gain any instrumental benefit (getting aid in catching the offender or stopping a situation from escalating), but because the police represent the law and order forces of the society and so should, in a moral sense, be informed. In these situations, the offence would also be 'handed over' to the police and, for watchers at least, the police would be expected to take the decisions as to how to proceed.

However, the police were also called to a wide range of other kinds of incidents, many of which were not concerned with crime at all. Sometimes, the police were used because they were thought to possess particular abilities or powers to deal with a particular kind of incident. It might be that watchers felt they could not cope with a particular kind of suspect (particularly an adult or a stranger). Or it might be thought that the police would be able to tie the incident up with others outside those particular small areas of watching, knowledge, and social obligation. However, the person calling the police would typically still have ideas as to what should happen to the suspect and what the police should do. Very often people did not know what the police actually did after leaving the scene (see Chapter 4). They then tended to suppose that offenders were processed formally, since this is still the image conveyed by the police (in spite of the fact that, for example, the majority of juvenile offenders are now cautioned). On the rare occasions on which they did find out what happened, they might not approve. People hated to criticize a body for which they had considerable respect (see Chapter 8). Yet there often remained a discrepancy between what happened to a case and what they felt should happen. This manifested itself in expressions of unease about the practices of the police.

The assistance of the police might be sought when informal options had been tried and failed – or where the problem seemed to be getting worse. It seemed that, in any one particular area, certain groups of youths would start to indulge in a wave of, say, vandalism of public and private property over a period of months. It would take time for this to become apparent to the residents and business people in the area, for them to pinpoint the group involved, and for the initial responses of telling the youths off and talking to their parents to be tried without apparent result. These 'waves' or 'spasms' of problems seemed to have affected most villages at some time and to exist in urban areas as well (though knowledge might well be less coherent there).

Approaches to the police on this kind of problem were not only of a formal kind. Where there was a known, local officer, an informal chat on the street corner was often the method employed, and people known to have a personal relationship with or some form of privileged access to him or her, might be 'briefed' to talk about the problem. The parish council secretary would be one person in this position in a village, as would the teachers of the local school. Business people fulfilled the role in both the urban area and in Southton. In Northam, where there was no known, local officer (see Chapter 9), contacts had to be more formal, with invitations issued to attend meetings.

Finally, people might call on the police simply because they couldn't think who else to call. This is not the positive decision to call on a body whose actions are predicted (even if wrongly predicted or disliked), but the result of a lack of any more appropriate response. Jones, Maclean, and Young (1986) have suggested that the police are, inappropriately, called upon to deal with many problems of a social-service nature which should be handled by other statutory or local agencies if these possessed the capacity to respond quickly at all times of the day and night. We are not so sanguine that other agencies could provide an adequate response on their own. Problems for which the informal resources of the area are insufficient often require at least the threat of force for their resolution – and the police have a monopoly over the legitimate use of physical coercion. In our study, the lack of further action options in the urban area was not mitigated by a localized presence of any of the other social agencies. More frequent recourse to the police (often for what they would term 'rubbish calls') and greater disregard for worrying problems may well have been due both to the lack of informal options for further action and to the lack of a local presence by the statutory and voluntary agencies.

The typical victimization survey asks merely why people did not report offences to the police. It is clear from the above discussion that the standard answers – that the offence was too trivial, that the police were not the appropriate agency – do not start to do justice to the very complex processes of interaction and decision-making which people go through when they become watchers, victims, or responsible people in respect of suspicious incidents and problems. Intervention is a stressful and difficult matter. It is bounded by views of appropriate action and by powerful ties of social obligation and custom which produce the social order that exists in neighbourhoods. The reports of intervention and its results are also the raw material for people's perceptions of the need for crime prevention and their concern about crime – matters to which we turn in the next chapter.

7
Concern about crime

Crime itself is no longer the only problem faced by residents, business people, and policy-makers. Fear of crime and concern about the amount of crime taking place in neighbourhoods are significant problems in their own right (Hough and Mayhew 1985; Ministerie van Justitie 1985; Mayhew forthcoming). There is a feeling that fear of crime is so high among certain groups, particularly women, that they are imprisoned in their own homes, leaving the streets empty and more tempting to criminals. Some say that in high-crime areas disorder, crime, and fear act in concert to encourage those who can to move out of what are seen as increasingly undesirable areas, further tipping them downwards and again encouraging criminals to move in (Wilson and Kelling 1982; Skogan 1987). When talking about problems in a neighbourhood, we have to consider not only crime and disorder, but also fear and concern.

Concern and fear are also relevant to crime prevention. When taking decisions on crime prevention programmes, a delicate balance has to be struck between, on the one hand, persuading people to take crime (and crime prevention) seriously and, on the other, alarming people, thereby increasing the level of fear. Winkel (1987) has shown that even seemingly innocuous crime prevention publicity campaigns can 'overshoot' their mark and encourage unwanted crime prevention action. Some susceptible people take the message so much to heart that they start purchasing firearms or ferocious dogs, or think about wiring their boundary fence to the mains.

The connection between concern, fear, and crime prevention is crucial. Crime prevention, to be effective, needs to reach those who are likely to be victimized. More pertinently, it needs to be tailored to people's environments and targeted on the specific kinds of victimization that people are likely to experience. Publicity on window locks is no good to those living in rented dwellings who are not allowed to alter their structure. Publicity on how to avoid street attacks will only alarm those who never go out. In our study, we have tried to explore people's beliefs and concern about the particular kinds of crime that affected them and to see what lessons emerge for crime prevention techniques and for people's views about their areas.

Concern, worry, or fear?

The term 'fear of crime' has often been used loosely to cover everything from not being prepared to go out alone at night to people's overall view of the amount of crime in the country. There are many aspects to concern, worry, and fear. At least eight have been identified in large-scale surveys, such as those of Hough and Mayhew (1983, 1985) and Skogan and Maxfield (1981):

1. people's opinions about the amount of crime in society;
2. their opinions about the amount of crime in their own area;
3. their perceptions of the likelihood that they will be victimized;
4. their overall concern about crime as a problem;
5. their concern about the problems posed in their areas by specific forms of crime;
6. their fear about going out of doors;
7. their avoidance behaviour;
8. the precautions they take.

Each of these appears to have slightly different associations with such personal and socio-economic variables as sex and age.

From our small-scale study, we cannot hope to tease out further the complex relationships. We did, however, ask our respondents a large number of questions designed to separate the different aspects. We can also relate people's answers to their knowledge about crimes that had occurred in their own area and the actual extent of victimization and so try to see what is supporting their beliefs and feelings. This, however, will not be a simple task. Indeed, it is likely to be much more complex than people's responses to suspicious incidents and their decisions to intervene. Intervention, typically, was a decision made relatively quickly, with its prime determinant being the total character of the incident. Fear and concern are likely to be of long standing for an individual, with any accompanying preventive and avoidance behaviours having become habitual. Their roots may lie far in the individual's past (see Stanko 1987) and may no longer be remembered.

We asked people about their views on burglary and assault, and about their more general views on crime. They tended to see the two types of crime in quite different ways, each of which was also different from their general views. We are, therefore, forced to present all these findings separately, though this may appear rather a long-winded way of going about things.

Concern about crime in the neighbourhood

When we asked people how much crime they thought there was in their area, those from the villages gave a totally different picture to those in

Table 7.1 *Estimates of amounts of crime, by area*

| | Urban areas | | | | Rural areas | |
| | 1 | 2 | 3 | 4 | Northam | Southton |
	%	%	%	%	%	%
A lot of crime	0	15	5	9	0	0
Quite a lot of crime	29	22	25	29	10	0
About average amount of crime	13	15	10	26	2	6
Not much crime	52	33	58	29	36	38
Almost no crime	7	15	3	9	52	56

Table 7.2 *People considering they were very likely or quite likely to become a victim of burglary or assault*

	Urban area %	Northam %	Southton %
Burglary	24	1	1
Assault	16	4	8

the urban area (Table 7.1). In Southton, for example, no one thought that there was more than an average amount of crime. Rural business people shared the residents' perception of a low crime level. In general, estimations of the likelihood of being burgled followed very closely perceptions of the amount of crime in general (see Table 7.1), whereas their views on assault were rather different (Table 7.2).

The only characteristic of interviewees that was related significantly to perceived amount of crime was what we have called 'opulence' – the researcher's judgement of the quantity and value of consumer goods owned. Perceptions of the amount of crime in the area were highly related to perceptions that one's own house or business would be burgled. Both residents and business people were acutely aware of the value of their possessions and their presumed attractiveness to thieves and burglars. Other socio-economic variables, such as sex, age, class, length of residence in the area, race, and whether a person lived alone, did not show any significant relationship (though of course, in a small-scale study, only very major effects will show up as significant).

How accurate were these beliefs? For each area, we know the amount of recorded crime and we also have an incident log for the year prior to the study (see Chapter 4).

Beliefs about the amount of crime seemed to reflect the gross differences in recorded crime that existed between rural and urban areas. Skogan (1987), in an integrated analysis of data from forty American neighbourhoods, also shows that people's beliefs about the extent of crime problems are strongly related to the amount of recorded crime and the amount of disorder in these fairly large areas. However, in our study, beliefs about the amount of crime did not seem to reflect the local pool of knowledge. The number of incidents in the incident log for the villages was of the same order of magnitude as the level in the urban area (see Chapter 4). The number of incidents that had occurred in the villages and which someone knew about was the same in the rural as in the urban areas. Moreover, when we look more closely at the recorded crime rates for the two urban beats, the relationship between perceived crime and recorded crime does not hold up. Urban areas 1 and 2 were in urban beat 1, which had over twice the amount of recorded crime as urban beat 2, which contained areas 3 and 4. But people's perceptions of the amount of crime were highest in the most opulent area – area 4.

Recorded crime levels seem to be good predictors of gross differences between areas in beliefs about the level of crime. They fall down in more subtle, local comparisons. What other factors might be influential? Possibilities include differences in people's definitions of what is a crime (if more things are regarded as 'nuisances', rather than 'crime', then crime levels will be thought to be lower); differences in personal experience of crime; and differences in personal knowledge of crime in that particular area.

DIFFERENCES IN DEFINITIONS

We saw in Chapter 5 that residents had different ideas about what they considered to be 'crime', and that, particularly, there were variations between rural and urban areas. 'Real crime' was a very circumscribed category as far as most villagers were concerned – and when villagers were answering the question: 'How much crime do you think there is here?', they understood it to mean 'real crime': 'From a crime point of view, it's very quiet here. From our point of view, there are little bursts of petty crime' (Northam).

In the town, by contrast, definitions of crime tended to be slightly more inclusive (though they would still not cover the whole spectrum of the criminal law). In area 4, particularly, some included vandalism within the term 'crime' – and were aware of the activities of the local vandals. This then is one possible explanation for the differences in beliefs about the amount of crime. But the slight differences in definition do not match the magnitude of the effects we observed.

Table 7.3 *Personal experiences of crime*

| | Urban areas | | | | Rural areas | |
| | *1* | *2* | *3* | *4* | *Northam* | *Southton* |
	%	%	%	%	%	%
As a victim	76	67	46	69	27	16
As a witness	18	27	32	19	12	9
Noticing damage in the area	67	79	68	86	68	70

DIFFERENCES IN PERSONAL EXPERIENCES

There are several ways in which people can experience crime – as a victim, as a witness, as an offender, or through noticing any visible after-effects of crime. The proportions of people in the urban and rural areas who said that they had been touched by crime in at least one of these four ways in the last year are shown in Table 7.3.

Not surprisingly, the percentage of those interviewed who said they had been a victim of a crime in the last year was much smaller in the villages than in the urban area. However, as we noted above, the differences between urban areas were not in line with those relating to beliefs about crime levels. Businesses in the urban area were much more likely to say that they had been victimized than were individuals (85 per cent of businesses in the urban area had been the victim of at least one crime in the last year) – and businesses were most prevalent in area 2, with some in areas 1 and 4. There was no such difference in victimization of businesses in the rural areas. So, if beliefs about crime are related to business victimization, then some of the difference may be explained.

People were far less likely to have witnessed a crime than they were to have been a victim. The percentages in the urban areas were very similar to those in the Dutch national victimization study (Steinmetz 1983). There was no difference between business people and residents in the likelihood of having been a witness, nor did it relate to personal characteristics such as sex, age, or household opulence, nor to victimization.

Seeing damage to property (one of the most common forms of seeing the after-effects of crime) was very common, despite the rapid repairs carried out in the villages, particularly Northam. Levels in the villages were of the same order of magnitude as those in the urban area, showing that the similar magnitude of vandalism in the incident log was accompanied by people noticing its after-effects.

Few people admitted to having been an offender in the previous year (though they did acknowledge past misdeeds). There were only eleven admitted offenders in the urban area, two in Northam, and one in Southton. Most of these offences related to assaults or motoring offences rather than property offences.

We can correlate people's beliefs about the amount of crime with their experience of victimization, witnessing, offending, and noticing damage. We find that, within the urban area, the correlation between high estimates of the amount of crime and noticing damage was highly significant (p<.004) and that with personal experience of victimization approached significance (p<.07). In other studies, both victimization and witnessing have been shown to be related to beliefs about the prevalence of crime (Hough and Mayhew 1985; Skogan 1987).

DIFFERENCES IN KNOWLEDGE ABOUT CRIME

Knowledge about crime comes not only from personal experience, but also from the media and local gossip. Media coverage tends to follow the levels of recorded crime, with well-known biases towards over-reporting of violent and sexual crime (Ditton and Duffy 1982; Smith 1984). In our study, the media did not appear to be picking up either unreported or unrecorded crime. Nor did people seem to have any idea of what had happened to crimes after their reporting to the police (Chapter 4). Neither residents nor business people mentioned the media as a source for their beliefs about the occurrence of crime in their area, though newspapers were an obvious source of reference for their views about crime and society nationally and for some people's fear of crime.

Gossip in the local area, however, did seem to be important. Residents picked up knowledge about incidents of crime in their local area from their neighbours and, particularly, from local shopkeepers, publicans, garage hands, and roundsmen. 'Crime' in this sense was normally defined as 'real crime', and the largest proportion of this was burglary. People's knowledge about burglary varied considerably between areas. In urban area 4, people's awareness of others' burglaries was quite widespread, though no one knew who was doing it:

'There's a lot of burglary, petty thieving, and break-ins over the walls. At a party at Christmas, someone said that there had been thirty break-ins within this triangle of houses within several months. We find it very strange that it's been going on for years and no one has any idea who it is.'

In area 1, by contrast, the number of burglaries was as high or even higher, but the spread of knowledge about them was much more limited and the suspected culprits were known to many of those aware of the burglaries: 'It's mainly petty – just one of those things – mainly the kids around here.' Beliefs about the amount of crime in one's area does, then, seem to be related to knowledge about the occurrence of local crime, particularly burglary.

CRIME IN ONE'S OWN NEIGHBOURHOOD

People's judgements and beliefs about the amount of crime in their area mostly concerned 'real crime'. For the villages and for the majority in urban areas 1, 2, and 3, this did not include vandalism, and was exemplified by burglary. Possession of valuable items that might be burgled tended to heighten fears of victimization and beliefs about the amount of crime in the area. Experience of victimization and noticing damage in the area seemed to be related to views that there was more crime around, as did greater local knowledge of actual incidents through gossip. Businesses were a particularly powerful focus for passing on this knowledge and their own victimization was influential in creating beliefs about crime. In area 4, opulence, more inclusive definitions of crime, and worried businesses came together. In area 2, there were many businesses with high victimization rates. In area 1, knowledge about burglaries was relatively poor, people were distinctly not affluent and definitions were tightly drawn. In the villages, burglaries (though not vandalism) were rare, and definitions of crime were the most exclusive of all. Knowledge of crime was relatively widespread, but the infrequent occurrence of burglary, and people's beliefs that they knew what was going on, encouraged the view that crime was rare.

Perceptions of crime tended to form a coherent whole. So people who thought that there was a large amount of crime were also significantly more likely to think there had been an increase in crime in the last two or three years and to think that they had a higher chance of being burgled. This coherence is also apparent in the much larger, more statistically sophisticated, American studies, such as those by Skogan (1987) and Skogan and Maxfield (1981).

Concern about assault

It is in the area of assault that we come closest to so-called 'fear of crime'. However, even here it is necessary to distinguish between fear and beliefs about crime, including perceived likelihood of victimization (Maxfield 1984; Skogan and Maxfield 1981; van Dijk 1978). Equally, it is necessary to distinguish between fear of assault and fear of other crimes, such as burglary. We shall explore people's beliefs about how likely they were to be assaulted in the area in which they lived, before going on to look at how emotionally charged those beliefs were, and whether there was a similar emotional charge to views about burglary.

People in Northam thought they were very unlikely to be assaulted (see Table 7.2): 'Perfectly safe — I've never heard of any trouble. There's nobody you need be afraid of.' Southton people were slightly more wary, since they felt that the glue-sniffing activities of the local 'gang' of youths made them relatively unpredictable. In both villages, people cited the lack of known incidents of violence, apart from at particular social events, like discos: 'It's not likely. I walk round the village in the evening for something to do. I've never met anyone. The discos have fights but I don't go to the discos anyway' (Southton).

Estimated likelihood of assault was significantly related to judgements about the overall amount of crime (p<.05 Northam, p<.004 Southton) and the chance of burglary (p<.002 Northam and Southton). Personal characteristics were not important. Beliefs were firmly grounded in local knowledge and events; newcomers to the village were as likely to share these views as those who had been there a long time. Even those who had come there from high-crime urban areas had developed a relaxed view very quickly.

In contrast, people in the urban areas accepted the possibility of violence occurring to them in their own neighbourhood. Their perception of their personal risk was related to their views about how attractive they thought they were likely to be to potential violent offenders. Some people thought attack was unlikely, provided no stupid risks were taken: 'Everyone has it in the back of their mind. We're not frightened, but we're wary.' Others felt more vulnerable: 'You could be attacked anywhere in town.'

Apart from urban area 1, where levels of perceived threat were lower, there did not seem to be great differences between the areas. Perceived vulnerability seemed to relate not to knowledge of local assaults, or indeed any known incidents or personal experience, but to people's personal characteristics. There was a vast range of beliefs and pet theories in all the urban areas: people living next door to each other might well hold completely different views about the potential violence in their street (see also Albrow 1982 for similar findings). People looked for support for their beliefs not to local knowledge, but to messages culled from the national and town-wide media. Their perception of their vulnerability seemed to be a facet of their suspiciousness of the world outside.

The statistical relationships reflected this. The perceived likelihood of assault was related not to judgements about the amount of crime in the area (or estimates of vulnerability to burglary) but to personal characteristics, particularly sex (women were more likely to think they would be assaulted; p<.05 level). Age, opulence, race, and time spent in the area were, however, not significant, the finding with respect to age replicating that of the *British Crime Survey* (Hough and Mayhew 1985).

Fear of assault

Linked with people's perceived vulnerability to assault is their emotional reaction to the possibility of it. We asked a number of questions to tap concern and fear about assault – perceived likelihood of victimization, feelings about going out alone after dark, patterns of behaviour, and how people were affected by feelings about crime. Previous work, unfortunately, has tended to concentrate on one particular measure: whether people say they feel safe walking alone in their area after dark. This is both exclusive and overinclusive. On the one hand, it asks about what may be a relatively unusual occurrence: walking alone after dark, as opposed to driving, or going out with others. On the other, it combines all sorts of reasons for feeling unsafe: not liking the dark, feeling unsteady walking on uneven pavements, just not liking to go out at all. The measure is called 'fear of crime' – but it could cover many other things as well. In our study, it seemed that fears about walking alone after dark tapped into a large number of beliefs, concerns, and worries. Our questions typically produced a long speech in which judgements about the prevalence of crime (typically assault), likelihood of personal victimization, preferred lifestyle, availability of cars and buses, fear of the dark, fear of spooky places, acceptable modes of behaviour (especially for women), and resulting habits were all intertwined:

> 'I would not now walk about even round here very willingly. After dark, I certainly wouldn't go in the back ways. I go by car. In winter I don't put the car in the garage, 'cos you have to get out and open the garage doors. Until two years ago, I wouldn't have thought of that. It's not because I've heard of it round here. It's just the town generally. Not the papers, but at work, what people say.'   (urban area 4).

We shall try to disentangle this package into its component parts of levels of concern or fear, places which evoke this concern, and resulting patterns of behaviour. However, we must remember that, for the person concerned, the package seems to be holistic and self-reinforcing. For once, attitudes and behaviour appear to be in synchrony.

LEVELS OF CONCERN AND FEAR

As Skogan (1987) has shown, people's levels of fear or concern as evinced by their answers to the question: 'How safe to you feel or would you feel being out alone in your neighbourhood at night?' do not relate closely to their individual likelihood of being assaulted (or robbed or sexually assaulted). In general, most people who report being fearful of crime have not themselves been victimized and many are not in a high-risk group as far as prevalence of victimization by assault is concerned

Table 7.4 *Feelings about walking the streets alone at night (fear of crime)*

| | Urban areas | | | | | Northam | Southton |
| | *1* | *2* | *3* | *4* | *Average* | | |
	%	%	%	%	%	%	%
Very unsafe	0	10	11	19	10	4	1
Unsafe	10	35	24	13	20	10	11
Average	0	7	11	13	8	5	6
Reasonably safe	19	14	13	22	17	6	18
Quite safe	71	35	42	34	45	75	63

(though there are disputes in relation to some street offences – see Jones, Maclean, and Young 1986; Hough and Mayhew 1983, 1985). However, when analysed at a neighbourhood level, fear of crime is related strongly and positively to crime rates (Skogan 1987; Maxfield 1984; Sparks, Genn, and Dodd 1977; Knol and Soetenhorst 1979). In other words, people who live in areas where there is a lot of personal victimization feel more afraid of being victimized (see also Jones, Maclean, and Young 1986). And this correlation does not seem to be due solely to the social or economic characteristics of the area, at least in the USA.

Our study found much the same patterns. Levels of fear or of concern about crime, as measured by the same question, differed between rural and urban areas according to the crime rate (see Table 7.4). And, at the individual level, fear of walking alone at night and perceived likelihood of victimization by assault in the streets were highly correlated ($p < .001$ in all areas). However, the rural–urban differences for fear of crime were much smaller than those for likelihood of assault or any other measure of actual crime (recorded crime, incident log) or perceived crime (overall amount, burglary). People were quite clear about whether they were afraid or not – there were very few 'average' ratings – but there were substantially more people in the villages who felt afraid than thought there was a considerable amount of crime in their area.

In multiple regression analyses of determinants of fear of crime, the most important variable in all areas was the sex of the respondent. Women were much more likely than men to say they would be afraid to walk alone at night, even if they also acknowledged that they were unlikely to be attacked. The second most important variable was having witnessed a crime in the last year (urban area and Northam). Witnessing seems to increase people's feelings that such things do happen in their area and also to make them think about their vulnerability if they were to be attacked. Age was also relatively important in the urban area (44 per cent of those aged over 60 felt unsafe or very unsafe, as opposed to 23 per cent of those aged 41 to 60). However, fear was not confined to the older age-groups. As many as 29 per cent of those aged 18 to 40 in the urban area also felt unsafe or very unsafe. In the villages, age was not a significant correlate of fear.

Fear of walking alone did seem primarily to be fear of assault, at least at the conscious level. Where people referred to crime, they referred to assaults – rape, mugging, threats, being beaten up. And, in the urban area, people were mostly concerned about crime, rather than falling over, or the dark, or spooky things. Of those mentioning a cause for their fear, 89 per cent spoke about crime. But in the villages, reasons were more diverse, with the dark being as likely to be a cause of fear as crime, especially for women.

Of course, these differences may relate to the acceptability of 'crime', 'the dark', and so on as reasons in different places. If it is generally accepted that crime is very unlikely – and you subscribe to that view – can you ascribe your fear to crime? Equally, if everyone is talking about the terrible things that happened on the next street, any unwillingness to go out can be put down to the likelihood of assault, with no social problems resulting. Indeed, such a reason may evoke social approval.

The assaults feared were not the most common ones – those by friends and relations – or even those by local youths, but the much rarer offences of serious, unprovoked physical or sexual violence by strangers (see Warr 1985 on American women's fear of rape). Stanko (1987) has suggested that violence against women is often hidden – taking place in the home, often unreported to the police, and not always regarded as 'real' crime, either by the women themselves or by the police. It would seem then that the kinds of images evoked by the question on fear of crime are not the typical or the known, but, generally, the unusual and the unknown.

FEARED PLACES: THE ROLE OF MYTH

The kinds of places to which most fear was attached also suggest a link with the unknown and the unusual. Almost all the places seen as most unsafe were out of the immediate area in which the respondent lived or worked (see also Skogan and Maxfield 1981; Skogan 1987). For urban people, places perceived to be unsafe were all in other parts of the town. One notorious place, mentioned by 38 per cent of all urban interviewees who identified particular places as unsafe, was a large park in the centre, which was not fenced and which had wide, well-lit walks through it. It was clearly easier for people to walk across the park to the very visible streets on the far side, but few would ever do so. They preferred to take the long way round – and many said they would not go anywhere near the area. Even police officers were wary of the park and would drive across at night, some with the car doors locked. By the time of our study, it had a fearsome reputation:

'Our girls [employees] don't like walking across the park and we agree with them. It is a muggers' paradise and the factory hours are set by the girls with darkness, muggers, and flashers in mind . . . so they can get home before dark in the winter. No one's had a problem, but it satisfies them.'

(business near park)

'I came across the park at 1.30 a.m. and I don't scare easy. I ran all the way.'

(male urban dweller)

'Walking along by the park, you do feel a bit things may happen.'

(male urban dweller)

Other areas feared by urban people were the town centre, especially at weekends (34 per cent – the town centre was also cited in Merry's (1981) study of an American city), back alleys (17 per cent), and another park outside our areas (6 per cent). In the villages, the kinds of places people mentioned were similar: the notorious urban park, the town centre, and dark alleyways in the villages. However, an individual's level of fear of crime was not tied to their nearness to these particularly horrible places. Those who were fearful seemed fearful of everywhere beyond the view from their own windows. Nor were these accounts of fearful places accompanied by any examples of specific incidents that had happened there, in contrast to the findings of almost every other part of the interview. It was an appeal to what 'everybody knows', a fear of the unknown, fed by reports which were usually second- or third-hand.

It seemed to us that really feared places had achieved the status of myth. Taking the town-centre park again as an example, it was true that, many years earlier, there had been some attacks, including muggings, in or on the outskirts of the park. However, at that time and since, there had also been equally bad attacks, in greater numbers, in other parts of the city. We checked the crimes that were reported to the police as having occurred in or near the park during the period of the study and the year before that. There were very few of any kind, and those there had been were largely thefts of wallets from the clothes of people playing football, minor disorder at events in the sports pavilion, and the like. In other words, the reputation of the park was undeserved. The fear had become a myth – so powerful that even the police supported it.

The nature of that particular fear seemed to have more links with totems and folklore than with experience of or knowledge about criminal events. Perhaps this is not surprising. Fear of crime, as opposed to concern about crime, seems not to be rooted in or tied to actual happenings. Just as a phobia transcends its original cause, so fear of the park had evolved far away from any initial reported incidents. It had become a place not to go to, a place populated by monsters – the modern equivalent of 'dragons live here' on medieval maps. No one could describe the kinds of people that might be found there, except that they would be strangers, and very likely disturbed or mad. And since people avoided the park, there was no easy way to change its reputation for being dangerous. If people frequent a place, then what happens to them there can be easily monitored. If no one goes there, then lack of trouble there is likely to be seen as a result of prudence in staying away, not lack of monsters. Only the passage of long periods of time, or determined and brave action by individuals, supported by leaders of public opinion, will change this powerful, though mythical, status.

These kinds of places seem to exist in many different societies. In urban ones, they are often lonely, dark places, with some 'undesirables' hanging around (drunks frequented some of the areas round the park and occasionally the park itself). There is a possible 'social control' function of having these as mythical horror places, peopled by formless monsters (Stanko, personal conversation). The monsters may have to be formless, because they are what is pointed to as the worst in that society, and the fear is of what might happen to people if they were to behave in socially disapproved ways. We no longer have workhouses to cite as the probable destination of the feckless and irresponsible. Maybe we need to make up a place that will perform this function, one which we people with the kinds of monsters that are particularly horrific in our society – no longer the indigent, but mad criminals. If there is truth in this analysis, then fear of crime performs a social-control function. And the best that people will be able to do when asked to cite why they think that park is an unsafe place will be to give examples of other parks from the national media or to say that 'everybody knows'.

The social-control function of using fear to keep women off the streets has been expounded by a number of feminist writers. However, we think it is important to differentiate carefully between the mythical fear of particular places already discussed (for which the social-control element is not just directed against women), the heightened fear of crime that some women have about many unfamiliar places, and the concern about crime and personal safety that all residents of high-crime areas and many women in other areas show. Mythical fear, we think, may well have a basis in the social-control needs of society. Concern about crime and safety is a very different matter.

Concern was linked to personal experiences in the area and to knowledge about the things that had happened to friends, relatives, and work colleagues. In our particular areas, crime was not an everyday occurrence for people and concern was of an appropriately low level. However, for some people, the vast majority of whom were women, concern had become magnified and, we would argue, qualitatively changed, into fear. This fear was no longer tied to everyday occurrences. It had permeated people's views and lives and, as we shall see below, altered their patterns of behaviour. It was a fear of monsters, of strange things that would reach into your life and hurt you if you ventured from your usual paths. It uses the real-crime stereotype taken to its ultimate extreme – crimes are very serious, offenders are strange adult men, victims are powerless, the only option is avoidance, not prevention, deterrence, or confrontation.

Why then are women more prone to succumb to this fear? There is a vast literature on the subject, in which rationality (or its lack), vulnerability, the kinds of acceptable conduct for men and women, and power groups in society have all featured. We cannot solve the question, which is likely to have many correct answers. Fear is a societal construct, as well as a disaster for the individual, and its target will reflect the patterns and beliefs of the society. However, our study does support the kind of analysis put forward by Stanko (1987) and, in a different way, by Skogan (1987). This suggests that continued contact with minor forms of crime sensitizes people to become aware that their environment is unsafe. This leads them to take precautionary measures, some of which, because they reduce the social activity of the individual, can increase isolation and reinforce the new patterns of response (if you become less victimized, or witness fewer crimes, then you conclude it is due to the change you've made in your lifestyle, not to the intrinsic rarity of the acts). In addition, there is little pressure from the media to combat fear, since news is not about safety and order, but about crime and disorder. A positive feedback loop may develop, which may lead on to a phobic-like fear. Stanko cites the level of sexual harassment of women and their consequent need to negotiate what they perceive as an unsafe environment. Skogan talks about the levels of crime and nuisances, incivilities, or disorder in a neighbourhood as affecting fear. Hope and Hough (1986) found from the *British Crime Survey* that there was a strong relationship between the level of disorder and fear of crime at an individual level, even when controlling for victimization. In our study, however, petty crime and signs of damage did not seem to have a direct influence on fear, but on people's perceptions of their area and the success of its attempts at social order. Pressure in higher-crime neighbourhoods, harassment, crime, disorder committed by unknown and uncontrollable offenders – all of these may cause more people there, particularly women, to suffer from fear, rather than concern.

Fear of burglary

Talking to people about the likelihood of their being burgled was often a very distressing experience for them. We had constantly to reassure them that burglary was a relatively uncommon occurrence and that just talking about it would not make it happen. Known burglars, in fact, evoked very little concern. There were several convicted (and active) burglars living in the villages. In parts of the urban area, people were well aware of local thieves. The general attitude towards them was one of caution and concern, rather than fear: 'We do have a resident burglar – is he retired now? No, he's in nick again. He's small and timid and thinks everyone's having a go at him, even if you smile at him' (Northam). 'There are three youths who seem to be involved in a lot of the crime in this area. The black youth does it. I clipped his ears when he was young' (urban area 1). 'I think I know who it was who burgled us last time. You get a couple of families up the street and if there's any bother it seems to end up being them' (urban area 3).

In the urban area, however, relatively few people thought they knew who the burglars were. Those who ascribed known incidents of burglary to outsiders were more likely to think they would become victims and were also the ones to show most concern. Hough and Mayhew (1985) have also found that, although everyone seems to exaggerate the risks of burglary, those who express most anxiety overestimate it most.

A few people in the urban area did not just express concern about burglary, but showed definite signs of fear. Like fear of assault, fear of burglary tended to dominate their lives: 'I'm petrified. I'm terrified on my own here. They have broke in all round here' (urban area 2). 'I'm sending my video back because four went in this area. I keep the place guarded – I sit in at night. A lot of people think like that. They're just sitting in in the evening' (young man from urban area 1).

Compared to fear of assault, fear of burglary has only rarely previously been cited in the literature (but see Allatt 1984). In our study, it was confined to a few people in the urban area – but the urban area we studied was hardly a high-crime area for Britain. And where people had developed this fear, it showed many of the same characteristics of fear of assault – burglaries were ascribed to strangers, their occurrence was grossly exaggerated, references were often to incidents or newspaper articles about other places, though data were also adduced to show that the neighbourhood was unsafe. However, those who were afraid of burglary in our study were almost all men, and the response it provoked was rather different – protective and preventive, rather than an attitude of avoidance. People stayed in to protect their property from attack, rather than fleeing. Of course, this also tended to reduce people's freedom of movement and the numbers around on the street after dark.

Table 7.5 *Prevention of assault and inconvenience of measures taken*

| | Urban areas | | | | Northam | Southton |
| | 1 | 2 | 3 | 4 | | |
	%	%	%	%	%	%
Some prevention, some inconvenience	16	30	28	23	14	9
Some prevention, no inconvenience	9	30	22	34	12	9
No avoidance or prevention	75	41	50	43	74	82

The effects of concern and fear: avoidance and prevention

Concern, anxiety, and fear can lead people to change their lifestyles in order to prevent a particular problem from occurring or to avoid the possibility of its occurrence. As a very general rule, we found that people who were concerned about the possibility of crime of a particular sort tended to take some preventive and/or deterrent measures (not necessarily terribly effective ones). And these measures would be specific to that offence and people's stereotypes of its perpetrators. Where anxiety was high or had turned into fear, prevention seemed to have given way to avoidance. People arranged their lifestyles so as not to have any possibility of getting into the feared situation.

For example, people who were concerned or anxious about burglary tended to have installed locks and bolts, to watch out for strangers, and to take what they regarded as crime prevention measures. We discuss on pp.128–32 their habits of and views about crime prevention and its likely effectiveness. The few people who displayed fear of burglary, however, had completely altered their lives. They sat in their houses all evening or paid people to sit there for them if they had to go away. They did without property such as videos which they thought might be attractive to burglars.

Concern about assault also caused people to take preventive measures. The proportions of people who took such precautions are shown in Table 7.5. Mostly, prevention involved avoiding what were seen as the most problematic places (though not making long detours), taking the car rather than walking, or going out with friends. Both men and women showed some avoidance behaviour, but only women were substantially inconvenienced by it. For men, avoidance merely entailed a rearrangement of their social lives. Women who showed concern rather than considerable fear were in fact just as likely as men with the same scores to go out at night, whether in the urban area or in the villages. Women who were more afraid, however, significantly curtailed their social lives (see also Warr 1985). They were unlikely to go out at night at all, even to post a letter. They went with friends if possible, took the car for safety (rather than for convenience), or just didn't go out.

Though not a significant influence on avoidance behaviour, age did compound the problems of fear, particularly for those in remote areas. The elderly and the young seldom had access to a car which, in villages especially, was often the only alternative to walking along unlit roads. Poverty also removed the option of alternative transport and confined people in inner areas of the city to their homes. For them, to get out in the evening meant either walking through the feared town centre, or depending on friends with cars to go further afield.

For those who were really afraid of assault, and these were almost all women, avoidance extended to the daytime as well. One woman was so worried that she would not use the front room of the house if her husband was not at home, in case someone saw her alone and decided to break in. Some with cars would not drive through particular parts of the town. Others would lock all the car doors and try not to get caught at red lights. They honestly believed that youths waited at traffic lights to leap into cars and mug or rape the occupant. They cited American newspaper reports to back this up. No incident of this type had been reported to the police in our urban area in living memory.

THE EMPTY STREETS

From our data, we are able not only to explore people's beliefs about crime and what they said they did as a result, but also to look at whether people did actually walk in the streets at night. We conducted periods of observation in all our villages and urban areas, covering all the major streets and public places. During these, one or both of us sat in a car or on a bench and noted down all the cars, vans, bicycles, pedestrians, and animals that passed or were visible during a set period (see Appendix). This was sometimes a very uncomfortable occupation, as the periods of observation stretched from the depth of winter to the height of summer, and took place at different times throughout the day and night. Most of the time we were left entirely alone, sometimes surrounded by mothers picking up children from school, sometimes with only the owls for company at dead of night. Sometimes in the villages we were seen as suspicious people and were approached and asked what we were doing (informal action in operation). No one, however, called the police.

The result of all this activity is that we are able to estimate the relative levels of traffic and pedestrian use in the evening and at night, compared to the daytime. Obviously, the percentage decreases show considerable variation between different locations, but there were several clear findings. Traffic in the evening period, from 5 p.m. to 7 p.m., was not significantly different to that in the morning (percentages varied from 60 to 120). The figures for the urban area were at the bottom end of that range. Evening use by pedestrians, however, was significantly lower than morning use everywhere but urban area 3. It became particularly low in urban area 4. Use by women dropped off more sharply than use by men. In urban area 4, there were no women walking the streets by the early evening.

By night-time (10 p.m. to midnight), there was a further marked drop in activity. Traffic was down to 20 to 60 per cent of morning levels. Pedestrian traffic in Southton (with its several pubs) and the urban area remained at early evening rates, though Northam went dead. But almost all these pedestrians were men. There were a few women in the villages, but none at all in any of the urban areas.

This is a startling finding. First, it indicates that, for women in the urban area, our question about walking alone at night was an entirely hypothetical one. Women did not walk alone in that area – we were asking about very abnormal behaviour. (Equally, surveys using only this question to tap fear of crime are referring to a non-existent activity – a very unreliable measure.) Our urban area was not an inner-city area, or part of a very large city. Yet individuals clearly did not go out at night and this was a response, not to 'something good on the telly', but to their fear of crime. In particular, many women had already curtailed their lives to exclude the possibility of going out. The habit had been infectious. The streets were empty of women at night. It will be extremely difficult to reverse this process. In its consequences, fear of crime has already had a far more substantial, restrictive, and painful effect than crime itself. It could be said to be the greater social problem.

THE EFFECTS OF CONCERN: CRIME PREVENTION AND PROPERTY CRIME

The response to an increase in crime has often been, in policy terms, to attempt an increase in deterrent or preventive measures. In practical terms, this has meant substantial publicity campaigns and regional and town-wide initiatives. Much of this effort has tended to assume that people are not sufficiently conscious of their risk of victimization and that even if they are, more publicity will jog their minds in the right direction. Advocated solutions have included the installation of security devices, setting up Neighbourhood Watch schemes, and encouraging surveillance. It seems to have been assumed that, once informed, people will hurry to do the 'right' thing. If they don't, there has sometimes been a tendency to blame the public for crime: they are irresponsible, lazy, even criminal themselves, and, almost, deserve what they get. The alternative explanations (the solutions are inappropriate to the area, household, or business; the devices are very difficult to use or fit or cost too much; people find a national approach irrelevant to their own local concerns) have only rarely been considered.

We thought it was important to find out whether people in our areas matched their concern about crime with concern about crime prevention and whether they were able to use the publicity to solve their problems. After all, as Skogan (1987) has suggested, if people are worried about crime and also about crime prevention, but find they can't cope with the suggested solutions, then despair and fear may set in and neighbourhoods will be seen as alien, crime-ridden places, to be moved out of rapidly.

The first thing to stress is that people, when thinking about crime prevention, did not think about crime in general. They thought in separate and different ways about burglary, assault, theft of cars, damage to cars, etc., and about different kinds of offender. As we found throughout this study, offences came in situation/offender/victim packages, not as legally defined entities. The words 'crime prevention' themselves tended to be associated with burglary, but this is likely to reflect recent national and local publicity and effort. Preventive beliefs and actions spread over most packages.

We shall concentrate upon burglary, because this was of great concern to individuals and because much information has been on offer. The people we interviewed often had quite definite ideas about their own likelihood of being burgled and about the factors that they thought would contribute to or diminish the risk. The most common ones (forming more than 5 per cent of all factors cited) are shown in Table 7.6. People tended to list things that prevented burglary rather than increased its likelihood. Their talk related to the action they themselves had taken or might take, rather than helpless worry or dependence on public bodies or the spending of large sums of money. People, both residents and business people, seemed to display a crime prevention set. Either people had always thought like this (so information provision was not necessary), or the message had already got across by the time of our study.

Were these factors likely to be effective in reducing the risk of burglary? There were differences between town and country (Table 7.6). In the urban area, design and hardware factors tended to predominate over surveillance. Villagers more commonly discussed surveillance, whether this concerned people watching or dogs barking. Unfortunately, studies on the effectiveness of burglary prevention measures anywhere are rare, despite the considerable amount of money being spent on security and other initiatives. The need to match measures to localities is only now beginning to be recognized (see Bottoms and Wiles 1986). Studies such as those by Bennett and Wright (1984) and Winchester and Jackson (1982) indicate that design factors, particularly the absence of

Table 7.6 *Burglary prevention factors*

	Specific factors mentioned as a percentage of all responses		
	Urban area	Northam	Southton
Bad access, especially at the rear	18	2	0
Possession of dog	13	10	25
Few valuables in property	13	11	10
Special locks or hardware	10	5	3
Watchful neighbours	9	21	11
Special alarm	5	2	0
People usually around on property	5	2	0
Property locked up	5	9	6
Isolated position (attracts burglars)	0	8	9
Valuables kept out of sight	1	7	3
Good visibility into premises (repels burglars)	2	5	4
Valuables in property (attracts burglars)	4	2	6
Double-glazing	1	2	5
Not many 'funny people' around	0	1	5
Total number of responses	175	130	79
Percentage of people citing any factor at all	67	77	66

rear access, do seem to be important in burglary. Surveillance by neighbours has also been said by burglars to deter them, though dogs only affect the decision to enter the house, not the decision to approach it. Hardware, unless as expensive and obvious as an alarm, does not seem so important. Locks that can only be seen to be present when right up against a building (like most forms of window locks) can have no effect on burglars' choice of houses to try. Equally, silent or internal alarms, unless widely publicized, seem to be designed more to catch burglars than to prevent burglary. In general, therefore, it would appear that our villagers had a more effective set of crime prevention beliefs than our urban dwellers. Urban people, perhaps because unaware of the current extent of urban surveillance (see Chapter 4), seemed to have rejected it in favour of rather patchy and ineffective beliefs about hardware.

Did people translate their crime prevention beliefs into action? For example, did they lock up their houses when they left home? Did they arrange for someone to look after the house or business when they were away? Our interviewees' answers are shown in Table 7.7 which indicates clearly that people were lax in locking up. Even in the urban area, there

Table 7.7 *Crime prevention behaviour*

	Urban areas				Northam	Southton
	1	2	3	4		
	%	%	%	%	%	%
Locking door of house or business						
Always locked when out	74	86	100	89	52	40
Not locked if out briefly	13	0	0	3	30	17
Not locked sometimes	13	14	0	9	17	43
Locking windows of house or business						
Always locked when out	65	76	87	53	27	35
Not locked if out briefly	15	5	0	9	36	21
Not locked sometimes	19	19	13	38	37	44
When going away Inform neighbour or friend:						
for crime prevention	36	27	40	39	38	11
to feed pets/water plants	23	15	0	25	27	15
other reason	0	8	13	24	7	23
Total	58	50	53	89	71	48
Inform police	0	0	0	7	4	8
Keyholder scheme/someone around	26	19	25	4	16	27
No special precautions	16	31	23	0	9	17

was a considerable minority of houses and businesses that were not locked up. Windows were even more likely to be left open (though in urban area 4 the percentages include second-floor windows which were likely to be beyond the reach of burglars).

This laxness was not due to a lack of awareness about the need for crime prevention. In urban areas, everyone was concerned. When people went away, for example, considerable precautions were taken. In urban area 4, everyone we interviewed had asked someone to look after the premises. Not locking up was not attributable to an irrational lapse, but to a combination of judgements about the prevalence of burglary, the presumed *modus operandi* of burglars, and the inconvenience of using the devices installed in the premises or available on the market. Where crime prevention aids were fiddly to operate (for example, many forms of window lock and garage door locks), they would not be used.

However, in the villages, the low known levels of burglaries produced some doubt about the need for constant security: 'I leave the milk money on the doorstep – I couldn't leave a £5 note out in town, but I do here. I wouldn't leave a £10 note out though' (Northam – honesty has its limits!).

People in all areas also had complete blind spots about particular parts of their property: 'I've enormous faith in the bolt on the gate, so I forget about the windows' (Northam).

The worst blind spot was the back of the premises – back door and windows. While the front of the house was considered a public domain to be protected, the back was private and invasion was not considered. In fact, of course, the back of houses and businesses is one of the most frequent routes of entry for burglars. But people did not know this. Their beliefs about the ways burglars operate, like their picture of who burglars are, were very inaccurate. This is hardly surprising. There was almost no feedback to people about crime in their areas. The actual frequency of victimization by burglary is still so low that it will be unusual for someone to be burgled in every house they live in. So their own practices of crime prevention are not likely to be tested. Knowledge about local burglaries was not widespread in any area – far less so than crime directed against public property. So the gossip network cannot play a substantial part in improving security practices. National crime prevention campaigns and police information up to the date of the fieldwork had only produced a general awareness of crime prevention – not any specific targeting of good practice to people's own property (see also Riley and Mayhew 1980 for an evaluation showing similar negative results on action). Contact with police crime prevention officers or local police officers about crime prevention was extremely rare. Businesses seemed to gain most of their advice from insurance companies or specialists. The police were not seen as obvious sources of information about crime prevention – a finding confirmed by the lack of messages regarding crime prevention in our analysis of calls on police services (Chapter 3) and the low number of people who informed the police when going away. In fact, were the police to be used by individual businesses, let alone householders, the present complement of crime prevention officers would be overwhelmed. Many times the current numbers would be needed.

Of course, crime and crime prevention were not constantly the most important things in people's lives. Employment and personal affairs usually filled that place. There were, however, certain times at which crime prevention seemed to come to the fore of people's consciousness.

The three most obvious ones were when people were going on holiday, when moving into new premises, and immediately following the commission of a burglary. Officers attending reports of burglaries did try to give some crime prevention advice – but the CID officers who were often involved were not specially trained in new crime prevention possibilities – nor did area officers often take it upon themselves to follow up the immediate response policing by helping and supporting victims. People tried hard to ensure the safety of their own and others' property when it was empty. Even neighbours whose prime duty was to feed pets or water plants would take on a crime prevention role as well – drawing and opening curtains several times a day, taking in deliveries, and switching on and off lights. Indeed, asking someone to 'feed the cat' was a polite way of asking them to look after the property. The prevalence of these social networks in the urban area was another pointer to the relative vigour of informal social control there.

When moving into new premises, people tried to think about crime prevention. Businesses in particular thought about hardware and security practices. But people just didn't know what to do. Insurance companies were willing to suggest specialist advisers (interestingly they didn't ever seem to suggest contacting the police), but they didn't advise directly on any remedies, and it was almost unheard of for them to insist on any particular precautions in business or residential property (though we had no high-risk premises such as chemists' shops or banks). There was no publicity available that was clearly targeted on the kind of premises an individual or business inhabited. Even with the current plethora of information which seems to be available, it was clear that people's particular needs were not being met – and that the publicity was not being put out at the most advantageous time.

Increasing crime prevention and combating fear

What might be done to help people make their areas safer? We have deliberately headed this section with the two concepts of increasing crime prevention and combating fear, because we are sure that, unless any potential initiative is judged in terms of both aims, it is likely to have unintended deleterious consequences. Fear of crime is already a serious problem, as is its correlate the likely decrease in surveillance which will render informal social controls more ineffective.

We have also expressed the question in terms of what people themselves might do. By this, we are not implying that people should take the whole responsibility for crime prevention and community safety upon themselves. In our view, it would be a dereliction of state and local public responsibility for promoting order if individuals were held responsible for the whole of crime prevention. People have neither the means nor the power. For example, every new car sold in the country comes equipped with moderately easy-to-use locks. We don't expect people to provide locks for their cars (though the corollary – that state pressure should play a role in improving car security – has only just been taken up by the Home Office (Home Office 1985–6)). Can we then expect people to remedy the defects in security hardware in their homes, particularly if they do not own their homes, or if these defects are ones in structure and design which will take vast expenditure to put right? A reliance on market forces to compel builders and planners to attend to security is a very slow, painful, and uncertain strategy. It can only immediately affect new building – and we are now out of the era of wholesale demolition and rebuilding. It presumes freedom of movement, ignoring patterns of employment and unemployment, housing policies, and, often, the lack of choice between housing designs in many areas.

However, a reliance on public initiatives imposed on local people would also, in our view, be unsuccessful. Fundamentally, the power of informal action, when directed effectively, is much stronger than that of formal agencies. David Smith (1987) has illustrated this powerfully by citing what happened when smoking was banned on the London Underground. From day one, smoking almost disappeared (at least until 10 p.m.). Social pressures, felt and overt, had made a previously common practice disappear. No state-imposed policing could have done the same.

Another reason for the limited usefulness of state or local-authority initiatives alone is the localization of crime and disorder. Problems are local, knowledge about problems is local, contacts are local, informal action is local. Effective solutions and initiatives are also likely to have to be local. But public bodies are, in general, not local in the same sense of being based at street level. They cannot know very effectively exactly what to do and to try.

The remaining solution is a partnership between state and individuals, public and private. This is a commonly advocated solution – one that has become almost a slogan or panacea. We argue that it is the right path to follow, but that not any partnership will do. It is not sufficient to announce that a partnership will be formed. It will not magically appear, not while neighbourhoods, particularly those with high crime rates, are fragmented, worried, distrustful, and without a structure that promotes further community action possibilities (see Chapter 6). Nor will it have crime prevention as a major facet where people do not have that constantly on their minds. Hope and Hough's (1986) findings that interest in neighbourhood watch was greatest in middle-crime, middle-disorder, middle-worried areas are significant here. So are Bennett's (1987) and Rosenbaum's (1986) findings that neighbourhood watch schemes seem to be set up in areas without very considerable crime problems. Equally, they show that interest in neighbourhood watch is only maintained where there is an existing informal network of support, and that where schemes are imposed, they do not seem to be effective.

We shall address the broader questions of community organization and inter-agency co-operation in Chapter 10, but here we can set out a number of pointers that might help to prevent crime, without increasing fear. First, it is necessary to make crime prevention measures relevant to local people. They need to stem from local people's concerns and the crimes they suffer. They need to fit in with people's lifestyles. They need to be targeted to be relevant to local property. They need to be followed up and evaluated, so that, as local conditions change, so do the initiatives.

Secondly, they need to fit in with patterns of informal action. Publicity should reach people when they are particularly interested in and able to do something about crime prevention – i.e. when they move into property and, where necessary, after they have been victimized. Publicity initiatives need to give out the same messages as the day-to-day work of the police and other agencies. In particular, it would be relatively simple to prepare leaflets about crime prevention possibilities – one for each type of housing or business property in an area. The right one could then be delivered to the house when people move in – for example, with the electricity/gas change of user messages. For businesses, insurance companies could do the same. The leaflets should address not only security hardware, but other local efforts and community programmes which concern fear, disorder, or crime. Recent initiatives by councils, NACRO, and the Police Foundation (the latter to install security hardware) are examples of the approach we have in mind.

Thirdly, people have some very strange misconceptions about crime in their area. Here, the messages have to be very carefully worded. The result of telling people that criminals look just like their neighbours can be a very fearful, estranged community. The solutions again have to be localized. Bottoms and Wiles (1986) have demonstrated clearly that the package of measures for areas with high victimization rates and high numbers of resident offenders must be different from the packages for areas with either one or the other or neither. We shall return to this again in Chapter 10. However, local newsletters have been produced in some American towns (Pate *et al.* 1986), giving details of crimes committed in the area, yet avoiding scaring people and making them more suspicious of their neighbours. And without greater knowledge, people really will not be able to do anything. At present, people suffer crime and disorder and, when they cannot cope, they pass the knowledge on to official agencies. Unfortunately, that knowledge is never returned in a manner that will help people to cope in the future.

In sum, we are arguing for a sensitive, local approach to crime prevention and fear of crime that places people themselves at the focus of activity. Official agencies should be there to support, to facilitate, and to guide informal action, being prepared to take over when solutions are outside the power and the means of people themselves, but also being required to report back on what has been done – servants and agents, not masters or unaccountable entrepreneurs. We are talking about a concept of 'community safety' (Osborn 1987) that places that community in the pivotal place.

8

What the public get and what they want

That we have a police force is no more than a fact of modern life. That it should 'do something about crime' was and remains a central political issue, put into the spotlight in recent years by the falling crime clear-up rate. How the police should set about this task, and to whom they should be accountable, are also the stuff of political debate, aired most recently in the run-up to the 1987 general election.

But real life is often more complicated than politicians make it appear. The police, whatever they do about crime, are also called upon for a wide range of other services (see, for example, Southgate and Ekblom 1984). What then do members of the public want from the police, from 'their' police officer? Several studies (Hough 1985; Jones, Maclean, and Young 1986; Jones and Levi 1983; Kinsey 1984) indicate strong desires to see more police on the beat and also to see serious crimes solved – desires which many police officers see as being in contradiction, since, they argue, serious crimes are rarely solved by the PC on the beat. Are the public ill-informed or do they have a different view of the nature of policing to that held by the police?

Moves towards 'area beat policing', 'community policing', 'neighbourhood policing', or any other of the apparently interchangeable synonyms – to invert a phrase coined by Robert Reiner, the move back from Darth Vader to Dixon of Dock Green – have resulted in a re-emphasis upon, or at least a greater stress in rhetoric upon, local, more informal 'community policing'. This has raised the question of 'community policing on whose terms?' This cannot be answered without, first, considering the basis on which the public know about policing and what it entails. How much contact do people have with the police, over what matters, and what impressions of policing does this contact give rise to?

Being policed: the public's experience

THE POLICE PRESENCE

Hough (1980) notes that only 35 to 40 per cent of police officers are engaged in patrol duties of some sort. Yet it is this minority of officers that, outside the television images of demonstrations, strikes, riots, and baton charges, shape the public's experience of policing. Broadly

Table 8.1 *Public opinions about the form of policing they would like to see*

	Urban areas %	Northam %	Southton %
Would like police house	11	31	24
Would like officer involved in local affairs	8	12	0
Would like a local and known officer	40	28	0
Would like a local officer	8	2	6
No change from current policing	32	26	66
Less contact preferred	2	0	0

speaking, our data suggest two things. There was an overwhelming demand for a police presence which could be typified by a local and known constable whose actions would not be out of place in Dock Green. Yet the public saw relatively little of the police and what they did see was characterized as a form of patrolling which did not appear to correspond to their expectations and preferences.

The strength of feeling about having a known, local police officer was enormous (Table 8.1). Two-thirds to three-quarters of those in the urban areas and in Northam wanted an officer 'closer to home', either living locally or having some connection with neighbourhood affairs. In the urban areas the demand was simply for a local officer, while in Northam a substantial minority (43 per cent) wanted to see a local police house with a local bobby living in it.

This strength of feeling can be seen against a backdrop of how people thought policing was in fact being conducted in these areas (see Table 8.2). In Northam, the 'local' police – that is, those who patrolled or who arrived in response to calls – were based in a village some miles away. They were neither seen often nor known personally by many villagers. The two urban beats each had three 'area beat officers' who were supposed to spend the whole of their working time in those areas, but over half our sample there either had not seen police officers in their neighbourhood, of if they had, did not know them personally and did not know whether they were 'ABOs'. The difference between these two beats in the proportion of people who had seen no police in their neighbourhood was probably due to two factors. Urban beat 1 was nearer the police station to which cars came and went using the rear vehicle access, set on a back street; urban beat 2, its boundaries defined by main roads, had no 'short cuts' through it and police cars would ordinarily use the main roads unless called to the area. In part, too, the difference may

Table 8.2 *Varieties of police presence seen in areas*

	Urban beats		Rural areas	
	1	2	Northam	Southton
	%	%	%	%
Knowledge of police seen in area				
Seen local beat officer for area, known to interviewee	23	20	18	90
Seen local beat officer for area, not known personally to interviewee	13	24	23	10
Doesn't know of a local beat officer, has seen a personally known officer	5	0	1	0
Doesn't know of a local beat officer, has seen an unknown officer	49	30	35	0
No police officers seen locally, or known to interviewee	10	26	22	0
(Number in sample	61	76	94	87)
Kinds of patrol seen (where this detail was given)				
On foot or bike	57	28	4	2
By car	23	25	53	10
On foot or bike and by car	9	13	13	87
No police seen in area	11	34	30	0
Perceived frequency of patrols (where this detail was given)				
Often	38	21	6	92
Occasionally	51	45	64	8
Rarely/never	11	34	30	0

have been due to the force's styles of uniform. The policewomen working beat 2 wore uniforms so dark and plain that they were practically invisible after dark.

In Southton, the local PC lived in the village. Villagers knew that he *was* the local officer and almost everybody knew him, though not necessarily personally. He was often seen walking or driving around. Many people wanted no change from their current policing. The difference in contacts and in beliefs was not one between rural and urban areas, but between those areas which had a highly visible police presence with a visible local base and those whose police appeared to be more remote. Yet even the situation at Southton was not enough for a substantial minority of people. A quarter of those we interviewed pointed out that he was not simply responsible for the village, but for the beat as a whole, including a large number of outlying hamlets and smaller villages; and he 'covered' an equally large adjoining beat when the officer there was off-duty. He was not, in their view, a 'local bobby' as such and could not pay enough attention to his home village because of his other responsibilities.

The call for a more local presence was also expressed in complaints about the difficulty in getting access to the police. In the urban areas and in Northam people had to telephone the nearest police station, which, as far as Northam was concerned, 'is such a long way away, it seems ridiculous'. In fact, the nearest station was only a few miles down the road, but was only manned between roughly 6 a.m. and 10 p.m., and outside these hours calls to it were diverted automatically to the station that people *described* as their nearest station – thus betraying their perception that a station which is closed overnight simply is not a 'proper' police station. In Southton, residents could in theory call or leave a note at the police house. But the force policy was that police houses should be ex-directory, and residents took the view that the police intention must, therefore, be that they should not call their local officer directly – even though he made a point of giving his number to many villagers. Many residents were highly critical of the need to call a town about 20 miles away simply so that a message could be passed back to the officer who effectively lived only 'down the road'. Local policing, in this conception of it, meant the ability to contact the local officer direct in the same way that in the past one might have contacted the local doctor or the priest – say between about 8 a.m. and 8. p.m., if necessary until about midnight, but later than that only in dire emergencies.

The reality of the police presence in our areas can be summed up by the observation that in three of our four areas, over half our residents set eyes on a police officer less often than once a week. This clearly was not the kind of frequency of police presence that was considered ideal, and we must question whether in fact, in any area except Southton, the police could be said to maintain anything more than an irregular and occasional presence. Neither was this level of perceived presence an effect of residents 'living in the back room' and not noticing the street life. In forty-seven hours of street observation, we logged only four passing police officers: two in Southton, one in Northam, and one on one urban beat.

This level of police presence was, however, probably more than it had been in the past. There had been a force reorganization in 1983, one aspect of which was an increase in the numbers of foot patrols and area beat officers, especially in the urban area. In fact, two-thirds of those we interviewed said that they had noticed some change (usually that there were now more patrols), while many others knew that this change had occurred even though they had not themselves noticed any difference in the frequency of patrols (see van Dijk *et al.* 1982 for a Dutch experiment showing similar results).

Table 8.3 *One-off contacts between public and police*

| | Urban areas | | | | Rural areas | |
| | 1 | 2 | 3 | 4 | Northam | Southton |
	%	%	%	%	%	%
Contact by interviewee to police	42	53	45	53	37	29
Contact by police to interviewee	32	40	33	9	17	21
Both forms of contact	10	13	18	9	7	10
No contact	35	20	40	47	53	60

ONE-OFF CONTACTS WITH THE POLICE

At some point in most people's lives, their contact with the police ceases
to be that of casual observer, becoming one of direct involvement. They
call the police or the police call on them about a matter which is typically
concluded in a brief space of time. We have termed these 'one-off
contacts'.

Our 'message pad' data (calls made by the public to the police,
discussed in Chapter 3) suggest that people in rural and urban areas
called on the police over similar matters, but that those in the urban areas
called more frequently. Our interview data cannot be compared directly
with the message pad data for various reasons, not least being that some
people did not contact the police switchboard (where the message pads
were written), but spoke to individual officers. On a count of whether
or not our interviewees had contacted the police in the year prior to the
interview, between 28 and 31 per cent of residents had done so, with the
exception of urban beat 2 in which the figure was 58 per cent (see Table
8.3). There was an even spread in age and an even split on sex among
those who had contacted the police, though in the urban area professional
middle-class people were slightly more likely to have made a call. In all
areas, the figure for businesses was around the 60 per cent mark. These
figures compare with the *British Crime Survey* estimate of 43 per cent
of residents who had initiated contact with the police (Southgate and
Ekblom 1984).

The most frequently experienced contact initiated by the police was
first apparent as a blue light in the rear-view mirror. Stops of cars were
the commonest form. The second was enquiries about crimes – or what
were assumed to be such. For example: 'A detective constable from

Sussex came to interview me because I have a red Porsche. He was interviewing all owners of red Porsches as part of a murder hunt. Very friendly chap' (Southton). 'The police turned up here last week to ask if we'd seen anything of next door's burglary' (urban area 3). 'Two police came here about a motor cycle. They wouldn't tell me what it was about – I told them I didn't have one and they went away' (urban area 2). Thirdly, there was a range of contacts for the purpose of checking gun licences (in the urban as well as rural areas), updating business keyholder lists, serving witness notices and summonses for court appearances, and the like – items described generically by police officers as 'process'.

Around one in five of our residents, both rural and urban, had been contacted by the police in the year prior to the interview. The rural business people had a similar level of contact. Urban business people were more often contacted. Over half had had some police-initiated contact, a proportion which may be explained by routine visits to second-hand shops (a way of tracing stolen goods) and by the use of car dealers and scrap merchants to dispose of abandoned vehicles.

The proportion having no contact of any kind was quite high – around 50 per cent in all areas except urban area 2. These figures fit quite well with others' findings. Smith, Small, and Gray (1983) and Southgate and Ekblom (1984) both suggest that about 50 per cent of residents (though a much higher proportion of black youths in inner cities) have some contact with the police in any one year.

CONTACT THROUGH WORK AND VOLUNTARY WORK

We have so far discussed the extent to which people saw and were seen by the police on a day-to-day, street-based, or routine basis. However, some people also had contacts on a more long-term basis through work, membership of an organization, or other spare-time activities. Around a third of those we interviewed had some work-related contact with the police. Some shopkeepers, for example, had officers drop in to buy a paper and ask after the local gossip. Among organizers of societies and voluntary organizations – most of whom were in social classes I and II – there were occasional contacts over the arrangements for fêtes, charity collections, and the like. Such organizations were usually village-based. Those we interviewed who were involved in Asian and West Indian associations in the urban areas were often also members of police liaison committees or were involved in aspects of police training. These organizational contacts were, in contrast to the day-to-day ones, usually with the more senior officers who dealt with the permissions that voluntary societies needed, or who serviced or sat on the liaison committees.

Support and concern: expectations and opinions of the police

Many surveys, including one carried out within the police force we studied, have found that the police in Britain do, broadly speaking, enjoy the confidence of large sections of the public. It is still fair to characterize much of the policing in this country as policing by consent, despite relationships that 'are tense and conflict ridden with the young, the unemployed, the economically marginal and blacks, especially if they fit the other three categories', as Reiner (1985: 81) notes.

Reiner's discussion of consent, however, regards it primarily as the acceptance of *de facto* power by those at the receiving end of police actions. Comparatively little is known about what people feel they are consenting *to*, especially if they are ordinary citizens who have little contact with the police from one year to the next. This shades into some broader questions. First, what kinds of things are the police expected to do? Second, under what circumstances is this general support and confidence, tapped by so many surveys, actually qualified or withdrawn? Third, do people try to influence the way in which policing is carried out in their neighbourhood, and if so, how?

CONCEPTIONS AND EXPECTATIONS ABOUT POLICE ACTIVITY

A general discrepancy can be found between what people thought the police should have been doing and what it was inferred, from observation, that they were doing.

What was desired seemed to be, as we have said, very much based on *Dixon of Dock Green* and *Juliet Bravo*. Reiner (1985) captures the flavour of this in his description of 'community policing', in which 'the keynotes . . . are an emphasis on the harmonious relations within the police force, and between it and the wider society'. Hampshire Constabulary (1984) illustrate it more specifically in their advice to constables to walk calmly, confidently, and slowly, and to stand in places where they can be approached. This manner, they argue, will reassure the public. The role the public were fashioning for the police harked back to Sir Richard Mayne's (1829 – cited in Scarman 1982) definition of the police role as 'the prevention of crime, the protection of life and property, the preservation of public tranquillity'. In particular, the demand for a local bobby was also a demand for a 'traditional' conspicuous patrol. As well as being a visible and symbolic reassurance that public order existed, the local bobby was envisaged as a deterrent to unruliness and minor crime. Two of the shopkeepers we spoke to mentioned that occasionally one or other police officer would call in and be offered a coffee. One went on to say:

'They said they wouldn't come in regularly because it would frighten the clientele. I said if any clients are frightened off by you, they're not ones I need. They do come in very occasionally and in fact some youths have stopped coming. But that's probably to the good.'   (urban area 2)

And one village resident remarked: 'It is a deterrent, you feel you're being looked after. The PC gets round in his car, and he's seen even if he's just on his way elsewhere, it puts him in mind' (Southton).

What were these hypothetical, non-directed patrolling officers expected to be doing? One way of illustrating this is to indicate what Northam residents felt had been lost when their local PC was withdrawn many years previously:

> 'We used to have a village bobby. My mother used to have the policeman round all the time, every day he'd tap at the window and say "all right?" It would be nice to have one, it would stop all the village kids going round in that little group.'

> 'He was a policeman that people respected – and he had a case of straying animals against my dad, but he told him why – why he didn't just put them back in the field.'

> 'We used to have a village policeman who would go round on a bicycle – that was a great thing, because if you suspected something you could have a quiet word. These Panda cars, they don't even look at you, let alone stop, let alone speak to you.'

Let us now turn from the ideal to the reality. Except in Southton, in general, the two bore little relation to each other. The police were not seen as 'patrolling' but as coming to the area 'only if something happens' or if they had specific business with offenders, victims, or others: 'you never see any foot patrols – they don't patrol, they just go from place to place.' Police in cars were seen as simply 'going somewhere else'. Northam people shared this view. They described officers as 'driving in and out' of the village and 'then they're gone' – patrolling from behind a steering wheel was not seen as 'proper policing' at all.

The exception to this scenario was Southton, where 'Dixon of Dock Green' still ruled. The local PC was described as 'wandering about', but also stopping the kid with the noisy motor bike, stopping children playing on the road, and the like. In short, his role was not seen as 'just going from one call to another' but as peacekeeping in the classic sense. Yet this officer was in fact doing very similar work to his urban colleagues who were also working as area beat officers. The difference was that he was highly visible as a 'local bobby' with a distinct base. He was known in the area, his actions were commented on, and people felt that they knew what he was doing (though their interpretations were in fact often wrong). And he was 'wandering about' on patrol when 'nothing' was happening as well as dealing with what did happen. He was 'doing police work' by his mere presence. This suggests a symbolic role for policing which we shall discuss in greater depth later.

Despite this lack of fit between the ideal and reality, the police in our study areas did enjoy a great deal of support. At the most general level, almost three-quarters of the Southton and half the Northam interviewees thought the policing in their area was 'good' or 'all right' (the other two categories we used were 'not good' and 'unsatisfactory'). Almost three-quarters of the urban responses also fell into the 'good'/'all right' categories. How can this pattern be explained?

Recent personal contact with the police (of any kind) and personal acquaintanceship with police officers were not significantly related to these assessments. Individuals appeared to be responding to the question with reference to a holistic concept of the police role and performance; a concept expressed through three themes, namely stretched resources, the idea and aims of local policing, and politeness. The judgement of policing in general as 'good' or 'all right' seemed to be made against what people saw as an underlying reality of stretched resources, which in turn removed the possibility of achieving the public's ideal conception of local policing, and excused some – though not all – of what was seen as 'unwarranted' or 'impolite' police behaviour. In this context, the high levels of support are explicable, while the lower level in Northam was due to what was perceived as a complete lack of policing without the corresponding perception that no policing was necessary.

The theme of stretched resources was touched on by many interviewees. For example: 'The police are very stretched – they can't do a lot about the yobbos and drunks, they can only move them on and they go round the block and that's it' (urban area 1). 'There's not much need for them here but they've deteriorated. You don't get the service. . . . They're undermanned, they can't keep up. . . . No, you can't have them on tap' (urban area 4). 'The police can't be here. They're just there to do a mopping up operation. Local people have to deal with things themselves' (Northam).

In the light of this, and in the villages particularly, it was explicitly accepted that many problems should not be referred to the police since their resources could not cope. This impression of stretched resources was seen as partly excusing the police from providing the more community-based approach which was desired, though there was still a substantial demand for a style in which personal and informal links could be made between a local bobby and residents – in other words, for a form of local policing. People wanted a face they knew, not a voice on the end of a phone with whom they could not negotiate informal solutions: 'We would like to be able to contact the local police direct – I don't suppose the police would want it' (urban area 4). 'If we had a local PC we could get them to keep an eye on the house if we go away. We wouldn't think of doing it now – our expectations are lower than they used to be' (urban area 3).

A certain politeness was expected in officers' dealings with the public, but this was sometimes not found. People who called the police for whatever reason, or who simply opened the door to an officer making door-to-door enquiries, expected a courtesy which was sometimes lacking (and other studies note such complaints are common among victims – see Shapland, Willmore, and Duff 1985). People who were being 'policed against' or who encountered officers on the street complained of unnecessary unpleasantness. The incidents recalled were on occasions several years in the past, but memories had lingered on and now touched all their views on policing:

> 'The police came a few years ago to ask to do an observation on someone across the road they suspected. They set up upstairs with a radio. They raided his house and that's the last we saw of them. They didn't say thank you or anything.' (urban area 1)

> 'In one of the murder hunts the police issued a description. I knew I'd seen [the victim] just before he went missing . . . I called the police and two CID came – but when I said oh, you've come about the [name] killing they said how do you know he's been killed, we only said he'd been found dead. They went on to accuse me virtually of killing him. In the end I got my tape recorder and recorded the interview. I couldn't get over how hostile they were, I'm not surprised they never found the murderer. It didn't put me off phoning the police but I'd think twice before naming anyone.' (urban area 3)

Unnecessary unpleasantness was often mentioned (by adults as well as younger people) in the context of younger age-groups. The essential complaint was that the police made no distinction between 'troublesome' and 'respectable' young people, and frequently tried to impose their authority by using an overbearing manner. Village teenagers commented:

> 'He harasses the teenagers; he even harasses me – he told me to stop loitering after a parish council meeting [which she had attended]. If you're in your teens you see him much more than if you're an adult.' (Southton)

> 'The police don't have any respect for young people, so young people have no respect for the police. One was arrogant [a CID officer], he swore, he threatened my friends but he was nice to me 'cos I'm a girl. No one wants them involved – to be anywhere near them. One [named] is an absolute brute – he's throwing his weight around and getting nowhere fast – even to the parents of [named, well-behaved young children].' (Northam)

It is sometimes said by senior officers that any police–public contact is an opportunity to improve police–community relations, and that crime enquiries and 'process' are occasions which enable police to spend time talking to 'ordinary members of the public' and to get to know people in their area. As far as young people were concerned, though much of this work was not directed *against* the individual who cited it to us, both it and the 'street policing' were seldom conducted in a manner that endeared the officer to the member of the public.

The most difficult area of relationships was almost certainly between the police and urban black youths. At an institutional level, the divisional superintendent and the leader of at least one black youth club had a very good working relationship. But the youth leader and others quoted a number of instances where thoughtless actions on the part of individual officers – some in the course of attempts to improve race relations – had actually tarnished the police image. Beyond this again, the superintendent, the youth leader, and others were aware that the relations between black youths and police formed only one element of what Pryce (1977) describes as 'endless pressure' – pressure in every aspect of these youths' lives. One consequence of this, it was said, was the appearance in some youths of symptoms of general aggression and mild dementia. Where these began to develop, one further consequence was said to be the vicious circle whereby the youths behaved in a way that brought them constantly to the attention of the police, who were then very easily characterized as unduly aggressive and discriminatory (see also Gaskell and Smith 1985).

DOING JUSTICE BY USING DISCRETION

Public expectations of the policing role essentially comprised a concept of local policing, which should allow informal contact and be conducted through something recognizable as 'patrolling' – that is, walking the beat rather than simply responding to calls or dealing with 'process'. But this rather homely image says nothing about actually catching criminals and bringing them to justice – a demand which is also very strongly made in some recent surveys (Kinsey 1984; Jones, Maclean, and Young 1986). Our own data suggest that there is indeed a desire to see wrongdoers brought to justice. However, we found a fairly clear distinction in people's minds between things that were described to us as 'real crime', which deserved strong police attention, and things that were offences but were for a range of reasons not considered serious wrongdoing.

We have listed the kinds of offences and problems that constituted 'real crime' and 'other crime' in previous chapters (see Chapters 4 and 6). There, however, we were concentrating on police responses to public demand. Proactive policing could also be 'unwanted policing'. In the urban area, for example, a number of people felt aggrieved because the night car crews had seen fit to issue parking tickets at 4 a.m. to cars facing the wrong way on the street. In Southton, it was argued that cars with expired car tax were usually parked on side streets and were doing no harm – the owners would get round to taxing them sometime; the local PC's inflexibility in reporting offenders without giving them a reminder first was considered irksome. There were, however, differences of expectation: some people thought the police should simply overlook these sorts of offences, while others felt it acceptable that they should deal with them if they happened to come across them but unacceptable if patrols filled in empty hours seeking them out, or, particularly, if individual officers suddenly mounted personal campaigns about car tax, worn tyres, and the like.

FOUR ROLES FOR THE POLICE

In one final attempt to sum up what people wanted from the police, we shall simply state, quite programmatically, what it was that our interviewees thought the police should be doing. There were four specific roles which, together, and in the minds of those we spoke to, constituted the normal, everyday police function.

First, it is beyond question that they wanted a speedy response to 'real crime', together with clear investigative effort and, where pertinent, prosecution. And, in general, a speedy first response *was* provided, often by the 'immediate response vehicles'. Problems with this role began after the police arrival, with some officers being apparently dismissive or uncaring; they went on to include broken appointments by CID officers, and the difficulties victims experienced in subsequently finding out what progress had been made – all points highlighted in other studies (see Shapland, Willmore, and Duff 1985; Burrows 1986).

Rural CID officers in this particular subdivision were very atypical in having adopted a team policing approach whereby rural CID work was allocated to officers on a geographical basis. Each detective constable would work on a continuous basis with four or five area beat officers. This seemed to work to the satisfaction of both uniformed and CID officers. Indeed, there were fewer problems of communication and liaison here than in the urban area, despite the greater distances to be covered and the large numbers of different stations and police houses out of which officers worked.

It seemed to us that, just as a call to the police transfers a problem from public to police 'ownership', the effect of a crime report was to transfer the crime to CID 'ownership'. Yet the local beat officers had a great deal to contribute to the investigation of 'real crime', particularly burglary, in both rural and urban areas. Offenders were often local; most primary detections for burglary are through neighbours' and victims' reports

(Burrows 1986; Hough 1987) and the area beat officers had some access to the informal watching systems in all our urban areas. But, in the urban area, house-to-house enquiries were often not conducted, nor were local officers consulted. We believe, in short, that CID officers working alone do not have the right approach to the investigation of burglary. Their undoubted concern for victims is, unfortunately, not accompanied by knowledge of local problems and they are not attentive to the possible inputs of local officers. This raises the question of closer liaison within the police, perhaps by decentralization of CID and the importation into urban areas of something like the team work approach adopted in our rural areas. This possibility is discussed in greater detail in the next chapter.

The second role which the police were expected to fulfil was that of dealing with problems and 'other crime'. By the time the stage of calling the police had been reached, the major demand was that the problem should stop – and while residents did not make specific demands about police methods, they clearly saw some 'rules' about police behaviour as important. In many problems to which the police were called, there was not a unanimous view about the seriousness of the problem or about what should be done. None the less, many of the local officers whom we interviewed and whose work was talked about by residents routinely 'solved' problems, at least temporarily, in ways that met the demands of interested parties, whilst remaining within any relevant demands of the law (see Lustgarten 1987, on the wide range of options within the law open to officers in many common situations). Women officers and young officers only a short time in the service were as, or more, effective than the more mature men often pictured as ideal for such posts. However, the police organization – training, support, supervision, and even the types of written records used – did not appear to be geared to this kind of 'problem-solving' policing. The skills of local policing had been eclipsed over the last twenty or so years by other styles. They were being resurrected, but the rusting memories and recollections were often being applied without any systematic thinking to fit changed circumstances.

The third role was that of 'ear': the public assumed that they could pass on information about disorder and longer-term problems against the day when some of it might 'fit together' into a solution for a problem, or even point to a suspect for some offence. This view also yielded some power to the police, who might for example decide on the basis of a number of scraps of information that a particular problem was so large that action should be taken. It was hoped that decisions of this kind, and their results, would be communicated back to the neighbourhood. Unfortunately, however, police work is generally geared towards immediate response and action. Local officers tended either to take immediate action or to dismiss the information. As we emphasize on pp.167–8), the facility for digesting and recording information – if only in the form of a diary – was not part of the paperwork structure of the organization.

The fourth and, probably, most important role which the public demanded was the symbolic one of, by their very presence, proclaiming a state of order. This was the root of the wish, noted in many other studies, for more foot patrols. 'Panda cars', or their latter-day equivalents, provided the public with little reassurance.

Many studies have concluded that foot patrols do not constitute an effective use of manpower. Soetenhorst (1983) among others points out that the public have unrealistic expectations of the deterrent effects of patrols and we would endorse that view. This assumes, however, that the effectiveness of foot patrols should be measured in terms of crime reduction (see Hough 1987). Our rural and urban residents and business people rarely cited specifically deterrent aims. Many simply thought that the possession of one's own local police officer was a kind of benchmark for a state of order and a way of achieving the necessary communication between locality and police that would promote the second and third roles. A greater emphasis on decreasing fear of crime would thus also suggest the use of foot patrols (see Skogan 1987).

In our view, this symbolic function of policing could quite adequately be fulfilled in rural areas and in suburbs (lowish-crime areas) if policing were primarily to be done by local beat officers who would conduct at least part of their duties walking around their area (with back-up from an immediate response vehicle for the relatively rare, really urgent calls). The local gossip networks would be quite sufficient to spread news of the officer's presence if he or she were, about once a month, to walk round village centres and visit the focuses of activity in urban neighbourhoods and talk to residents and business people.

Setting agendas: neighbourhood accountability and control

Debates about police accountability in this country are usually set at the level of who should have policy control and who should have operational control over policing. The position is, broadly speaking, that chief constables of forces may be asked to provide accounts of their actions to police authorities, one for each force, composed of local councillors (now often from different councils) and magistrates. There are a number of recent innovations, not least the police–community consultative committees, mostly set up at district level. But operational control still lies with chief constables, and police authorities have comparatively little influence over issues which do not directly involve budgets and expenditure. (For a fuller account of these arrangements and recent debates, see Jefferson and Grimshaw 1984; Lustgarten 1987; Morgan and Maggs 1985; Reiner 1985).

All of this leaves local residents with a problem. How, in the absence of a formal mechanism for telling the local police officer to stop Johnny skateboarding in the street, can local people direct what they see as the 'right kind' of police attention to such local issues? The first point is that it is hard to do so when one has no idea who the local officer is, or there just isn't one. One cannot 'send the right messages' to an anonymous police officer or civilian who may well not know the neighbourhood. Hence, so far as we could tell, there was no informal mechanisms in the urban areas for attempting to control the police, at least in the sense we describe below. But where there was a known and local policeman, it was possible to display a range of small (though not necessarily effective) signals that one might prefer certain things to be done or overlooked.

We observed three such strategies. The first and least sophisticated was to hint to the officer that particular actions by him or her were disapproved of. Second, information was manipulated in various ways. When a crime was reported or a complaint made, individuals would withhold items of information in attempts either to change the way in which the officer would see the situation or to conceal the identity of their suspects. This last was particularly prevalent where local youngsters were thought to be involved and where it was feared that the police would prosecute first offenders. (Since it was rare that anyone ever learned what happened to a specific incident they had witnessed, these fears continued unchecked.) Third, villages are blessed with parish councils which, in our areas, from time to time decided that something should be done about rubbish bins being damaged or windows broken, for example. One strategy was to call the police and to ask if they might take the matter in hand. The presence of a known local officer was not essential for this to work, though it was helpful and tended to encourage an earlier, informal approach with negotiated action by both parties to stop the nuisance. Both Southton and Northam parish councils made such calls on the police during the study period, concerning vandalism, 'youths', and what was perceived by some parish council members as a rising crime rate.

These strategies could not be used without problems for police and public. First, many calls were of a non-crime nature and related, as we have already stressed, to little Johnny and his skateboarding or similar annoyances. The police typically have few legal powers useful to the resolution of such matters, and must rely on negotiation. Successful negotiation and conciliation (the regulatory, rather than prosecution mode of law enforcement, see Hawkins 1984) rely on personal relationships and long-term contact. They are also facilitated by the possession of some back-up powers (such as those held by factory inspectors to issue improvement and prohibition notice). People knew this, and felt on the one hand that the police ought to have some statutory powers that could be exercised to stop little Johnny. On the other hand, they also knew that such power would be draconian and double-edged – useful if you want to have someone controlled, but invidious if one is being controlled. Second, Christie's notion of disputes as 'personal property' was highly relevant (1977). People had to be sure, at the moment of involving the police, that they no longer wished to influence the outcome of the problem, since, once the call had been made, the potential for influencing the manner in which it was dealt with and its outcome became very restricted. Third, and related to this, it is clear that the only way in which people could set the level of 'police tolerance' of minor offences was through their decision whether or not to report the matter, while offences which came to police attention in any way other than through public reports were not even open to this form of influence.

These few points are germane to recent moves on the part of the police forces to introduce more 'neighbourhood' or 'community' policing. It seems clear that where more police are returned to the beat as local area officers, they will be exposed to the various informal strategies designed to control what the officer does on his patch and how he does it. As more Dixons of Dock Green emerge on to the streets, the likely pattern for the future will be the rediscovery of how Dixon managed his affairs, got to know the local community norms, and negotiated his way through them. Community policing is not a one-way process in which the public co-operate with the police. The reality will be that the police will also be expected to co-operate with the public. This will almost certainly include demands on the one side to attend to matters such as vandalism which are, from the policing point of view, difficult to solve and often unrewarding (will the PC want a reputation in the station for always nicking vandals rather than burglars?). And they will include, on the other, expectations that certain levels of illegality should only be noted – or informal words spoken – at least until the offence is repeated. Here the local officer will also be expected to act as an intermediary between the public and other less familiar aspects of policing, such as the involvement of specialist officers. This point is taken up in the next chapter, which discusses the police view of policing in urban and rural environments.

9

Police views of policing

In this chapter we consider how the day-to-day concerns and views of police officers, their perceived priorities, and the organizational demands of policing shape the character of their task and affect the public's experience of the police. The two sections at the end of this chapter lay out the framework for a means of bringing public expectations and police 'service delivery' closer together. Since our own work reflects the specifics of one police force and its organizational structure, we shall where possible point out how our own findings complement or contradict those of others.

Occupational cultures

The day-to-day concerns and views of officers are often described in terms of an 'occupational culture'. Reiner's (1985) recent and comprehensive work summarizes his own (Reiner 1978) and other studies of the subject. In his view, eight 'core characteristics' of the culture are:

1. a sense of mission. Policing is seen as a way of life with a victim-centred perspective as its main justification;
2. cynicism about the prevailing state of order and pessimism about likely developments. These attitudes, says Reiner, derive from extreme commitment to a sense of order;
3. suspicion. Officers whose day-to-day work concerns potential dangers and confrontations develop 'finely-grained cognitive maps of the world' in which many events are clues about potential disorder;
4. isolation and solidarity. Seeing themselves as remote from 'civilians' who do not share their concerns and values, the police form a strong group solidarity. In part this is expressed through a typology of civilians. Relying on the work of Holdaway (1981) and Lee (1981), Reiner suggests seven categories: good-class villains (professional criminals who share many game-like understandings with the police), police property (for whom the police are the dominant mode of social control, such as vagrants, alcoholics, and prostitutes), rubbish (people whose calls on the police are unworthy of attention, for example those in domestic disputes), challengers (doctors,

lawyers, and social workers – whose profession gives them the power to challenge police actions), disarmers (the very young, very old, and women, whose apparent vulnerability can lead to complaints against the police being taken seriously), do-gooders (for example, civil rights groups), and finally politicians, whose attitudes to the police depend on the prevailing climate of opinion;

5. conservative moral and social (though, in Britain, not necessarily political) views;
6. machismo, perhaps a reaction to and way of releasing the tensions, in particular the moral tensions, of police work;
7. racial prejudice. Reiner cites several studies, including Smith, Small, and Gray (1983), which suggest racial prejudice exists at least to the same level as in the general population, though he notes that there is little evidence to suggest that discrimination on purely racial grounds occurs in practice;
8. pragmatism. The desire to get the job done with the minimal fuss and paperwork. Reiner refrains from saying how this might affect day-to-day police work, noting only that it tallies with conservatism and resistance to change.

Having presented this list, Reiner goes on to suggest that the ways in which individual officers adjust to and live within the culture can be described broadly in terms of a fourfold typology. This comprises: the peace-keeping 'bobby', the disillusioned time-serving 'uniform-carrier', the crusading 'new centurion' for whom law-keeping is paramount, and the public-relations wise, managerially orientated 'professional'. This categorization is essentially similar to other typologies proposed by both English and American authors. Finally, he argues that some variation along these lines may be seen in different police specialisms; the 'new centurion' may be more common among CID while police managers (presumably inspectors and above) are more likely to have the 'professional' outlook.

We have concentrated upon Reiner's summation because, in our view, it best sums up the results and philosophy of much of the sociological work on the culture of policing in Britain. All these observations and studies, however, are essentially broad generalizations about 'police' as a unitary concept. They stem from observational work on, and are essentially based on studies of, urban police. They say nothing about potential variations between rural and urban police styles and views. Cain (1973) appears to be the only British author to have considered this point, though her study of rural, town, and city policing preceded recent moves back to neighbourhood policing. Rural police, she found, tended to work with community values in mind, saw themselves primarily as 'peace-keepers', worked in co-operation with police on neighbouring beats, and sought public co-operation while keeping a social distance from citizens. Police in small towns paid less attention to community norms and tended to compete with each other rather than co-operate. The city police had no regard for community norms and little incentive to develop good community relations. Their work was largely characterized by monotony, so far as routine patrolling was concerned.

A plurality of cultures?

The literature distinguishes, then, between officers 'on the ground' and their managers, and identifies broad strategies by which officers adapt to the job. But our own data suggest that there is also wide cultural variation in officers' conscious approaches to their work and their motivations, which are discernible in different areas of police work and which are only beginning to be discussed (though see Cain 1973 and Fielding 1985). We are not alone in this view: Brown (1981), for example, describes a yawning gap between the ideologies of response work in cars and foot patrol work ('law enforcers' versus 'peace keepers'). But we would argue that the situation is actually more complex than this, and that the occupational culture may be more appropriately considered as a series of more or less discrete subcultures, which bear clear relationships to each other but are none the less quite clearly differentiated.

First, however, we need to set out briefly the organizational pattern of policing in our rural and urban areas. Northam fell into parts of two rural beats, covered by two area beat officers (ABOs) with cars who worked either from a police house in a nearby village or from the local police station in the small town (open part of the day). The officers covered a wide area. When they were not on duty, incidents would be dealt with by immediate response vehicles (IRVs) working over the whole of the rural area, by officers in cars sent out from the local station or the divisional station, or by rural ABOs from any one of five or six beats up to 20 miles away. Southton had, as we have described, its own rural beat officer living in the village, who 'paired' duties with the officer from the adjoining beat. IRV crews and officers from the nearby small town filled any remaining gaps as regards urgent calls. CID officers were largely geographically localized in their workloads and based on one of the small towns.

In the urban area, response policing was largely decentralized. In fact, though residents complained of not seeing enough of their officers, the structure of policing there was orientated far more towards area beat policing than it was in almost the whole of the rest of the country at that time. Each beat was policed by three ABOs. They were intended to work together as a team, though their duties would usually be at different times unless they had organized a particular operation. They were backed up by a small number of IRVs and by CID officers based on the main police station.

ABOs in both rural and urban areas were the main police resource and dealt with the whole of the non-urgent police workload – reactive and proactive. They were expected to deal with crime, as well as promote community relations.

We interviewed fifty-three officers, from constable to superintendent, all working in or responsible for the areas we studied (see Appendix). We asked about day-to-day work, approaches to it, the concepts and contexts which informed what was done, and how and why it was done. Outside the interview situation, meals in station canteens and work on police files also gave us a great deal of informal contact with a range of officers. We set out below our own typology of police work, looking in turn at the ABOs, the IRV drivers, the CID, and lastly at the supervisors and supervisory processes.

AREA BEAT OFFICERS

One or two of the urban area beat officers (ABOs) for each beat would normally be on duty between 8 a.m. and 2 a.m. every day. They patrolled on foot, dealing mainly with matters that the radio controller, using the 'call grading system' operative at the time, selected for a 'delayed response'. They also dealt with follow-up calls and 'process'. All emergency calls, and urgent calls between 2 a.m. and 8 a.m., were dealt with by IRVs (see next section). Of the twelve we interviewed, six either were working or had just stopped working as local area beat officers for the two urban beats we studied. Thumbnail sketches of the work they did included:

'all the out-of-time enquiries – traffic warden follow-up enquiries, general crime and messages that come in that are delayed response. The general run-of-the-mill we get – all the time on foot, walking round.'

'Everything really – but more crime-oriented. You come into contact with people, then they get to know you and come out and see you rather than phone up the station. And school talks, cycling proficiency . . . just being seen and walking about and talking to anybody – trying to put yourself into the community.'

Three themes characterized the urban beat policing. First, the ABOs remarked that, unlike other officers, they could organize their working day more or less rationally, without rushing from incident to incident. Second, they saw themselves as having a high degree of public contact in situations ranging from domestic disputes to cycling proficiency tests. Third, the two beats were seen as very socially mixed: 'To look at, you think what an area. Working-class vagrant types we come in contact with; there's a strong contingent of Irish and Asian. And a good mix of business, residents, shops' (urban beat 1). 'An urban area, with low-class dwellings, none really bad – depends if they're owner-occupied – also medium class and high class. Large West Indian, Asian and Irish communities; family life, and bedsits, and hostels. Businesses and factories, etc.' (urban beat 2).

This mix was said to 'help make life more varied', despite the perception that much of their time was spent with a small number of people who 'must regard us as bad news because we're always dropping something on them'.

Another six officers interviewed worked beats in the rural subdivision. One was the Southton PC; two others worked the beat which included Northam, and the remaining three covered nearby beats. The beats were quite large, and where the working patterns required a constable on duty to 'mind' the adjacent beat for his off-duty colleague, the area he covered would easily measure about 10 miles across – large enough for the officers to be slightly concerned that while 'we're supposed to be community-involved', some villages 'only see us go through . . . you only go down there if you're sent down'. Again, we collected brief descriptions of their work: 'Everything from fires to cats up trees. It's not just eight hours a day, I'm up at 3.30 a.m. with people banging on the door. In [my last village] if I heard a burglar alarm I would get out of bed and go – you're a doctor/social worker.' 'Anything and everything. All police matters, some advice in civil matters, rescuing animals, attending fires, attending road traffic accidents, helping people get into their houses, assisting at trees being cut down, etcetera. Basically attending anything where we can assist.'

The rural ABOs characterized their work differently. While they too said they could organize their working day rationally, this was seen as the consequence of generating a significant amount of work for themselves: 'Town officers' work is largely assigned. With rural it's 50/50 assigned and self-generated. I have a workload that's not immediately obvious, and when I'm off-duty I still notice things.'

A second theme emerged from this. Much of what they generated, and probably much of what was assigned, was described as 'not real police work'. 'Real' policing appeared to mean crime, 'process' enquiries, and possibly traffic accidents. In contrast, much of their work concerned matters that the public, in such ways as were open to them, indicated should be dealt with unofficially or which – like felling trees – people simply thought 'needed' a policeman to be around in case 'anything happened'. Though they did not, in their terms, do 'real police work', they saw themselves as the 'coalface workers' for a wide range of problems, in an environment that required careful treatment. This range of work was valued:

'You need a wide smattering of criminal and traffic law, there's a wider variety of things happening. Civil law – domestic cases. You know about the other emergency services more. Farming, and a feeling for people's emotions. It's not so cut and dried out here. In town you can go to an incident and lock everyone involved up – out here no.'

Rural officers also talked about the benefits of having an area to oneself, whilst urban ABOs tended to talk about the benefits of discussion with colleagues (when they were perceived as interested in ABO work!). As one rural ABO said: 'I rely heavily on experience to stop antagonism which could result in requiring another PC rather quickly.'

There were, then, clear differences in what the officers valued about the kind of work they did. But there were also similarities:

'There are two ways of policing. Aloof and separate, or as one of them [villagers]. As one of them is far the easiest – not too familiar though I join in social acts – there's always a cup of coffee.' (rural ABO)

'I try to make a point of going to every street in the area each week. There are several places for cups of tea – I find out what's going on.'(urban ABO)

'A cup of tea is a good thing. It's a cross-section. You talk to anyone, the local shopkeeper, parish council, postman, old dears down the road. Even isolated people know about things because everyone goes to talk to them. You get more info that way. With pubs, they have to protect their clientele, but some publicans will talk. Postmasters know an awful lot. Some won't talk. Some farmers will, but they farm such large areas. You've got to speak to farmers.' (rural ABO)

'I pop into major employers and little businesses and homes – I know a few people and go and have a natter.' (urban ABO)

Urban and rural area beat officers seemed to share a model of community policing which relied on getting information along with cups of tea. What was done with such information was sometimes, in a strict sense, to 'cuff' it – that is, not to report it. And that was what people often wanted. Equally, the model put 'solving the situation' prior to 'law enforcement', with its attendant recourse to arrest and other official procedures (though none flinched at arresting and prosecuting where they thought it was needed). It saw this kind of emphasis as being in line with public demands. The extent to which this squares with public concerns about 'police property' is discussed later. Finally, this model was held by both urban and rural ABOs to contrast with the kind of work expected in the city centre (where policing was organized using the shifts/sections more common elsewhere in the country, rather than ABOs):

'It's different from the city centre – there it's one shoplifter after another. This is self-motivated work – you give advice on domestic problems, it's not things you're sent to. In the station they give you some jobs, but you're self-employed whereas IRVs are sent to one job after the next. The sergeant said when I came here: "You're going to have to slow down" – in town you're immediate response on legs. It took me ages to adjust – there's still a lot of work but the pace is different, you don't run.'   (urban ABO)

IMMEDIATE RESPONSE POLICING

The force we studied deployed what in their jargon were known as 'immediate response vehicles' or IRVs. These cars – sometimes known as 'jam sandwiches' due to their livery – were usually single-manned. They provided, as the jargon suggests, rapid response to calls from anywhere in the subdivision to which they were allocated. In theory, three such vehicles were available at any one time in the urban subdivision (which covered nearly one-half of the city). But vehicle servicing and tasks outside the subdivision frequently reduced this coverage. Bearing in mind ABOs' hours, it was possible for the police presence on the streets of the subdivision at, say, 3 a.m. to comprise in total one or two such cars.

Local beat police were often disparaging about IRV work, saying that it consisted of charging about and never finishing off any job properly. Urban IRV drivers agreed with the description but not the evaluation:

'Burglar alarms, accidents, domestics, assaults, obvious traffic offences, breathalysers, the occasional car with criminals in it. And all the 999s – they're about half our load. The original idea was, for example, if we got the prisoners and brought them in, we could leave the paperwork for the General Duties boys and go back out on the street. But it's like the old panda system, but there's more RTA [Road Traffic Accident] work 'cos there's no traffic cars in town. And if a PC's not on his beat we may get his delayed response jobs.'

'We do minor things, taxi work – mostly with traffic and nearly all accidents because if we go to a crime then CID come and take over.'

In contrast to Holdaway's (1983) picture of fast driving and dramatic incidents, our IRV officers sound positively pedestrian. Their 'bread and butter' consisted of traffic accidents, routine enquiries which filled the slack times on patrol, and a great deal of paperwork, this latter often used to fill the times when the shortage of cars left drivers kicking their heels at the station. The high number of traffic accidents they dealt with, in both urban and rural areas, is explained by the smallness of the traffic division, which concentrated mainly on motorway policing. In effect, the IRVs were the force's major traffic control element. The lack of 'real' police work, such as burglary, came about because after the initial response such matters were passed on to CID.

The urban IRV drivers were, as a consequence of their shift patterns, comparatively isolated from the ABOs. And they did not pass work on to them:

'All accident paperwork, minor crimes, you don't pass on to anyone else – only if it's burglary or serious assault. We don't pass stuff on to area officers – sometimes we fill out the crime report and manage to do the follow-up ourselves.'

Neither would they see ABOs at incidents, since if the incident required an IRV in the first place it was also likely to be serious enough for the CID to take it on. This lack of contact had some interesting results. For example, ABOs complained that they would not hear about serious crime on their 'patch', because the IRV drivers and CID did not tell them what had been going on. Consequently, ABOs sometimes found themselves in embarrassing situations:

'That is a problem – IRVs get briefed on parade. We don't. I rummage around and look in at the station but other chaps are just given the work waiting for them and relying on their partner and they're not told. But if things have happened on that duty or when I'm off-duty and people talk to me, I'm their local policeman – it's embarrassing.' (urban ABO)

Happily, both rural and urban subdivisions had acquired a microcomputer just prior to our research, and the weekly print-outs of crimes for each beat were much appreciated by the ABOs for the basic information they provided. Indeed, the speed of adaptation from fear of computers to eagerness to demand new analyses had to be seen to be believed! The rural IRV drivers were by no means so isolated, ironically because the large area covered by them and by the ABOs made it necessary for the distinctions between the two to be blurred. The response to a call was made by whoever was nearest, or, for 'delayed response' calls, whoever would be passing the address in the next day or so. Thus the rural IRV drivers saw their work in such terms as:

'You follow it through more out here – you're not running from job to job . . . in the city you get a burglary but it's passed on as a crime report. Here you see it through, and there's self-generated work. I like seeing the end-product.'

'We go to the more serious incidents – but the rural men to a degree do the same job as us. The area is so large that if there's one IRV on, the quickest car there might be a rural beat man, so we haven't really relieved the rural beat man that much.'

If IRV drivers, especially in the urban areas, saw themselves as excluded from 'real police work' and operating as a quasi-traffic division, what value did they get from their work? Primarily, they seemed to enjoy the 'fire brigade' aspect of the work and the professional skills required from being the first on the scene at major incidents, being called into action at a moment's notice, and living with the uncertainty of what the next call would involve.

THE CID

Criminal investigation has a chequered reputation. On the one hand, many police consider that this is the essence of police work. On the other, some researchers (for example, Ericson 1981) report that 'detection' seems largely to consist of waiting for information to emerge, rather than generating it; that 'pursuing enquiries' often means spending time in cafés and bars, ostensibly looking for informants; that much 'detective work' in practice boils down to 'cooling out' victims whose crimes have not been solved, and that a specialized detective squad is probably not the most efficient means of detecting crime.

In the force we studied, the CID was expected to process and solve 'serious' criminal offences. Their bread and butter comprised domestic and commercial burglaries, business frauds, robberies, violent offences (including woundings and serious sexual assault), and offences resulting in death. In consequence, they dealt with only a minority of reported crimes, the majority being handled by the ABOs and, to a limited extent, the IRV drivers. Indeed, in the urban area, the CID attempted to guard the 'boundaries' of their work and discourage the referral of certain types of case:

> 'CID doesn't investigate crime, but deals with it when it comes our way. The area men are pretty good – they approach us for advice, it's good – they like to deal with their own problems. But sometimes, like when the IRV's got stolen DHSS books and wanted us to deal with it – his attitude was he'd done his job – we feel put upon for minor stuff.'   (urban CID officer)

The urban and rural CID must, however, be described separately since there were substantial differences in their approach and organization.

Urban CID. One summary of the pattern of urban detective work was:

> 'The 9 to 5 shift deal with prisoners. The 4 to midnight shift covers everything. There's one night DC who visits burglaries initially, and leaves a report for the early turn. Burglaries are allocated to the early turn DCs, 8 to 4, because they tend to be reported at night. There are more house burglaries than factory or office breaks, and with house-to-house enquiries it's say 65/35 house to business contact.'

The allocation of cases created a caseload of around thirty to forty 'jobs' per detective constable (DC), of which typically about one-third were judged by DCs as offering enough information for any detection to take place; the remainder were, in the jargon, 'no-goers'. In principle, each DC and detective sergeant was attached to a 'zone' comprising two or three beats. This system, only recently introduced, was intended to promote liaison between CID and ABOs who could then jointly create a localized knowledge of 'their' neighbourhoods. However, the CID caseloads were, at the time of the study, in no way allocated on the basis of this zoning:

'I've got two frauds, one deception, one enquiry from Edinburgh and numerous burglaries from all over town. But the beat system isn't working. In theory I'm supposed to have crime from one area only but I'm getting anything from everywhere.'

'In principle the DS (detective sergeant) liaises with the area officers on particular beats, that's existed for six months, but no such liaison exists in practice. . . . All you could do is take an interest in crime occurring in that area but you can't afford to concentrate on it. . . . It's not at all structured – just the way it works out. . . . So I'm pessimistic. We're very busy, at saturation point and sometimes beyond it. We could do double the overtime.'

The zoning principle was being resisted by senior CID officers, who felt it more important that DCs should specialize in specific kinds of offence and that, in any event, the organization should remain 'flexible'. This appeared to mean two things. First, the CID saw themselves as so overloaded that any system of allocating cases would be overruled to meet short-term demands. Second, senior officers wanted a 'contingency reserve' of officers who could quickly be made available if a very serious offence occurred.

Given this lack of enthusiasm for liaison, lack of it in practice is hardly surprising. Little information beyond that given on the crime reports seemed to pass into the CID; and very little seemed to pass back from CID to other officers:

'It's a sore point in my opinion. I have thought I'll use CID, for example, OK they can deal with so-and-so, he's difficult – but nothing gets done – so now I try to do it myself . . . you're considered the lowest of the low by CID. The top men think liaison is where it's at but it hasn't spread down . . . the CID is a boys' club – it's difficult. So I go through one of the [uniformed] ex-CID people for contact. Maybe I shouldn't.'   (urban ABO)

'They are worst at keeping secrets as to what's going on. Lots of things that happen on your area you accept that IRVs have dealt with and not thought to tell you – but CID have burglaries or are interested but very rarely you find out about it. . . . It would be a good idea to have localized CID.'(urban ABO)

All of this suggests that CID saw itself as a specialized group with relatively tenuous links to other forms of policing. This distance was maintained in at least two ways. First, the boundaries between what the CID saw as 'their business' and 'other people's business' were themselves well-policed. Second, the flow of information was mainly to CID from others and much less in the other direction. What, then, did this specialized group do to process or solve crime? Two brief observations are pertinent.

The first relates to methods of detection. The urban CID had begun to adopt a strategy of 'targeting' known criminals on the assumption that it was they who committed most crime. Targeting involved keeping surveillance on individuals selected on the grounds that, for example, they had just been released from prison. The rationale was that sooner or later, evidence of an offence would be generated. The form of surveillance often left the person in no doubt that they were being watched. At the time of our study, this policy was being reconsidered, since the offenders involved seemed to regard it as a 'change in the rules of the game', and retaliated by refusing to admit to any offences other than those for which evidence existed. This decline in 'offences taken into consideration' had reduced the clear-up rate for the subdivisional CID.

Secondly, while the research was being done, the urban CID were concentrating their efforts on offences of burglary, and justified this strongly to us and among themselves in terms of the serious financial loss and emotional harm experienced by victims. Yet these victims did not, so far as we could see, obtain much support from the CID. The initial visit was usually made by IRV drivers who would say the CID would call next day. But detectives often did not call for several days and even then commonly missed their appointments (see Shapland, Willmore, and Duff 1985; Maguire 1982). And, in keeping with Ericson's (1981) findings, it was rare for the urban detectives to seek out witnesses or check with the ABO – both courses of action that would be likely to improve their detection rate (see Burrows 1986; Clarke and Hough 1984; Eck 1983). Our own conclusion was that the ABOs may have been equally if not better able, even in serious cases, to detect offenders by concentrating on witnesses rather than on known offenders, as the detectives did.

Rural CID. The rural situation was markedly different. The kind of work they dealt with was similar to the urban CID, though caseloads were lower and the approach more victim- and offence-based. In part, the rural detectives saw the difference in approach as necessitated by the large area they had to cover:

> 'We have a smaller caseload here than in the urban area, so we work more thoroughly. It's not so cursory, we give each one more attention. . . . But caseloads are still high because of the way the establishment is worked out. . . . In the urban area, it's easier to clear crimes because there are "nests" of criminals and enquiries are easily done. Here there are travelling criminals and geographical dispersal.'

The practice of allocating cases also differed, as did attitudes, with rural officers seeing benefits in geographical rather than offence-based specializations:

'It's better having a local CID for an area as vast as this. You can't expect to pool the work. In the urban area they have an office which is a pool, and no one has a clue what's going on. It's better to give someone an area.'

Equally, the rural CID were less inclined to see themselves as separate from uniformed police, saying that detectives and ABOs were partners in a team:

'We contact the RBOs [resident beat officers] and they us. We do work with them. Some would rather give you the job and let you get on with it. I prefer it if they want to be involved all the way along. It's a good idea to have localized CID. You're more involved in the area – it's greater satisfaction.'

(rural DC)

'We've just had a roll-up [detection of a lot of similar crimes] with three kids breaking into sixty cars. That was a collective effort – the uniformed and me. And it's the stuff that annoys people in the villages. In the sticks we can do old-fashioned policing. They [urban CID] *say* they're doing house-to-house but they don't do it.'

(rural DC)

Uniformed officers still grumbled about lack of liaison, but grumbles and bitter criticism are leagues apart.

THE SERGEANTS

In principle, any officer on duty, on whatever shift, should be able to obtain advice, call his supervisor to a serious incident, and indeed be 'checked up on'. This made supervision arrangements somewhat complex. For a rural ABO, for example, the first line of supervision would be his 'section sergeant'. Each section sergeant had a 'portfolio' of beats, was responsible for all the officers attached to them, and checked their paperwork. Section sergeants did not, however, work the same shift patterns as many of those they supervised. If the section sergeant was off-duty, the next in line was the 'shift' sergeant, whose pattern of shifts would be the same as the ABO but who would not necessarily have routine oversight of his paperwork. If that sergeant too was, say, on leave, the third alternative would be a duty sergeant or the duty inspector at the subdivisional station.

The extent of supervision required and exercised in practice varied considerably. The urban ABOs said they usually saw their section sergeant once in every shift, though the shift patterns inevitably left periods when officers would not see them for several days and, with some combinations of shifts, for several weeks at a time. To counter this, some urban sergeants and ABOs had begun regular 'beat meetings' as a way of discussing common problems. In the rural areas, the shift system was more flexible and contact easier, at least in theory. Even so, the occasions on which the constable saw his or her sergeant were essentially those on which paperwork was exchanged, and while some rural constables saw their sergeant on most working days, others saw them only once or twice a week. The idea of 'section meetings' or 'beat meetings' had not taken hold.

Other constables, such as IRV drivers and the 'general duties' officers who manned the stations had much greater contact with their sergeants.

For ABOs everywhere, supervision in practice amounted principally to being given tasks and asking for advice on some cases:

> 'I see him once a day – there's not many days when I don't see one. We talk about work, what's on at the moment. For example cases where it's unclear if it's civil or criminal. If there's an arrest to make, he'll come with me.'
>
> (urban ABO)

The role of the section sergeant was largely one of handing out, receiving, and occasionally chasing paperwork, much of it originating from within the force or from other forces. Besides this, section sergeants dealt with queries, passed on information and instructions, and to some extent negotiated understandings about management practice between the inspectors who created it and the constables who were expected to follow it. There was a tendency among ABOs to organize their work so that they could seek advice from their own section sergeant, who would also know the characteristics of, and characters on, the beat:

> 'It can be a bit difficult, you think your own sergeant will help you more – I have very little contact with them apart from being given jobs, you're left on your own. You have to be your own sergeant. But they are all right, they will help, they will come down [to the beat].'   (urban ABO)

This was, however, more common among the urban constables, who were younger (three or more years' service) and felt less well-established in their beats.

In sum, sergeants did not, by and large, spend much time 'inspecting' or 'checking on' their constables out on the beat (see Chatterton 1985 for similar findings in other forces). It was not, they said, their job to tell the ABO how to run his or her beat. The only sense in which 'inspectoral' supervision was done was that sergeants were expected to use the paperwork relationship, and occasional visits to the beat, to assess whether officers thought they were coping.

SENIOR OFFICERS AND VIEWS ON MANAGEMENT

Describing police policy and management is a dangerous exercise. The pace of change is now so fast that the definitions of the 'management task' were almost entirely rewritten during the three years of our project (see O'Dowd 1987). The management strategy at the time of the study was to try to make explicit the hitherto largely unstated assumptions and principles which comprised the police definition of their objectives, to state them, and then to devise ways of ensuring that they were achieved (this approach is known as 'Policing by Objectives' or 'PBO': for an extended description see Butler 1984).

One area which featured strongly in these formal documents – improving community relations – appeared to be both an objective and a method of reaching it. The force had, among other activities, conducted a public attitude survey as an aid to this. But in day-to-day work, what was termed 'community relations' by officers appeared to mean relations between senior officers (many inspectors and almost all the more senior uniformed officers) and a range of groups and agencies. These latter included such diverse groups as youth clubs and parish councils and local authority planning departments. In addition, multi-agency committees had been set up, including joint panels with social services and education departments to consider juvenile offenders, while the Police and Criminal Evidence Act 1984 had required police forces to set up a police–public consultative process – in practice, division-based consultative committees. This new 'policing glasnost' was intended, ultimately, to be a two-way communication process. But at the time we saw it the process was at an early stage, and the police were talking more than they were listening, largely because those they were talking to did not know enough about policing to open a dialogue (see Morgan 1987a, 1987b).

Contact with local authorities was also sought over issues such as traffic flows, parking, and lighting, where potential solutions to what the police saw as a problem could only be achieved by council action. Such contact was only sometimes problem-free: 'It can be frustrating because we're dependent on the council responding to our identification of problems and sometimes they won't – we can wait up to three months for replies. Eventually I go to councillors through the consultative committee.'

A second part of the management strategy revolved around the perceived management need to set realistic objectives and monitor progress towards them. The scheme was built around an annual cycle of consultations between all ranks from constable upwards, resulting in the formulation of general aims and local, more specific, objectives, together with methods of achieving them. Constables were required to state how much time they had devoted to each local plan, and monitoring schemes were devised to assess what progress had been made. The uniformed constables at the 'sharp end' of PBO were cynical about it. They often claimed that they were doing more paperwork while pursuing the kinds of goals they had always set for themselves anyway, and saw the whole idea of identifying which goals had been pursued at what times as a cosmetic exercise. But there was some recognition that the scheme gave greater autonomy to constables who could define and pursue their own goals, while the process of committing to paper the local problems and potential solutions was seen by others as a useful discipline. DCs, in particular, appreciated the challenge of trying to make crime reduction plans, operationalized in terms of clear-up rates and amounts of recorded crime, difficult for officers from other subdivisions to massage so that the figures showed apparent successes! More senior officers saw more advantages in the scheme, though these were not necessarily the 'official' benefits:

> 'It's not changed things, but you can see the end-product. Before, we didn't evaluate – we still had blitzes on particular things but we didn't know what we'd achieved. This system brings to light failures. And also, the new system means more communication. You don't go to a superintendent's office on hands and knees and leave bowing and scraping. And the inspectors are much less likely to pull their punches with each other – there's more plain speaking, which is very good.'

Policing and ideas of community

Notwithstanding the very real improvements which were in train at the time of our research, the kind of policing in place in our areas was still relatively far from what the public appeared to want of their police (though, comparing our results with those of other studies, we believe that the public were very much more appreciative of the force in the areas we studied than in areas with more traditional, shift-based policing). Several factors encouraged the split between public wishes and policing practice.

First, and broadly speaking, senior officers did not regard area beat work as a specialism within uniformed work or even as a particularly skilled task, in the way that they saw IRV and public order work. Special training, meetings on good practice, and manuals of relevant skills were conspicuously absent – in contrast to the position in many other areas of police work. ABOs were thrown on their own resources, and were often supervised by sergeants who had joined the force at the time when patrols in panda cars were being introduced. These sergeants had now to learn what area beat policing was about at the same time as their constables were finding out how to do it. The result was ironic. The police themselves had precious little to draw on as a model other than television images of Dixon of Dock Green.

Second, while senior officers were heavily involved in 'community relations' work, this almost exclusively meant relations with groups and agencies. We argued in Chapter 4, however, that neighbourhood problems tended to exist at the much more localized level of streets and parts of streets. 'Community relations' might reasonably be expected to raise and solve neighbourhood problems; but the level of consultation was too general for this to be so (with the possible exception, in the rural areas, of parish councils). The extent to which local organizations could provide a fruitful 'way into the community' was questioned by one urban officer who pointed out:

'In this area the residents seem to be full of apathy – complete non-interest. We've had three residents' meetings organized by the Labour Party, they delivered invitations to every home. The first one fourteen people turned up; the second one one person turned up; it was redated and then ten people came. But it's very strong Labour politically.'

Not only the area officers questioned whether community relations could be pursued through organizations. In the rural area, the very existence of 'village England', with small, tight-knit communities looking after their own, was considered something of a myth. The consensus seemed to be that while it might be sensible to talk about community backing for specific projects, incidents and crimes were experienced by individuals as individuals, and the idea of a 'community response to crime' was simply not on. This view broadly fits with our own findings in Chapter 6.

In the rural areas, neighbourhood problems remained the province of *ad hoc* solutions by rural ABOs, possibly assisted by their sergeant. In the urban area, a further compartmentalization occurred. The ABOs were most in touch with local problems while organized neighbourhood liaison was the province of more senior officers or specialists – 'schools liaison' or designated 'community relations' officers. In the urban area, then, not only were there few local venues at which problems could be raised, but equally, those police officers who were most in touch with local problems were not those whose job was to liaise about them. Was this being hinted at by the officer who defined his role as 'in between the police and the public'?

This last point would have mattered less were a third problem not also present. Most senior officers had become very aware of the lack of communication up and down the force hierarchy and between constables: 'The area men have got a vast amount of knowledge and no one's tapping it – it's a weakness we've got.' 'We are totally incapable of briefing officers and passing information on, and it shows up particularly now we have flexible rosters.'

Information about problems and contacts remained largely in the heads of the ABOs, was not available to other officers unless they knew whom and what to ask, and was 'lost' as constables moved to other posts. Where it was held on paper, it was often difficult to collate together the various sources in ways that could give a good picture of the perceived problem.

Attempts were being made to remedy this deficiency. One was the microcomputer. A 'communications audit' had also been instituted to discover what means for presenting information were most likely to result in it being remembered by officers. But problems of liaison and communication are often embedded in the institution, so that a fundamental review of organizational structures and working practices is necessary to tackle them.

Policing communities: a model for local policing

In the last chapter, we argued that there is an identifiable public demand for local area constables. These officers should know the local manners and customs; patrol on foot; be open to informal approaches and allow people to define their own requests for action; be able to find informal solutions to problems which, in some cases, may legally constitute comparatively serious crimes; and, none the less, act quickly and formally in instances of what the public see as serious crime.

In the earlier sections of this chapter, we have shown that, while ABOs and, to some extent, rural IRV drivers, were seeking to act in these ways, they were hampered by a range of factors. In the urban area, the occupational culture isolated them from CID work (and the CID did not act in ways that supported the area men). The ways in which they should go about their task had not yet been thought through within the force. Lines of communication in the force, while improving, did not allow for a good flow of information to the ABOs, while recording systems did not allow information to be easily recalled. The division of responsibilities for 'community relations' led to those officers who knew most about the neighbourhood having little input into the way the police related to it. Lastly, the very idea of 'community relations' rested upon an inadequate concept of the nature of community.

What was lacking, and what is needed, is a model based substantially on local policing by area beat officers. We feel that area beat policing is one of the major initiatives for the future and that it should be accorded status as a major specialization with appropriate skills. It does, of course, require a wide range of skills and an acceptance that 'real police work' includes work that the police are asked to do. But in many neighbourhoods area beat policing is the front line of policing and the type of police work in which good and continuing police–public relations matter most. Our own model for local policing, based on police and public experiences in our areas, is outlined below.

First, the pattern whereby one officer is attached to a rural beat and two or three to an urban beat seemed to fit the public demand and the practicalities of shift working (given the use of a minimum number of IRVs as well). The rural officers could cover for, and where necessary work with, officers on adjoining neighbouring beats. Shift patterns in the force we studied provided area officer coverage every day from 8 a.m. to 2 a.m. However, on the assumption that fast cars will always be needed to deal with emergencies, there is no intrinsic reason to define shifts so rigidly. Area officers are primarily required to talk to people during the working day and early evening; their presence is sometimes needed at, for example, pub closing times; they are occasionally concerned with, say, keeping night-time observations; and from time to time (apart from change-over periods) two or three of them might be required to work in concert on one job. All this militates in favour of allowing them considerable leeway within fairly wide limits in organizing their own hours of work.

Second, the 'how to do it' recipe knowledge of local beat policing needs to be reinvented and systematized. Before the ill-fated 'unit beat policing' model, such knowledge was probably the life blood of constables. Certainly official and unofficial beat manuals were produced, and if historical accounts are to be believed, beat lore was passed from constable to constable if not from sergeant to constable. The substance of this lore dealt with everything from potential troublespots to which premises were to be checked to ensure that they were locked, and from the local gossips, drunks, and vagrants to where a quiet cup of tea could be had. From what we saw in our areas, officers had some of this knowledge and some beats were starting to produce, unofficially, the same kinds of books. However, they primarily relied on their 'process' workload (summonses, licences, etc.) to bring them into contact with both residents and businesses. Consequently, some of those who might be most useful, from both police and public points of view – those we have characterized in Chapter 5 as the 'watchers' – had no contact with the police. Moreover, the occasion on which an officer calls to check licences or make enquiries is perhaps not the best time for him to open up conversations about the local grapevine. There is room for more development, training, and teaching of beat craft. Constables may need to be taught whom to talk to and how to find out about local problems. Skogan (1987) has shown that citizen contact card initiatives in the US, in which officers were instructed to find certain groups of people and ask them their views, were very successful in alerting officers to local views.

Third, the role of CID must change, despite – or even because of – their attachment to their current style of work. It does not make sense to have a specialist unit whose day-to-day work is so out of touch with what should be one of their prime sources of information. CID officers should be attached to beats and work in liaison with local ABOs. There seems little logic to the argument that this would prevent detectives from being drawn in to conduct enquiries on large cases.

Fourth, we see a need for beat officers who work together or cover for each other's beats to have a common information base and a method for liaison. This suggests a common office near their beats. A range of possibilities exists, from offices to police houses (where they still exist, though this option tends to disrupt domestic life) to police boxes (some of those we saw were quite roomy and comfortable) to a small shop or part of some other building. The methods for recording information are more difficult to envisage. Once computerized beat-based information came on stream, even officers distrustful of computers found it useful (when they had realized that a 50 per cent increase in crime was not a disaster if it was a rise from two crimes to three). There is clearly a role for more computer-based information, including the use of software mapping to indicate trends. But low-tech alternatives – wall maps, beat logs, and the like – would be equally useful. One further point worth noting is that while the criminal side of police work and 'process' are accompanied by a great deal of paperwork, there are no official documents on which to file 'beat work in progress' or 'state of play' for continuing problems. As moves towards minimization of crime and process paperwork gather steam (Cozens 1987), we hope that it will be possible to introduce a means of recording problem-solving without the general groan that any talk of 'another form' produces. No current form suffices. Message pads are merely records of 'who responded and what they found', useful primarily to controllers. A similar lack can be observed for CID in regard to crime enquiries. The most illuminating document in a crime file is normally the general summary by the officer in the case, but this is compiled after the event. Records of what is in progress are often scrappy notes literally on the backs of envelopes and intelligible only to their writer.

Fifth, the point at which the public began to see offences as serious, 'real' crime is higher than that in law, in police practice, and in decisions to prosecute. In some measure the definition of a crime as 'real crime' was also informed by who the offender was. Changes in the past ten or so years, including the development of diversionary measures such as cautioning and the promulgation of the Attorney General's guidelines, have begun to create greater distinctions between types of offences and between types of offenders. Yet the current opinions remain inadequate. In some forces, offenders can still only be unofficially warned if the offence is not recorded (this creates a risk for the officer if the offence has been reported by a member of the public). Or they can be formally cautioned, or reported for prosecution (this latter is not the decision of the constable). But other options are possible and may be more in tune with what the public want of the police. For example, officers in our study had arranged an apology to the victim, or conveyed a wish for some form of restitution. Formal diversionary schemes currently exist for juveniles in, for example, Northamptonshire and Devon and Cornwall. There should be further moves to create such possibilities.

Equally, recording a crime on a 'crime report form' is an obvious necessity for statistical reasons. But, once such a form has been completed, the tendency is to regard it not simply as information, but as determining procedures and outcome. Certain paths have to be followed, most involving CID as ultimate decision-makers. And the obvious outcome is prosecution. Decisions not to prosecute have to be justified, whereas decisions to prosecute are seen as the norm. So the tendency of officers is only to record as 'crime' incidents which might justify prosecution. Others are never put on paper. This restricts information about an occurrence to the one officer concerned and thereby lowers problem-solving effectiveness. The recording of incidents which are legally crimes needs to be separated from the process of decision-making on their outcome. From this simple step, new ideas and measures of 'success' in policing are likely to emerge.

It will be apparent, lastly, that the proposals outlined above will place new demands on sergeants. Whatever their current job description, they are currently largely tied to retrospective supervision of paperwork and constables' requests for advice. Yet if our proposals or something like them were to be implemented, it would be sergeants who would negotiate flexible timetabling for constables with them and senior officers, ensure that information was being passed between constables, maintain oversight of case disposals, and encourage the development of beat craft. All this, in addition to continuing to attend serious incidents, having oversight of the implementation of force objectives, and continuing to deal with paperwork and requests. The expansion of their role has been seen as a threat in comparable initiatives in the US. But sergeants we have spoken to in several forces in Britain have tended to regret the current change in philosophy and the effective diminution of their role consequent upon promotion from constable. We believe that British sergeants, despite some apprehension, might welcome the change.

The local policing approach we advocate is susceptible to three major problems. First, what happens if a local beat officer is not suited to the work or does not get on with the locals? And what happens if the greater discretion which would be given to officers is abused? A team approach (several ABOs, CID, sergeant) will at least avoid what happens at present in rural areas if the sole officer falls sick or is otherwise unable to cope – that the area receives very little policing of any type. It may also mean that a rogue officer would be pressured and possibly offered support by his team mates. But it may mean that the whole team develops informal practices which undermine the ethos of local policing. Solutions can only be found as problems emerge, and only good supervision will ensure that, where there are problems, they will emerge. The risk, however, can be minimized by including substantial experience of local policing with ABOs in probationer training, and developing the idea of area beat work as a specialism for which potential beat officers must apply. Ironically, the way to give the work status would be to give it a mystique and then limit access to it.

Second, a move to localized policing will inevitably result in dilemmas of local justice (see Chapter 10). The archetypal example cited by police is what to do about cannabis-smoking in public in heavily Rastafarian areas. Constables are also well aware that, since any neighbourhood contains many groupings whose interests may diverge, contradictory demands on the police will result. The result is often the assertion that officers should seek to enforce the law in a way that is consistent among them and across localities. Any such assertion – and it can be heard from some police as well as politicians – ignores the very real differences in policing styles and law enforcement that already occur, are considered necessary by senior officers, and are promoted by large segments of the public in their wish to make policing ever more local. The philosophy of local policing acknowledges that there are differences between areas and dissensions within neighbourhoods. Rival views about what constitutes social order exist even within a single street – often tied to age-groups, social classes, and racial groupings. There are no final answers to such difficulties – only provisional, constantly renegotiated understandings. This is a thorny road, but there is no longer any possibility of avoiding travelling down it. To deny its existence is not only to continue to travel down it blindly, but to create long-term and serious problems of public consent to policing.

Third, and perhaps most gravely, there is a problem which is both operational and political. The recent history of public order policing seems to have led in the direction of arrangements for large numbers of officers to be summoned to particular locations at short notice. If public order policing of this kind remains a major part of police work – and we suspect it will – then, without planning and forethought, disruption on the beats will be crippling, given the need for local knowledge and local understandings. The way round this is worthy of a book in its own right. However, despite myth to the contrary, emerging research findings tend to show that such demands are generally predictable and are a consequence of political demands and solutions (Johnstone and Shapland 1987; Morgan 1987c). Disturbances requiring large numbers of officers usually revolve around foreseen events – football matches, demonstrations, and industrial disputes, for example. Plans for these are drawn up well in advance. Public disorder that springs up from nowhere and requires more officers than the subdivisional strength on duty at that time is very rare indeed. Where disorder is predictable, the officers to be used can be selected in advance – there is no need constantly to rob the same beat. A team approach to local policing can also allow for abstractions of officers from their normal duties to police major events etc. and retain the passing on of information that is necessary for continuity of effort. At least some of the crises where public order has broken down have been the consequence of bad relations between police and public which will take years to improve and, we suggest, will only improve if local policing becomes more prevalent.

10
Policing by the public?

At the beginning of the book, we posed the question: are villages becoming the desert wastelands of crime, disorder, and community breakdown which already form the stereotype of urban living? Quite clearly, our villages were not. They suffered from vandalism and other occasional excesses by their local youth, and sometimes from crimes such as burglary and theft, but levels of recorded crime were far lower than in urban areas, and people felt they were still relatively peaceful, ordered areas.

But our urban areas didn't fit the stereotype either. It is true that if one looks solely at recorded crime statistics and calls upon police services, the urban areas had much higher crime rates than the villages. It is also true that more urban dwellers felt wary about walking around their neighbourhoods than did villagers. But the difference of degree did not amount to a difference in kind.

Villagers had problems – and urban dwellers and business people seemed to have the same problems, usually comprising vandalism, noise, youths, parked cars, and crime – the consequences of a number of people with different views and habits living close to each other. Wherever they occurred, they caused complaint, were attributable to the same kinds of local people, were very localized, and were usually dealt with in the same ways. In other words, informal social control was alive and well and living in towns as well as villages. Watching out for things and noticing disorder were regarded everywhere not as spying, but as neighbourly, protective, and helpful. Trying to do something about disorder was not regarded as vigilantism, but as implying a series of possible steps to be taken by particular people and regulated by social pressures.

Nor was there any sign of the imminent demise of informal social control. It is possible that there has been a decrease in 'community' in rural areas, accompanying an earlier decrease in urban areas and a greater emphasis on individual rights, as Clarke (1987), for example, has proposed. But this is extremely difficult to prove. We have very little data on informal processes today, and almost none on those of the last century or earlier times. However, where historical and contemporary data do co-exist, the problems of disorder – and the mechanisms for their control – have often been found to be very similar (for example, O'Connor 1986). In addition, increasing emphasis on people's rights in the recent past is likely to affect the formal mechanisms of social control far more than the informal. Where control is based on coercion and punishment, it may conflict with the protection of individual rights. Where control relies more on prevention, example, and coping with the after-effects of disorder, individual rights are unaffected.

If informal social control is still so active, can the 'official' guardians of the peace afford a more relaxed attitude to crime and disorder? Or, if not, can't the balance between formal and informal control, police and public, be left as it is now? The answer to both these questions must be a resounding 'no'. Informal social control cannot cope by itself and, by its very nature, will never be able to do so. However, neither can formal methods of control succeed by themselves. And, while formal and informal are not on speaking terms, their joint endeavours will be uncoordinated, ineffective, and, on occasion, counterproductive. The police and the public will annoy one another and their mutual incomprehension will fuel further criticism and misjudged action.

In the rest of this chapter, we shall explore the dilemmas of matching formal and informal social control. We shall start by setting out the limitations of informal social control – the questions of 'what community?' and 'whose order?' These lead on to the fundamental problem of controlling the controllers – the questions of 'whose police?' and 'whose crime prevention?' since official policies seem to be at times at variance with informal action. The last section of the chapter argues that, while specific solutions must be found locally, there are practical ways by which this can be accomplished – providing the willingness is there and, equally important, a new accountability emerges.

What community?

Neither villages nor towns are now, if they ever were, groupings of people with identical lifestyles who feel that they are all the same as each other and belong together. People live different lives, are of different ages and income levels, and have different beliefs about what constitutes 'their community'. But, at least as far as our study was concerned, they also all agreed on the existence of the same problems of crime and disorder. Who you were affected how seriously you regarded a particular problem, but not whether it was seen as a problem *per se*. And, at least as far back as the memories of the oldest residents could take us, the same kinds of problems had existed, waxing and waning over time as the age-mix and housing condition of the area changed.

Notwithstanding the similarities of definitions of 'what the problems are', the divisions within neighbourhoods produce difficulties for informal social control. Can a victim or watcher exercise any control if he or she does not know the offenders or suspects, of if they come from a different 'community' within the neighbourhood? This is a complex

question. It contains a number of different components, often wrapped
up together in the word 'community', but which we shall have to unpack
if we are to find the limits of informal social control.

It was certainly true in our areas that people differed in their lifestyles,
their views of the seriousness of problems, and their preferred solutions
to them. However, informal social control could cope with the divisions
between people over solutions, largely because action in respect of any
particular misdeed was considered the responsibility of its particular
witness or victim. Others might gossip privately but would do no more,
and so informal action did not tend to increase conflict within an area.
The actions of formal bodies such as the police, however, were seen as
ripe for comment by anyone who heard about them.

Informal action was, however, intrinsically limited in the kinds of
responses that were perceived as appropriate. It was primarily aimed at
coping with problems, rather than at deterring or preventing them. There
was some deterrence and some prevention, largely practised by organizations in the villages. But there was no hint of direct punishment for
misdeeds or of vigilante activity. A prerequisite of punishment is certain
knowledge of who did the deed (see, for example, the 'trials' and harsh
punishments meted out by the informal 'courts' in the black townships
of South Africa (Burman, undated)). In our areas, this certainty was only
achieved by the formal agencies – courts, police, social services. People
in both rural and urban areas were very wary of pointing a finger at an
offender unless they had direct, eyewitness proof. And since much
disorderly and problematic activity (vandalism, for example) was
unobserved, conclusive evidence was very rare.

Watchers could, of course, decide to take no action about what they
had seen. Sometimes, this was because people just did not see the incident as sufficiently serious. Sometimes it was a result of not feeling any
social obligation towards the victim. Social obligation was rarer in town,
though still remarkably prevalent. It extended to businesses as well as
dwellings. Sometimes, inaction was due to fear of retaliation, though
known offenders tended to evoke little fear (except for a few, notorious
ones). In general, people were less willing to intervene in the town.
Informal social control is not very effective against unknown offenders
– and so it is dependent upon watchers' and victims' spatial areas of
knowledge and social obligation.

It is also dependent upon the localization of offenders. Watchers,
unlike the police, do not feel they can operate at a distance from their
homes or businesses. We did have one example of a woman who
followed a gang of youths for over half a mile, watching their deprada-
tions and waiting until they returned home. But this was very rare and
even she felt extremely uncomfortable when she was on the offenders'
estate and off her home patch. Most offenders were very local, and so

informal social control could, in principle, be effective against them. What was problematic was if offenders (or their parents) would not acknowledge the fact of their wrongdoing. In the villages, if a victim, say, approached the local gang of youths and made a complaint, they might just laugh and carry on. It was then possible for that victim or others to go to the parents of the youths, or to one of the village organizations. Since disorder of this type was not normally a single, isolated incident, but part of a wave of offences against several victims, organizations could use preventive or deterrent tactics. In the urban area, few victims or watchers knew the relevant parents – and there were no possibilities for further action through organizations. There, the limits of informal social control were reached much faster.

It might be argued that it is all different in higher-crime areas. There, we would expect crime to play a more prominent role in lists of problems (because it is more prevalent, though not necessarily more serious), but other problems to continue to be represented. Morgan's (1987a) list of the topics raised by the public in police–public consultative committees in both inner-city, high-crime areas and more rural ones tends to bear out this prediction:

> For, unlike the police, they generally (though this varies from area to area) do *not* talk about serious crimes. Apart from the reassuring presence of more foot patrols, typically they want the police to do something about nuisances, incivilities and inconveniences. Traffic problems – speeding, parking, abandoned vehicles and the absence of pedestrian crossings – figure prominently. The behaviour of youths – their noise, their intimidatory street corner habits, their cycles on footpaths, their motor bike racing, their foul language, graffiti and minor acts of vandalism – are perennial topics. And the quality of the environment – litter, dog-shit, uneven pavements, poor street lighting, uncollected rubbish, unrepaired street furniture, insecure council housing fittings – these are the matters members raise and about which they seek action.
>
> (Morgan 1987a: 35)

The *Islington Crime Survey* (Jones, Maclean, and Young 1986) and the *Merseyside Crime and Police Survey* (Kinsey 1985) found crime, vandalism, and noise (together with the euphemism for youth problems – 'not enough things for young people to do') to be high in people's perceptions of problems. People in all sorts of areas seem to agree on what disorder looks like.

In our urban areas the limits of informal social control were reached more quickly than in the villages. Some other areas, in big cities, are likely to be even less able to cope (though some areas, with even higher crime rates, may well have stable and effective social networks (Baldwin and Bottoms 1976; Bottoms and Xanthos 1981)). Our urban areas at least had businesses and service industries which acted as foci for neighbourhood communication. Residential housing estates with no facilities will lack even those. But our urban areas, in common probably with many others, had no structures or organizations through which people could discuss the solutions to their problems and which could act for them, whether by themselves or in conjunction with the police and other formal agencies. In the town, people had to act by themselves, or with occasional *ad hoc* groups of friends, or keep quiet. Many kept quiet and just worried.

Whose order? The dilemmas of informal social control

Informal social control is not only limited in its effectiveness and scope, but also suffers from a number of intrinsic problems, all of which revolve around the question of 'whose order?' If someone is complaining about their neighbour's noisy party, should the complainant's definition of noisy be accepted? If older people object to youths hanging around a bus stop, should the youths move on or should the old fogeys put up with it? Informal social control can refer to no laws passed by Parliament limiting or defining, even partially, what kind of order should exist in neighbourhoods. Social order is continuously being constructed and negotiated. And, where problems, knowledge, and action are very localized, solutions are likely to be as well. Informal social control carries within itself the seeds of a very local justice and the potential for constantly varying standards of expected conduct within each village and each town. We can illustrate this with respect to just one of the subgroups within each area: businesses.

THE ROLE OF BUSINESSES

The businesses within each of our areas played an important role in defining and maintaining informal social control. In the first place, they suffered substantial amounts of victimization. Of our sample of urban businesses, 85 per cent said that they had been the victim of some form of crime in the past year. Skogan (personal communication) and Baril (1984) have found similar high rates among the North American businesses they studied. Businesses could be said to be sinks of opportunity for crime for the (predominantly local and youthful) offenders in the area. Their crime prevention practices and attitudes substantially affected people's views of the amount of crime in the area, since incidents of disorder on public property and against business premises were the most widely known.

This effect was heightened by the communication role played by some service industries, such as shops, newsagents, garages, pubs, restaurants and take-aways, second-hand dealers and street vendors. These businesses formed foci for the exchange of gossip and information about what was going on in the area – and one of the major topics of conversation was any recent incidents of disorder or crime. Business people were also often active watchers and active interveners. They spent longer in their area every day than did many of the residents. Residents would look after business premises at night and at weekends, whereas business people would look after the street in the daytime.

But business people appeared to have different views on informal action from residents (see also Baril 1984). In respect of incidents affecting residential property near them, or private individuals, those who were active watchers would be more likely to take direct informal action (and, if the incident was 'real crime', would be more prepared to contact the police). However, if something had happened to their own business premises or to their employees, the decisions they took seemed to be motivated by the consequences each course of action would have for the economic health of the business. Any preventive hardware to be installed had to be cost-effective (or insisted on by the insurance company); reporting of incidents to the police would occur only if it would be useful (because of making an insurance claim or encouraging police patrolling to deter future predators). So, for example, one large factory in our urban area used its full-time odd-job man to repair the numerous broken windows it suffered. None was reported to the police (despite the fact that the old lady living opposite had discovered that one main culprit was not, as suspected, a drunken youth on his way back from a town-centre pub, but a middle-aged man with an iron bar). The factory also lent its employee to neighbouring businesses to repair their windows. There was extremely little reporting of any crime committed by insiders. Employee theft, supplier or distributor fraud, or bad cheques would be dealt with either by cutting losses and ensuring that it could not happen again, or by using the civil law. None the less, the volume of crime committed against businesses meant that they were one of the principal customers of the police. Businesses accounted for 29 per cent of the recorded property crime in our urban area and 53 per cent in the rural area.

Businesses, then, played a major part in constructing and maintaining the social order in their areas – but according to their lights and their views of how it should look. Where business people were fearful and worried about disorder (a rare occurrence in most of our urban area), so were the many customers who patronized them. Where they were merely occasionally exasperated, people remained confident about the ability of the informal mechanisms of the area to support its particular brand of order. Where there were no businesses at all, there was a dead feel to the streets. Knowledge of incidents was rarer, but so was knowledge of the identity of suspected offenders. The areas seemed less confident in dealing with what did occur.

CONTROLLING INFORMAL SOCIAL CONTROL

There will be a constant tension within each area as to whose order will predominate. Leaving active intervention to victims and watchers puts the area in the hands of whoever tends to suffer disorder the most. In the villages, any wave of disorder by any particular band of youngsters tended to hit public property as much as or more than private property. Public property was in the hands of the organizations, who could try to produce a graded response to the problem. Attacks on individuals, often relatively powerless or timid individuals, would often come to the notice of the organizations as well.

In the urban area, this was less likely, though racially motivated incidents (bricks through windows, damage to doors, verbal harassment) were often reported to the relevant community groups, who would engage in the same process. Many residents, however, did not have this possibility of communal support and were left to deal with any disorder on their own. Equally, there was little opportunity for control of their decisions by others in the area. The unifying factors were indirect: a common appreciation of what the problems were; some agreement on the likely offenders; common perceptions of the usefulness and likely responses of the police; a fairly lively gossip network (though mediated through only small networks of friends). These factors can promote consensus, but they cannot attain it, or control any action disapproved of by others.

Informal social control is by definition diffuse. There may be no 'community leaders' with whom the police can consult. There may be little scope for promoting it or curbing its excesses. Almost all the information gathered by official bodies, such as the police or the local authority, is given to them by local people or organizations, who can decide to withhold it. And there is no guarantee that the order achieved will be very tolerant of, say, minority groups or strangers, or will fit neatly with the 'official' view of what 'order' should be. Descriptions of order and its maintenance in societies are descriptions largely of their informal social control. The intolerance of strangers documented by Baumgartner (1981) in an American suburb, the vicious punishments meted out by the informal 'courts' in South Africa (Burman, undated), and the entrepreneurial semi-criminal culture of businesses in the East End (Hobbs 1988) are all their forms of social order.

We shall discuss later how to promote informal social control. Here we need merely comment that, once it has been promoted, it can only be controlled by official agencies to a small degree. The direct powers which agencies possess for control are largely repressive. They can withdraw support if things seem to be going 'wrong' in their view. They can take criminal proceedings if matters go that far. But these are very blunt weapons and they also have the consequence of depressing the very phenomenon that the agencies were originally trying to create or improve.

The results of many 'community' initiatives have been disappointing (for example, neighbourhood watch (Bennett 1987; Rosenbaum 1986)). They only seem to expand, and not be taken over by a small group, if they achieve broad-based support within the area, and knowledge of their existence is disseminated and consultation promoted on a broad scale early in their life (see NACRO 1987a). Several writers have stressed the dangers of the police creating a social order that dispossesses and drives out the young, the poor, ethnic minorities, and those in industrial conflicts with their employers (see, particularly, Jefferson 1987; Jones, Maclean, and Young 1986). Others have commented that the police do not have the powers to enforce social order on the problems of disorder about which we are writing (for example, Morgan 1987a). Jefferson (1987) argues that justice and social order must take into account the interests of the policed – those who routinely and most commonly interact with the police. We suspect that, if neighbourhoods were left to police themselves and to construct their social order entirely by themselves, it would not be the policed who would determine that order. It would be those with the most informal power within an area – probably business employers, the middle-aged, men. The result might not be an order very tolerant of different lifestyles. The police may, ironically, sometimes act as the protectors of diversity.

Whose control? The role of formal agencies

Of course, in practice, people are not left to get on with informal social control themselves, or abandoned totally to their own resources. The informal social control we found operating in our areas was crucially tied in with the activities of the police and other agencies of formal social control (such as the various tiers of local authorities and schools). We found informal and formal control each to be dependent on the other and, at the same time, each to be antagonistic to the other's demands.

The dependence of the police on the public to do police work is now accepted without question (see Jones, Maclean, and Young 1986; Shapland, Willmore, and Duff 1985). The vast majority of police work consists of reacting to demands made by the public. The limitations of informal social control and the use that residents and business people made of the police have been documented above and in previous chapters. The police were essentially expected to perform four roles: first, to respond to, solve, and prosecute instances of 'real crime'; second, to attempt to solve the problems presented by some instances of disorder and other crime; third, to note and process information about all instances of minor disorder mentioned to them (but not necessarily to do anything about them unless suspects were found or indicated); and fourth, to be around in the area as a symbolic presence of formal order and as a resource for roles one to three (see Chapter 8). However, the police were not expected to find problems for themselves. Proactive action was usually not appreciated. Moreover, people wished to continue to be involved in things they had reported to the police – to know what was happening, to continue to be able to make some input, and, occasionally (though not in instances of 'real crime'), to be able to control events.

The police did not see things in quite this way. They have always reserved to themselves the final power to decide the outcome of anything they take on. Both they and local councils have also always felt that they have the power to impose a particular conception of social order. Councils do this most obviously through planning and housing decisions, but also regulate social and community provision. The police have reserved to themselves, and jealously guard, their operational independence. The recent introduction of consultative committees is just that – a potential means of increasing consultation and widening the information base. They do not affect decision-making directly. Morgan (1987a, 1987b) has shown that:

> The police reveal aspects of their organisation, but do so superficially. They keep their operational cards close to their chests and do not generally reveal their managerial problems: they regard the arena of local politics, of which police consultative committees are becoming an integral part, as dangerous terrain where they are liable to be attacked. There is limited consultation about major police operations in some sub-divisions, but it is intermittent and partial.
> (Morgan 1987a: 40–1)

This imposition of social order by the police is visible in the decisions of every constable called to attend an incident (which person to believe? which party to support?), as well as in more major instances of public disorder. The job of policing is the policing of conflict (Smith 1987). Writers on this topic have tended to portray the police as a monolithic entity with one purpose, that of perpetuating the oppression of certain classes. We found the police to be very far from monolithic. Different officers in different jobs had very diverse views of the correct way to police incidents. However, taken together as a set of beliefs, those of the police were not identical to those of the residents and business people in our areas. More particularly, they were not those of the young or the radical (though nor were they those of business people, the rich, or the ultra-conservative). They could perhaps best be differentiated along a public–private axis. Police officers were expressing what they felt to be the best solution for the public as a whole. Watchers and victims were, generally, operating in their own private interests.

The difficulty is that the police were not particularly well-informed about the totality of public views and priorities in the areas they policed; nor, consequently, did they share the perspectives of the public; and the structure of the service did little to encourage them to take note of such views. Current patterns of patrolling and response deployment have relegated local beat officers to a minority position in most forces. Even in our areas, where most policing was carried out by officers at least nominally assigned to a particular beat, officers' contacts with the public were largely confined to responding to calls from victims and watchers. In general, police–public contact was low. It has been shown that, in many forces, patrol time is under-utilized (see Smith, Small, and Gray 1983; Kinsey 1985; Martin and Wilson 1969; Comrie and Kings 1974). In our rural and urban areas, the use of area beat officers as the major police resource had diminished the amount of 'dead time' – and officers' boredom! But lack of supervisory suggestions as to what officers might be doing in their areas still made police–public communication only minimally effective.

We can imagine two opposite scenarios – 'ideal cases' which define the ends of the possible spectrum for policing and its control. The first is separate policing – policing of an area by the police using their own principles, beliefs about problems, and methods and, entirely separately, policing of the same area by the public, with their own problems, beliefs, and methods of informal social control. The second scenario is policing with the public: policing by police and public together, using a negotiated, common set of principles, priorities, and methods.

Separate policing is likely to be ineffective policing – neither party in fact has the ability to solve alone even the problems they themselves define. The efforts of one are likely to get in the way of the efforts of the other, thereby promoting discord, misunderstandings, and hostility. Since each party will start to define the other as unhelpful, they will then try to meet their own needs out of their own resources. The public may have to resort to having civilians use coercive force on other civilians – strong-arm tactics or vigilantism. For the police, the advantage of separate policing is that they will be able to attain a reasonably uniform standard over different locales (since they themselves will be doing all the decisionmaking). At least for the more coercive, formal aspects of policing (riot control, prosecution policy), the public will be able to be pretty sure of what they will get. Policing may be decided according to the police view of the world, but at least activity will tend to be coherent and predictable. The disadvantages include reduced information coming in from the public and a consequently reduced ability to solve problems and detect those crimes that are still reported, and increasing hostility, particularly from groups which feel most strongly that their needs are being ignored. In its extreme form, this is the 'military' policing set out by Lea and Young (1984). As Clarke (1987) has commented, the police are 'currently having to confront . . . the impossibility of effective management of populations by crisis intervention on a more formal, bureaucratic and due process based model'.

Currently, we believe that we are much nearer separate policing than the contrasting collaborative model in which public views would be acknowledged to have weight in determining the scope and manner of policing, and in which decision-making would be a joint enterprise. In so far as local areas currently have any influence, it is at a highly indirect and informal level. Obviously, the level at which operational decisions are taken within the police varies with the task in hand – processions, football matches, and protests are the stuff of operational plans formulated at middle-management level in divisions and subdivisions; whereas how individual incidents are dealt with is normally the responsibility of one or two individual constables, with possible subsequent comment by a sergeant. But consultative committees only affect operational plans indirectly. Equally, 'taking account' of a neighbourhood is usually rated only as 'good beat craft', not as a necessary or even desirable part of policing individual incidents. Where specialist officers, such as the CID, are charged with dealing with particular kinds of incidents, all possibility of using the very local knowledge necessary and of attaining local participation in policing usually vanishes, since these officers are not assigned to jobs on a geographic basis.

Fielding (1987) has argued that a number of aspects of the structure of the police promote such distance from the public that there is no possibility of any joint activity. He says that in the police world of operational autonomy, arrests are valued as the primary means of control and orientation to crime; the public and their problems and priorities are given only a low value. We are not so pessimistic about the possibility of change, since we suggest that the whole official rhetoric of police–public relations has, until recently, reinforced this separation and the public's perception that the police are 'snatching conflicts'. The public have been told that if they see anything criminal or disorderly, they should immediately pass it over to the police, with the implication that the police will then deal with it. The rhetoric, at least, is now altering from this position.

Whose crime prevention?

The same distinctions between public and private, between state agency and private individual or group, arise in respect of crime prevention. The very words 'crime prevention' have in fact been used almost entirely to imply seeking an overall decrease in crime. This is an official or societal perspective, which seeks to exhort private individuals and groups to change their habits, start initiatives, or install hardware in order to accomplish its aims. Claimed reductions in crime in a small area are only 'successes' if there is little or no 'displacement' of that crime to adjoining areas. Where initiatives have failed, the public may be blamed – for not being sufficiently aware of crime or the need for crime prevention, for not implementing the initiative effectively, or for housing too many criminals within the local community.

If we look at crime prevention from an individual viewpoint, then the task is different. It is that of individuals protecting themselves against the kinds of problems or crimes about which they are worried, in such a manner that they can continue to live according to their preferred lifestyle, without having to give up too many important things. It is a balance between the perceived threat (its seriousness and its likelihood), the resources available to combat it (money, knowledge of solutions), and the consequences of adopting a particular solution (amount of crime reduction, retaliation, responses of the neighbours). A similar equation can be struck in respect of the small local areas we have been studying. Essentially, people there wanted solutions to their own perceived problems (which might not be the crimes focused on by official agencies) – solutions which were within their resources, fitted in with their lifestyles, and did not harm their community.

Again, in the current situation, official agencies (Home Office, Department of the Environment, local authority, police, crime prevention panel, etc.) appear to be completely separated from the public. Initiatives have been at a national or town-wide level. There has been little differentiation between areas. Even where models have stressed local participation and consultation and where efforts have been made to achieve these (for example, the work of NACRO and the Priority Estates Project), the local priorities which *have* been established have not always led to remedies fashioned from scratch to match the particular problems. It is all too easy to pull a 'solution' package off the shelf, without tailoring it to local circumstances. As Bottoms and Wiles (1986) have pointed out, and as we argued in Chapter 7, solutions cannot be the same for different areas.

Essentially, the problems are extremely localized, and solutions need to reflect this. Moreover, packages of solutions need to be put together which mix security hardware, methods of policing, information campaigns, design, housing and local authority management, and social initiatives for youngsters and others. The hardware should reflect the design of the buildings, the *modus operandi* of the offenders, the financial circumstances of individuals and public agencies, ease of use for the relevant age-groups, and the effect on fear of crime. Management and policing need to tie in with informal social control and to take account of local offending patterns. As Arthurs (1975) has said, the aim must be to help local neighbourhoods to cope with their own problems, and, for many high-crime areas, that means coping with their own local offenders, not attempting to shut them out, alienate them, or ignore them. The dialogue so far has tended to be with people as potential victims, not with the same people or their neighbours as offenders or witnesses. Equally, it has tended not to involve either local businesses in areas, or the security industry as supplier.

Proposals for change

The list of policing or crime prevention initiatives which have foundered or just not been evaluated is a long one. In fact, it seems hard to point to many successful ventures (Weatheritt 1986). What happens when something goes wrong is instructive. The tendency is *either* to blame the agency which was largely responsible for promoting the initiative, *or* to blame the public. The police have been criticized for being unwilling to change and for sabotaging, consciously or unconsciously, anything which looks likely to decrease their autonomy. They have also been slammed as possessing a workforce which is so independent that whatever the hierarchy says won't be done (see, for example, Fielding 1987). Local authorities have been portrayed as bureaucratic monsters with antiquated housing policies and management practices (NACRO 1987a). The public have been seen as lacking any sense of community (or, rather, any effective means of solving all their problems by themselves), as being uninterested in the altruistic attempts of agencies to help them prevent and solve crime, and as being a thoroughly degenerate, helpless, but stubborn and awkward lot.

The problem with these initiatives – and with many of the rather one-sided criticisms of their failure – is that they have tended to start with the solution, rather than with the problem. Someone has a bright idea and then proceeds to inflict it on an area, regardless of the local people's views. Sometimes, only certain types of solutions have been advocated (such as design changes, or starting youth clubs). Sometimes, the agencies have wanted to think only in terms of capital projects, rather than maintenance or management ones (Hope 1982).

We would argue that it is best to start with the problem. What happens then? The first thing is to define the problem, to consider whose problem it is, and to go and talk to them about their concerns, their suggestions, and their reactions to any proposed solutions (theirs or others'). The next stage is to consider who will have difficulties in solving the problem. There are four types of difficulties. First, there is difficulty in recognizing the problem – those suffering it and those engaged in its solution may well have different priorities and may not be able to communicate about either the problem or the priorities. Second, there is difficulty in finding solutions to the problem – those that are closest to it may not have the information, the skills, the contacts, or the methods of working to think of the best solutions or to evaluate their consequences. Third, there are difficulties in getting the problem sufferers (generally the public) and the problem solvers (generally official agencies) to work together. Since these difficulties often result from structural failures, they are usually by far the worst to overcome. Finally, since these are social problems, they are constantly changing. The solutions need to have, within them, the potential for change, as do the mechanisms for communication between agencies and public which will mediate these solutions.

Using our findings, we shall take the problem at the heart of our study – the management of social order within small areas – and try to see which kinds of solutions might meet some of the difficulties we have outlined.

The management of social order

RECOGNIZING THE PROBLEM

Threats to social order in particular neighbourhoods can be caused by very broad economic and social factors, such as unemployment, poor housing design, historical patterns of allocation of housing and planning of businesses, and government and local policies on taxes, benefits, and social facilities (see Skogan 1987 for a review of the American literature; an equivalent analysis for the UK does not exist). The local manifestation of problems with social order is at a quite different level. As perceived by residents and business people, problems seem to be drawn from a quite limited list of crime, disorder, and nuisance, with people citing a number of very localized instances (see Chapter 4). Official agencies seldom hear about these problems, but most come to the attention of at least one agency through at least one complaint from a member of the public. The agency which receives the vast number of these complaints is the police. It is also the agency to which both residents and business people look to solve these problems (even if they are at least partly someone else's responsibility).

The difficulty is that current avenues for communication between public and police (primarily consultative committees, interagency meetings, etc.) are at a different level from that of the problems. Problems are mostly at a sub-beat level (though more formal policing, such as policing of major public events, does affect much wider areas). It is impossible to envisage consultative committees for every street. They are just not the right mechanism for that kind of problem. Possible alternatives are either to create and maintain structures through which the public can funnel information about problems and complaints up to a level at which consultative committees, etc., exist, or to improve individual contacts between residents, business people, and their local police officers so that information is passed on and reaches up through the police to those taking operational decisions. Some areas have structures for the public such as residents' and tenants' groups and parish councils. They can be helped into existence in housing estates, for example (see NACRO 1987b). It would be possible to create parish councils in towns – and these might also help to give further possibilities for action by informal social control groups. But areas with many problems tend also to have a high level of disorganization, making it very difficult to create structures (as Alderson 1979 and Dahrendorf 1985 have, in their different ways, advocated). Here, structure-building can only be regarded as a long-term aim, the success of which probably presupposes alleviation of some of the problems through other means.

In all areas, but especially in high problem areas, it will be crucial for the police to make effective use of information. This implies not only analysing, monitoring and using message pad data in particular, but also setting out to acquire information on what people see as problems, communicating it to all officers who deal with an area, and passing information back to the area about its problems and what the police are doing. This is an information brokerage role: information is given to the police in trust to use effectively, account for its use, and pass back. There will be a temptation for the police to retain control over the information. However, in this case, though information is still power, it is not absolute power. The police cannot act on their own and, moreover, if trust is abused, the information flow may dry up and cannot be replaced.

FINDING SOLUTIONS

As we discussed earlier in this chapter, informal social control has severe limitations. It is dependent upon the decisions of particular individuals. It can usually only pick up the pieces after some untoward event has occurred, and try to prevent its recurrence, rather than finding and punishing an offender. It is very localized, and, in urban areas, there are the difficulties of lack of further possibilities for action and lack of communication between residents.

The problems of formal social control by the police seem almost to be a mirror image of these. Police officers are not generally trained to use negotiation and problem-solving techniques, rather than prosecution/formal warnings. They have few means to record the instances in which they do use these techniques. They are usually not supervised whilst doing so or rewarded for it. Policing is organized on a wide basis geographically and involves specialists who are normally even less localized. There are major difficulties with communication, liaison, and information management within police forces, particularly between different types of officer (see Chapter 9).

Formal social control by other agencies, particularly local authorities, is dogged by the same problems as control by the police. Even worse, there is a lack of realization within many local authorities and other agencies that social disorder, crime prevention, and so on are anything to do with them (NACRO 1987a). Both informal and formal approaches suffer from lack of specificity as to which solutions might suit which problems in which areas, and lack of information about their success in other areas (largely due to an almost total lack of evaluation of solutions and initiatives).

In this area of multiple and multiplying difficulties, we feel that it is not yet possible to produce solutions – or even to create structures to find the solutions. We are at an even more preliminary stage of trying to specify what the structures might look like and trying them out. We are, however, sure that the structures need to match the problems – that is, that they should be local and that they should involve communication between the sufferers and the solvers. Residents, business people, and police all suffer the problems; all need to communicate about specific remedies for them. We, therefore, strongly support a local team structure for policing, involving specialist officers as well as patrol officers. We also support decentralized team housing management and local authority services. We feel that solutions will have to be differentiated according to the demands of local areas, and that the contributions of different people and agencies will vary in consequence. But all will be needed at some time. And the mechanisms for their participation must allow for this.

LOCAL ACCOUNTABILITY: ACCOUNTABILITY TO WHOM?

Coping with social disorder essentially means matching problem and solution. Here all the difficulties pile up. Different definitions of a problem confront different advocated solutions. Skills, money, power will be at variance with both definition and solution. Perhaps the only basis for optimism comes from the realization that there is no perfect solution and that the optimum one will constantly change over time.

Social order is created by the actions and views of people who exist in an area, but who are different from each other. It is a compromise between different ideas of how the area should be, and will constantly change according to people's levels of tolerance of others' views. A problem, in the sense that our residents and business people used the word, comes about when one set of people do things which are sufficiently outside their immediate neighbours' views of social order for something to 'need to be done'. A number of instances of the same problem, or, more usually, several problems, can make both residents and agencies feel that social order is beyond their control. That point, which is correlated with more people suffering from 'fear of crime', seems to be attained less rapidly if people have some structure they can use for informal social control and if they feel that formal agencies are accountable to them at a local level.

We have used the term 'accountable' several times. Accountability is almost as much of a weasel word as 'community'. It has many different meanings, but it has been purloined in discussions of policing by certain groups and its definition limited to pre-emptive control of operational policing by democratically elected representatives of residents of a relatively large area (equivalent to that covered by district or county councils). We find this limitation extremely unhelpful to the discussion. Day and Klein (1987) express the essence of accountability as comprising agreement about what constitutes effective performance by a particular person or body; a common language of justification and explanation; sufficient control to demand the giving of accounts; and sufficient political control to demand change if the account does not satisfy. They comment, in our view quite correctly, that the police are not currently accountable in any of these elements to the public. There is 'multiple accountability with contested criteria' and 'a Babel of evaluative languages' (Day and Klein 1987: 105). We suspect the same could be said of other agencies of formal social control. The problem is not just one for the public, but a matter for the police as well. As Bayley (1983) cites: 'Most police forces in the world literally do not know what they are doing.' Day and Klein argue that, currently, the police are trying to resist taking responsibility for the consequences of policing – the amount of crime and social disorder – as indeed are the other formal agencies. Those consequences are supposed to be a problem for the public and a result of long-term social forces. Agencies, on this view, need only think about their managerial processes and, particularly, putting the right resources in; they do not need to think about outputs or outcomes.

Day and Klein go on to investigate the attitudes of members of police authorities towards accountability. Of course, only a proportion of such people are currently elected. However, even among these it seemed as though accountability was unproblematic. They did not worry about whether they were really representing their constituents and did not take steps to gather data on what the problems were in their area. It seemed that 'the fact of election, the constitutional myth that election *ipso facto* makes members accountable, washes away the contradictions involved in that role' (Day and Klein 1987: 228). In fact, all the members tended to internalize accountability as a 'general duty to pursue the public good according to their own criteria of what was right . . . their own ''civil super-ego''' (p. 229). And they judged what the police were doing according to individual cases that they had heard of. Unfortunately, the police, like other service providers, were able to make their general policy relatively invisible, especially since policing is delivered mostly 'on the hoof', rather than being made visible in buildings and institutions.

We have described the findings at length, because we think they illustrate well the deficiencies of relying solely on democratic accountability of the type that is normally proposed. The same deficiencies are clear in other fields, for example, in Boards of Visitors of prisons (Maguire, Vagg, and Morgan 1985) and in the health service (Day and Klein 1987). They include lack of relevant information, lack of indices by which to measure performance, inability to find out what is happening independently of the institution being studied, and unrepresentative control. Proposals for improvement have covered all these areas (see, for example, Jefferson and Grimshaw 1987; Lustgarten 1987; Morgan 1987b; Baldwin 1987).

We feel that the argument has been too restricted. The task of policing, its mandate, and its priorities are essentially undefined. There are a large number of different audiences for policing by the police, including police officers' peers, their superiors, the police authority and the local council, business groupings, the public in the area, individual victims, witnesses and offenders, the Home Office, Parliament, and so forth (see Shapland and Hobbs 1987 for a development of this argument). Each of these audiences seems increasingly ready to believe that, since it is in some way a consumer and/or supporter of police services, it has a right to look critically at and comment upon what the police are doing. Yet each audience has a different view of what police priorities should be and, necessarily, sees a different mixture of what the police actually do. In addition, the importance of the various audiences for the control of policing changes over time. The result of this indeterminacy is that there can be no permanent resolution of the task of policing and its control. It is and will always be a constant political debate.

The lesson for accountability in our view is that it needs to take place at different levels, to be directed at different audiences, to use different tools, and to employ different measures of performance according to the policing task which is being considered. Only then will each group of 'auditors' have any chance of appreciating what policing is being done. At the level of formal resource deployment and major operational plans, currently being decided upon at force headquarters or by senior divisional officers, a district council, force, or divisional structure for accountability seems to be the most appropriate. However, democratic election of 'auditors' from a base of individual residents alone will not cover all consumers, if that is the wish. Equally, the fact of election alone will not provide sufficient tools for understanding consumers' wishes, gaining information on policing activities, setting priorities (without much more discussion of what these might look like and what effects different prioritizations would have), or analysing and evaluating performance. Financial analysis is one means, but is more suited to resource deployment than, for example, to judgements of the success or failure of the policing of major disturbances.

At the level of the problems that residents and business people express about what is happening in their area, accountability of whatever form at the district level will not suffice. There needs to be local accountability as well – a local accounting by the police of what they do about individual incidents and more persistent problems in the area. The findings need to be given to individual victims and witnesses, concerning what has happened to the incident that they reported or were involved with. The ends of the stories must be told. But the accounting also needs to be made jointly by police, other formal agencies, and local groups. Priorities need to be communicated, action reported and plans concocted together. There is policing by the public – and it will continue to create and maintain social order. There is policing by the police, imposed upon the public. Perhaps one day there will be joint accountability.

Appendix: methods

Our project entailed the collection of data from a range of sources utilizing a variety of methods. We studied crime records and calls to the police; interviewed police officers and those living in the study areas; made formal observations to establish, for example, the extent of pedestrian traffic at night; and also conducted less formal fieldwork of an anthropological type in both rural and urban areas. This appendix first describes the need for such a mix of methods, the selection of the research sites, and the order in which the research tasks were completed. It then deals with each of the data sets – police records, interviews with residents and businesses, interviews with the police, and observations – describing what was collected and how, and discussing the principal strengths and weaknesses of each type of data.

Methods are related to research aims. Our principal objectives were threefold. First, we wanted to look at perceptions of social order and disorder and to draw as complete a picture as possible of the views of residents and business people in the study areas. Second, these views were to be related to the overall social composition and characteristics of each area. Third, since we wished to relate them also to police views and police statistics, we set out to gather data on this 'official knowledge' about disorder.

Eclecticism in methods, while dictated by our research aims, has advantages and disadvantages. Where more than one source of data bears on a particular topic, one data set can be validated, and indeed interpreted, through comparison with others. On the other hand, where different conditions in the research areas implied that differing sampling methods had to be used (as with the sampling of the residents to be interviewed), care had to be taken to ensure that statements about rural and urban areas were derived from comparable data sets. These points are discussed more fully below.

Selection of research sites

A number of practical criteria needed to be fulfilled in determining which area would be chosen. First, if all the research areas fell within the boundaries of one police force, crime reports and other police documentation on the areas would utilize the same format and be completed by officers with some degree of common expectations about the character of the administrative system within which they worked. For similar reasons, the areas we selected were coterminous with enumeration district boundaries to facilitate the use of Census Small Area Statistics.

Second, while the urban areas in our selected force were policed by a mix of area beat officers and 'immediate response vehicles' common to all the non-city-centre beats in the city, rural areas were policed in a less uniform way. In view of the current debate about the value of area beat policing (or 'neighbourhood bobbies') in urban areas, we wanted to select a rural area with a resident 'local bobby' and one without, in order to see what differences this made to residents and, more generally, to patterns of social order and disorder. This limited our choice, since the police force had in the last twenty years sold many of their houses and used others as, for example, local offices or to accommodate policemen not working in the area.

Third, the study aims implied the need for long periods of continuous fieldwork in a few places, with data being gathered through not only conventional interviewing but also observation and informal conversation – in short, through an anthropological perspective rather than a conventional survey methodology. We needed small areas in which we would be able to interview a large enough proportion of people to ensure that we collected data on any disagreement as well as any consensus about problems and their solution. Yet each area needed to be fairly typical of its district's social composition and housing and business structure. In particular, the urban areas should contain shops, offices, factories, and leisure facilities as well as housing of different types, thus ensuring their comparability with the rural areas (which contained a mix of uses) rather than offering the special features of town centres or housing estates. The areas finally chosen are described in some detail in Chapter 2.

The research time-scale

The research was conducted in two phases – the first concentrating on the rural areas and the second on the urban. The order in which research tasks were begun, and the way in which they were organized, varied between the two. The paucity of previous studies of crime in rural areas led us first to a study of relevant police records, so that a picture of recorded crime was created. Subsequently, interviews with residents and business people were carried out, together with periods of observation. We also made informal contacts and recorded events and conversations of interest in a field notebook. One researcher was able to live in the village studied for three or four days a week. The other had previously lived in the other village over a three-year period. The rural fieldwork comprised thirteen months in one site and nine months in the other, starting in January 1983. Following this, we interviewed as far as possible all the police officers who had any substantial contact with the public in either village.

In the urban areas, all these tasks were pursued simultaneously – partly due to pressure of time, partly because it was an efficient way of using the 'slack periods' between interviews, and partly because a consideration which influenced the rural fieldwork did not apply here. In the rural areas, we became comparatively well-known figures and our movements were, in all probability, the subject of gossip. We were careful not to be seen with police officers while we were dealing with the public, in order to avoid being labelled as 'grasses' or 'snitches'. In the urban areas we were in many ways more anonymous, and the police station, though near to our research areas, was not within them.

Police records

RECORDS OF CRIMES

Our study of recorded crime comprised an analysis of all the crime reports for the year from 1 September 1981 to 31 August 1982 for both urban and rural areas – 1,200 rural and 1,384 urban reports. A minor complication was that the force had been completely reorganized during 1982–3, with a new pattern of beats in the urban area introduced on 1 January 1983. Since we wanted to use the beat boundaries current during the fieldwork, all the crime reports for the urban subdivision were mapped on to the 1983 beat boundaries. This gave us the samples of crime reports for the district council area including our two villages and for the two beats of the urban subdivision including our interview areas 1, 2, 3, and 4 (the rural and urban areas respectively for the analysis in Chapter 3). We also subsequently extracted those reports originating from Northam, Southton, and urban areas 1, 2, 3, and 4 and continued our search into the crime reports for subsequent years in order to collect reports referring to crimes committed in the interview areas, or to crimes committed against individuals living there, or to crimes committed by residents of the interview areas. We thus created an index from 1 September 1981 to the end of the fieldwork of all the recorded crimes affecting the areas in which we were interviewing. The complete crime files relating to those crime reports were then also studied, so that a more detailed picture of policing and criminal activity in the interview areas was built up.

CALLS TO THE POLICE FROM THE PUBLIC: THE MESSAGE PADS

Messages from the public represent the largest single file from which the use made by the public of police stations can be gauged. In our study force, the 'message pads' (later redesignated 'action pads') were forms on which incoming messages were written. They included reports of most telephone calls made by the public to the police station, some of the visits made by the public to that station, and a few of the letters received from the public. Each contained brief details of the content of the message, the person making the call, and any immediate action taken by the police (advice given over the telephone, a police car dispatched, etc.). The officer 'dealing' with the message should also, at a later date, have recorded the result of the call and this was monitored by supervisors (sergeant and possibly inspector) and 'signed off' by them. Telex messages were also filed in the same sequence, though these we ignored, since they were in the main inter-force messages about crimes committed in far-flung parts of the country.

We collected four samples of message pads:

1. from the rural areas for seventy-two days in the period from 1 January 1982 to 30 September 1982 in runs of seven to eight days in order to acquire data from different days of the week and to follow up enquiries over the midnight boundary. Only messages received at Town 1 (the largest police station within the rural area) were noted, so those to Town 2 or to the police houses would not necessarily figure. A number of administrative messages (concerning the availability of officers and so on) also came over the telephone, though most arrived by telex. Telex messages were not included.

2. 'action pads' (the new name for message pads after the reorganization of the force) for the same seventy-two days in 1984 for the urban area. It was not possible to use 1982 material since action pads were destroyed after a period of time.

3. 'action pads' for twenty-three of the seventy-two days (from January, May, and September) in 1984 for the rest of the urban subdivision. This enabled us to check whether the workload and pattern of demand in the whole of the urban area were substantially different to those on the rural beats and to compare the quantity of calls arriving at the switchboards dealing with the urban and rural areas.

4. in the urban area, messages were often jotted down first in a 'rough occurrence book' and later transcribed on to an action pad form. We collected the entries in the 'rough occurrence book' for eight of the days in 1984 which also featured in samples 2 and 3. In fact there was very little difference between the entries in the rough occurrence

book and the message pads, so message pads have been used in the analysis in Chapter 3. If such a system was in use in the rural area during 1982, it was not formalized and the records had not been kept.

OTHER POLICE DATA

We also examined the police records of requests to check licences, serve summonses, and take statements about road traffic accidents (known to the police as their 'process' workload), and the summary statistics on crime produced by the police for the use of beat constables.

INTERPRETING POLICE DATA

The problems of analysing and interpreting police crime statistics are relatively well known (see Bottomley and Coleman 1981; Bottomley and Pease 1986; McCabe and Sutcliffe 1978). Essentially, the statistics deal only with recorded crime and neither unreported events nor reported but unrecorded events will figure; they are collected using counting rules which may be of some value to officials, but may differ from those which researchers would like; the counting rules are changed from time to time, and some evidence suggests that occasionally they may not be followed; and finally, they do not represent a constant index of crime, but may be subject to variation as different policing policies are applied.

The methodological problems of analysing and interpreting message pads are, by contrast, not well documented (though see Ekblom and Heal 1982; Manning 1980). As a record of a transaction between police and public, message pad data have several deficiencies. Since the forms are completed for internal police consumption, they present the message in a manner which enables it to be dealt with in police terms. The introduction of the new term 'action pad' was itself significant. The major pressure on the writer of the pads was to move towards action, which was to be accomplished in as short a time as possible, given the possibility of many more calls arriving in the next few minutes. The function of message/action pads was, therefore, to record that which directs attention towards action that 'needs to be taken'. The fact that the major exceptions to the norm of abbreviating the content of the message (in both rural and urban areas) were 'complaints against the police' and 'bomb/other threats' illustrates the normal nature of this police coding. Both complaints and bomb threats required the attention of a senior officer, who almost certainly would have wanted to know the callers' exact words.

The use of jargon and abbreviation on the forms created a problem for the researchers, which some police supervisors must also have experienced. Several of the abbreviations used were ambiguous in their meaning. The major example was the use of 'A/R' in the results section, standing for 'all regular'. This could mean that nothing was found to be abnormal at the time when the officer arrived; that nothing had occurred; or that the officer had taken action so that the situation had in his judgement calmed down by the time he left.

The new format of the document also seemed to make a difference to the amount of information recorded. The 'action pad' introduced in 1983 allowed the officer completing the form to pre-code the nature of the message, the resources used, and the result achieved, and so aid computer analysis of the demand on police resources. The codes were developed from intensive pilot studies of current police categorization and ease of use. The new form, though simpler to use, was to some extent more prescriptive than its predecessor, in that only officially recognized 'results' were included. Moreover, the introduction of these codes appeared to have a considerable effect on the amount of detail given. One content category, for example, was 'juvenile nuisance'. In the rural area forms, prior to 1983, the kind of nuisance and number of juveniles would usually be specified. In the urban area forms, after coding was introduced, the detailed content of the message might be, simply, 'nuisance by juveniles'. It is to be hoped that the officer answering the call was given more detail.

As often occurs in studies of organizations, especially the police (Weatheritt 1982), changes in practice like that mentioned above confound simple comparisons such as urban/rural. The new forms and the greater workload in the urban area must have had some effect on the numbers and types of incidents written on message/action pads. It is unlikely, however, that they resulted in the non-recording of large numbers of messages of the types we were concerned with (see Shapland and Hobbs 1987). The need for written accountability – to show that a call was received and correct action taken – was enormous. This feature of police life is also illustrated by the close correspondence between the incidents recorded in the rough occurrence book and those transcribed on to the action pads.

Interviews with residents and business people

Interviews with residents and business people in the rural and urban areas took between one and three hours and were semi-structured in nature. We asked about:

1. length of residence in the area, extent of knowledge of people living there, noticing strangers, nosiness, speed of communication about incidents, views about the area;

2. neighbourhood problems, action taken about them, and reputations of those thought to be responsible;
3. surveillance, expected surveillance and intervention by neighbours, kinds of people and events considered 'suspicious', self-reported intervention, and options for action;
4. perceptions of the amount of crime in the area, of the likelihood of victimization, feelings of safety, protective activity and crime prevention, fear of crime;
5. victimization, witnessing of incidents and self-reported involvement in offending in the last year, noticing damage in the area;
6. local big events, influxes of strangers, public order problems, and pubs; and
7. policing, contact with and visibility of the police, perceived changes in police practice and organization, opinion on policing of that area.

ACCESS TO RESIDENTS AND BUSINESSES

It was clear from the outset that random sampling techniques alone would not provide us with the data we needed from residents and businesses. Each village contained a number of social circles – Nonconformist and Church of England congregations, the users of particular pubs, sports associations, and so on, within which many issues were discussed and views formed. It was possible that different groups within a village held divergent views or widely varying accounts of, for example, the activities of local youths. Similarly, each village contained a number of 'key people' whose views on, and knowledge of, local events were respected or influential in certain circles. In order to discover, for example, the views of the parish council on vandalism – or the views of the vandals on the 'target hardening' of street furniture – we had to find and interview specific individuals identified by other villagers as 'key people' in these contexts. Consequently, our interview samples were constructed using a snowball method.

Initial access to the villages was less difficult than might be supposed. One of the researchers had previously lived in Northam, and was able to begin by interviewing people with whom social contact had been retained. In Southton, the initial contacts were more accidental. One researcher's car overheated during a visit to the village, and this was turned to advantage when a local publican lent tools, supplied water for the radiator, and incidentally introduced him to other customers. A rented room in a private house was later secured as a research base, and the researcher spent three or four days a week living there. The process of searching for accommodation led to a number of introductions.

Our initial contacts were interviewed, and they introduced us to others in their social circles whom we also interviewed. Where possible, we induced interviewees to refer us to other social circles where the process was repeated, and to those they identified as 'key people'. As a check on this process, we attempted to interview members of at least one household from every street in each village, and some of those in outlying properties. We also attempted to cover different occupations and age-groups. Since introductions were not forthcoming in a few parts of Southton, we did use random sampling to collect interviews from certain streets, sending an introductory letter and asking for an interview (where interviewees recommended individuals but could not arrange a personal introduction, this letter was also used).

We used the same methods for those running businesses in the rural area as for residents. While we have made a distinction at certain times between residents and business people, it must be borne in mind that some of those we spoke to ran businesses from home; the distinction between business and resident is thus less clear in the rural samples than in the urban.

So far as the urban areas were concerned, we anticipated that residents' social circles might not be restricted to the relatively small areas which we studied; people might know others living elsewhere, but few in their own street. The 'snowball' approach was thus replaced by a random sampling method. We obtained the electoral registers for each area and having set a target number of interviews for each street, used a random number table to decide which households we should approach, and a flipped coin to decide which individual within the household. We thus interviewed not only 'heads of household', but also other household members on the electoral register – sons, daughters, lodgers, and so on. The individuals selected by this process were sent an initial letter with a reply-paid slip, followed by a second letter if there was no reply within two weeks. If no reply was received within a further ten days, a researcher would call at their house. The major problems with this method were that the sample to be interviewed was limited to those aged 18 or over; that temporary residents were under-represented; and that the register available at the time of commencing the urban fieldwork was almost a year old, so that several potential interviewees had moved.

In the rural areas, the 'snowball' method had enabled us to interview shopkeepers and business proprietors without the need for a separate sampling system; but because the urban samples were drawn from electoral registers, a second method had to be employed in order to interview such people. We drew up a list of all businesses in the urban areas by walking the streets and noting down who was where. We used a quota system to determine the required number of businesses from each street and a random sampling method to pick the particular businesses to approach. Letters were sent to named individuals where possible, and otherwise to 'The Manager' or whatever other designation seemed appropriate.

Around one in three (35 per cent) of those in the urban areas to whom we sent letters agreed to be interviewed. This figure varied by area, with the largest proportion of acceptances in urban area 3 (48 per cent) and the lowest in urban area 2 (25 per cent). Of the remainder, 39 per cent replied to our letter with a refusal, though 12 to 15 per cent of the letters to areas 1 and 2 were sent to people who – we later discovered – had moved or died. In four cases the refusal concerned people whom it was impossible to interview (one being deaf and dumb). One in five (19 per cent) of the addressees proved uncontactable when we followed up the letters with doorstep visits. This acceptance rate is lower than that found in surveys of victims and may reflect people's diffidence about the importance of their views. It also illustrates how preferable was the methodology adopted in the rural area. The acceptance rate for urban businesses was higher – 46 per cent. When we followed up the letter, 35 per cent of the addressees proved uncontactable, often because the business had been wound up.

THE INTERVIEW SAMPLES

To summarize matters, we interviewed eighty-seven individuals in Southton and ninety-four in Northam and its neighbourhood; of these, five in Southton and twenty-four in Northam were local business people. The total urban interview sample comprised thirty-three individuals from urban area 1; thirty from urban area 2; forty-one from urban area 3 and thirty-seven from urban area 4: a total of 141. This included thirteen business people from urban area 1, fourteen from urban area 2, eleven from urban area 3, and two from urban area 4: a distribution which reflects the number of businesses in each area.

In some interviews, we found that other members of the households whom we had not approached also wished to be interviewed along with the chosen interviewee. While this may have meant that some answers were influenced by what the other person thought, the advantage was that the individuals could and did confer, and discuss their responses with each other. These discussions allowed us a great deal of insight into why people answered the questions as they did, for example in relation to the fear of crime; and also gave us some insight into the neighbourhood social networks, for example where one person present had heard of an incident and others had not.

Tables A.1 and A.2 compare the age and social class of our samples with those for the population of the areas, according to the *Census Small Area Statistics* for 1981. When looking at the tables, it must be borne in mind that the Census figures for social class are based on a 10 per cent sample of each enumeration district and thus relate to only twenty or thirty individuals in each area (less than our sample). However, this

Table A.1 *The interview sample compared to the 1981 Census Small Area Statistics on age[1]*

Age		Urban areas %	Northam %	Southton %
16 to 19	interviews	2	7	6
	census	11	8	8
20 to 29	interviews	17	10	5
	census	20	22	19
30 to 39	interviews	15	19	28
	census	15	25	18
40 to 49	interviews	19	23	12
	census	13	14	15
50 to 59	interviews	20	19	18
	census	12	11	15
60 to 69	interviews	15	6	18
	census	12	11	13
70 +	interviews	13	16	12
	census	17	8	12

Note
1. Individuals under the age of 16 have been omitted.

Table A.2 *The interview sample compared to the 1981 Census Small Area Statistics on socio-economic status of residents*

Socio-economic status	Urban areas		Northam		Southton	
	interviews %	census %	interviews %	census %	interviews %	census %
I	4	2	5	4	9	1
II	16	10	36	25	19	14
IIIN	17	6	6	20	6	14
IIIM	14	20	7	13	4	21
IV	7	10	4	6	3	19
V	3	6	0	2	6	3
Not economically active	40	46	43	30	54	29

comparison suggests that our samples tend to under-represent 16- to 19-year-olds in the urban area and those aged 20 to 40 in the villages. Social classes I and II are over-represented in our villages sample (though not in the urban area) and those not economically active in Southton are over-represented compared to those who are economically active. The results will, therefore, tend to be biased towards the views of the middle-aged and the old and those in managerial occupations in the villages. This last is likely to be a result of our focus on 'key people' within the rural sampling. Men and women were sampled according to their proportions in the Census figures.

Police interviews

We interviewed virtually all the officers who worked in or around the villages and the urban areas, or whose work in some way concerned them.

For the rural phase of the study, we thus interviewed twenty-six officers: the subdivisional deputy superintendent; the inspector who allocated shifts and reliefs; five sergeants who allocated work to and supervised the village constables; seven constables responsible for the beats in which the villages lay or who regularly patrolled there; five others whose work might take them there (including the subdivisional crime prevention officer and three drivers of immediate response vehicles – the cars which responded to incidents over the whole area); and six CID officers.

For the urban phase, we interviewed twenty-seven officers: the divisional superintendent; three inspectors (one the duty inspector, who allocated shifts); the two sergeants responsible for the city beats, and the woman sergeant in charge of the Women's Section; the six constables attached to the two beats we studied; four immediate response vehicle drivers; three constables who worked on the station front desk (since many calls on the police were reported in person here); the schools liaison officer; and six CID officers.

These interviews usually lasted about one and a half to two hours and covered the workload, supervision, the kinds of crimes and non-crime problems dealt with, relations between the police and the public, and the differences between city and rural policing.

Observations

The use of finite observation periods is not common in criminological work. However, they are a very useful tool with which to contrast the perceptions of residents and business people with actual occurrences. We utilized this method to:

1. illustrate the extent to which areas suffered particular problems, where these could be gauged by direct observation (and would also

be visible to the casual passerby). Examples were volume of traffic, cycling on pavements, groups of youths, loose dogs, and loiterers;
2. enumerate potential watchers who might be visible to offenders;
3. illustrate the effect of physical design features and amenities, such as shops, on street activity;
4. measure factors possibly related to fear of crime, such as the number of people, and in particular the number of women, walking around at different times of day and night.

Observations will, of course, only 'capture' easily visible street activity. They will not enumerate possible watchers hiding behind net curtains. They will not discover much actual criminal activity (crime tends to occur in private places and is, as far as the offender is concerned, hopefully unseen). But views about crime and disorder and their incidence in particular localities, and fear of crime, may be related to the amount and kind of visible street activity and its physical setting – the liveliness of the area, the amount of social interaction which takes place in public settings, signs of disorder and of lack of community control (mainly in respect of public property), and signs of repair and refurbishment.

The observations, particularly the charting of numbers of people and vehicles moving around at various times of day and night, also give a rough indication of the extent to which people or unattended property could be subject to surveillance by local residents and businesses; provide a quantitative base by which to assess interviewees' claims that they – or people in general – did not walk around at night; and enumerate the kinds of activities which take place in the street and who is involved. Thirty-nine observation periods of between forty-five minutes and one hour in duration were conducted at four locations in Southton and five in Northam, at different times of day and night and in both summer and winter.

In the urban observations, researcher fatigue became a problem because of the volume of traffic and individuals to be recorded. It proved necessary to limit the observation periods to ten minutes only, and fifty-one such observations were completed. At least two streets per urban area were covered, with observations again taking place in the morning, afternoon, and evening, and at night.

Interpreting these data requires the appreciation of certain methodological biases and problems. The figures are dependent upon the siting of the observation point and on whether all visible activity is included or only people or vehicles passing the observation point. Similarly, observations in the dark are more prone to error than those in daylight (especially given the lack of street lighting in the villages). The basis for counting events may also introduce bias; if a vehicle or person is counted each time they appear, passing traffic will tend to be over-represented and stationary people under-represented compared to the length of time they remain on the street.

One special aspect of interpretation is that it is important to consider what constitutes a 'busy' or 'empty' street for the residents in terms of the local range of variation. It is often helpful to use, for example, a ratio of night to morning traffic rather than the absolute figures. Finally, wherever possible, we have compared our observational data with that available from our index of incidents occurring in the areas (compiled from all the interview data) and with data from our informal observations in the areas.

References

Albrow, M. (1982) *The Fears of the Elderly in Cardiff in 1982*. A report prepared for Cardiff City Council.

Alderson, J. (1979) *Policing Freedom*, Plymouth: McDonald & Evans.

Allatt, P. (1984) 'Fear of crime: the effect of improved residential security on a difficult to let estate', *Howard Journal* 23: 170–82.

Arthurs, S. (1975) 'Community involvement and crime prevention' (Paper given to conference on crime prevention, Toronto, Canada).

Bailey, F. G. (ed.) (1971) *Gifts and Poisons: the Politics of Reputation*, Oxford: Basil Blackwell.

Baldwin, J. and Bottoms, A. E., with Walker, M. A. (1976) *The Urban Criminal*, London: Tavistock.

Baldwin, R. (1987) 'Why accountability?', *British Journal of Criminology* 27: 97–105.

Banton, M. (1964) *The Policeman in the Community*, London: Tavistock.

Baril, M. (1984) 'The victims' perceptions of crime and the criminal justice system: a pilot study of small shopkeepers in Montreal', in R. Block (ed.) *Victimization and Fear of Crime: World Perspectives*, Washington DC: US Department of Justice.

Baumgartner, M. P. (1981) 'Social control in a suburban town: a ethnographic study' (Unpublished Ph.D. dissertation, Yale University).

Bayley, D. H. (1983) 'Knowledge of the police', in M. Punch (ed.) *Control in Police Organizations*, Cambridge, Mass.: MIT Press.

Becker, H. S. (1966) *Outsiders*, New York: Macmillan.

Bennett, T. (1987) *An Evaluation of Two Neighbourhood Watch Schemes in London* (Final Report to the Home Office, Executive Summary), Cambridge: Institute of Criminology.

Bennett, T. and Wright, R. (1984) *Burglars on Burglary*, Aldershot: Gower.

Bittner, E. (1967) 'The police on skid row: a study of peacekeeping', *American Sociological Review* 32: 699–715.

Block, R. (ed.) (1984) *Victimization and Fear of Crime: World Perspectives*, Washington DC: US Department of Justice.

Bottomley, K. and Coleman, C. (1981) *Understanding Crime Rates*, Farnborough: Gower.

Bottomley, K. and Pease, K. (1986) *Crime and Punishment: Interpreting the Data*, Milton Keynes: Open University Press.

Bottoms, A. E. and Wiles, P. (1986) 'Crime and housing policy: a framework for crime prevention analysis' (Paper given to Home Office conference on Communities and Crime Reduction, Cambridge, July 1986, and to be published by HMSO).

Bottoms, A. E. and Xanthos, P. (1981) 'Housing policy and crime in the British public sector', in P. J. Brantingham and P. L. Brantingham (eds) *Environmental Criminology*, Beverly Hills, Calif.: Sage.

Bottoms, A. E., Mawby, R. I., and Walker, M. A. (1987) 'A localised crime survey in contrasting areas of a city', *British Journal of Criminology* 27: 125–54.

Bradley, T. (1983) 'Within the Double Margin: Poverty and Deprivation in Rural England' (Paper presented to British Sociological Association Conference, Cardiff, April 1983).

Brantingham, P. L. and Brantingham, P. J. (1984) 'Burglar mobility and crime prevention planning' in R. Clarke and T. Hope (eds), *Coping with Burglary*, Boston: Kluwer-Nijhoff.

Brogden, M. (1982) *The Police: Autonomy and Consent*, London: Academic Press.

―――― (1987) 'The emergence of the police: the colonial dimension', *British Journal of Criminology* 27: 4–14.

Brown, M. (1981) *Working the Street*, New York: Russell Sage.

Bulmer, M. (1986) *Neighbours: the Work of Philip Abrams*, Cambridge: Cambridge University Press.

Burman, S. B. (undated) *Beyond Apartheid's Courts: Reaping the Whirlwind*, Oxford: Centre for Socio-Legal Studies.

Burrows, J. (1986) *Burglary: Police Action and Victim Views*, Home Office Research Papers 37, London: HMSO.

Butler, A. J. P. (1984) *The Management of the Police Organisation*, Farnborough: Gower.

Butler, A. J. P. and Tharme, K. (1982) 'Social survey: Chelmsley Wood Subdivision', unpublished, West Midlands Police.

Cain, M. (1973) *Society and the Policeman's Role*, London: Routledge & Kegan Paul.

Chambers, G. and Tombs, J. (1984) *The British Crime Survey: Scotland*, a Scottish Office social research study, Edinburgh: HMSO.

Chatterton, M. (1985) 'Mouldy files, red pen entries and paper that bounces: issues in the supervision of paperwork' (Paper given at conference on the Police Foundation research programme, Harrogate, 12–14 December 1985 and to be published by Gower).

Christie, N. (1977) 'Conflicts as property', *British Journal of Criminology* 17: 1–15.

―――― (1986) 'The ideal victim', in E. A. Fattah (ed.) *Reorienting the Justice System – from Crime Policy to Victim Policy*, London: Macmillan.

Clarke, M. (1987) 'Citizenship, community and the management of crime', *British Journal of Criminology* 27: Autumn.

Clarke, R. V. G. and Hough, M. (1984) *Crime and Police Effectiveness*, Home Office Research Study 79, London: HMSO.

Clarke, R. V. G. and Mayhew, P. (1980) *Designing out Crime*, London: HMSO.

Clinard, M. B. (1978) *Cities with Little Crime: the Case of Switzerland*, Cambridge: Cambridge University Press.

Cohen, A. P. (ed.) (1982) *Belonging: Identity and Social Organisation in British Rural Cultures*, Manchester: Manchester University Press.

Cohen, S. (1985) *Visions of Social Control*, Cambridge: Polity Press.

Coleman, A. (1984) 'Trouble in Utopia: design influences in blocks of flats', *Geographical Journal* 150 (3): 351–62.

Comrie, M. and Kings, B. (1974) 'Urban workloads', *Police Research Bulletin* 23: 32–8.

Cozens, R. (1987) Paper on the work of the Home Office PRSU on minimizing paperwork in the West Midlands given at the International Conference on Crime Prevention, The Barbican 14–18 September 1987

Dahrendorf, R. (1985) *Law and Order*, London: Stevens.

Davidson, R. N. (1984) 'Burglary in the community: patterns of localisation in offender–victim relations', in R. Clarke and T. Hope (eds) *Coping with Burglary*, Boston: Kluwer-Nijhoff.

Day, P. and Klein, R. (1987) *Accountabilities: Five Public Services*, London: Tavistock.

Ditton, J. and Duffy, J. (1982) *Bias in Newspaper Crime Reports*, Background Paper Three, Glasgow: Department of Sociology, University of Glasgow.

Eck, J. E. (1983) *Solving Crimes: the Investigation of Burglary and Robbery*, Washington DC: Police Executive Research Forum.

Ekblom, P. and Heal, K. (1982) *The Police Response to Calls from the Public*, Home Office Research and Planning Unit Paper 9, London: Home Office.

Ericson, R. V. (1981) *Making Crime: a Study of Detective Work*, Toronto: Butterworths.

Fielding, N. (1985) 'Police socialization and police competence', *British Journal of Sociology*.

—— (1987) 'Being used by the police', *British Journal of Criminology* 27: 64–9.

Fitzmaurice, C. and Pease, K. (1985) *The Psychology of Judicial Sentencing*, Manchester: Manchester University Press.

Forsythe, D. (1982a) 'Primary School Closure in Rural Areas – Expectation and Experience' (Paper given to SSRC/BSA Rural Economy and Society Study Group, Oxford, December 1982).

—— (1982b) *Urban–Rural Migration, Change and Conflict in an Orkney Island Community*, North Sea Oil Panel Occasional Paper 14, London: SSRC.

Gaskell, G. and Smith, P. (1985) 'How young blacks see the police', *New Society*: 261–3.

Gill, O. (1977) *Luke Street: Housing Policy, Conflict and the Creation of the Delinquent Area*, London: Macmillan.

Greenberg, M. S. and Ruback, R. B. (1984) 'A model of crime victim decision making' (Paper given at Third International Institute on Victimology, Lisbon, 11–17 November 1984).

Hampshire Constabulary (1984) *Beatcraft*, Winchester: Hampshire Constabulary.

Hawkins, K. O. (1984) *Environment and Enforcement: Regulation and the Social Definition of Pollution*, Oxford: Clarendon Press.

Hobbs, D. (1988) *Doing the Business: Entrepreneurship, the Working Class and Detectives in the East End of London*, Oxford: Oxford University Press.

Hobsbawm, E. J. and Rudé, G. (1973) *Captain Swing*, Harmondsworth: Penguin.

Holdaway, S. (1981) *The Occupational Culture of Urban Policing: an*

Ethnographic Study (Ph.D. thesis, University of Sheffield).
—— (1983) *Inside the British Police*, Oxford: Basil Blackwell.
Home Office (1985–6) *Research Programme*, London: Home Office.
Hope, T. (1982) *Burglary in Schools: the Prospects for Prevention*, Home Office Research and Planning Unit Papers 11, London: Home Office.
Hope, T. and Hough, M. (1986) 'Area, crime and incivilities: a profile from the British Crime Survey' (Paper given to Home Office conference on Communities and Crime Reduction, Cambridge, July 1986 and to be published by HMSO).
Hough, M. (1980) *Uniformed Police Work and Management Technology*, Home Office Research Unit Paper 1, London: HMSO.
—— (1985) 'Demand for policing and police performance: progress and pitfalls in public surveys?' (Paper given to conference 'Police Research: Where Now?', Harrogate, December 1985 and to be published by Gower).
—— (1986) 'Counting crime: an overview of the British Crime Survey', in R. E. Mawby (ed.) *Crime Victims*, Plymouth: Plymouth Polytechnic.
—— (1987) 'Thinking about effectiveness', *British Journal of Criminology* 27: 70–9.
Hough, M. and Mayhew, P. (1983) *The British Crime Survey: First Report*, Home Office Research Study 76, London: HMSO.
—— (1985) *Taking Account of Crime: Key Findings from the Second British Crime Survey*, Home Office Research Study 85, London: HMSO.
Jacobs, J. (1965) *The Death and Life of Great American Cities*, Harmondsworth: Penguin Books.
Jefferson, T. (1987) 'Beyond paramilitarism', *British Journal of Criminology* 27: 47–53.
Jefferson, T. and Grimshaw, R. (1984) *Controlling the Constable: Police Accountability in England and Wales*, London: Frederick Muller/ The Cobden Trust.
—— (1987) *Interpreting Police Work*, London: Allen & Unwin.
Johnstone, V. and Shapland, J. (1987) *Classification of Public Disorder*, Report to the Home Office, Oxford: Centre for Criminological Research.
Jones, S. J. and Levi, M. (1983) *Police–Public Relationships*, Report to the Home Office, Cardiff: University College.
Jones, T., Maclean, B., and Young, J. (1986) *The Islington Crime Survey: Crime, Victimisation and Policing in Inner-city London*, Aldershot: Gower.
Kinsey, R. (1984) *Merseyside Crime Survey: First Report, November 1984*, Liverpool: Police Committee Support Unit.
—— (1985) *Merseyside Crime and Police Surveys, Final Report, October 1985*, Edinburgh: Centre for Criminology.
Knol, F. A. and Soetenhorst, J. (1979) 'Multi-level analysis: dimensions in the relation between community variables standing for the "social climate" and variability of behaviour concerning "going out in the evening"' (Paper given to Workshop Meeting of Research Committee for the Sociology of Deviance and Social Control, The Hague, 30–31 August 1979).
Lea, J. and Young, J. (1984) *What Is to be Done about Law and Order?*, Harmondsworth: Penguin.

Lee, J. A. (1981) 'Some structural aspects of police deviance in relations with minority groups', in C. Shearing (ed.) *Organisational Police Deviance*, Toronto: Butterworths.

Lejeune, R. and Alex, N. (1973) 'On being mugged: the event and its aftermath', *Urban Life and Culture* 2: 259–87.

Lustgarten, L. (1987) *The Governance of the Police*, London: Stevens.

McCabe, S. and Sutcliffe, F. (1978) *Defining Crime*, Occasional Paper 9, University of Oxford, Centre for Criminological Research, Oxford: Basil Blackwell.

Maguire, M. (1982) *Burglary in a Dwelling: the Offence, the Offender and the Victim*, London: Heinemann.

Maguire, M., Vagg, J., and Morgan, R. (eds) (1985) *Accountability and Prisons: Opening up a Closed World*, London: Tavistock.

Mangione, T. W. and Noble (1975) Cited in DuBow, F., McCabe, E. and Kaplan, G. (1979) *Reactions to Crime: a Critical Review of the Literature*, National Institute of Law Enforcement and Criminal Justice, Washington, DC: Government Printing Office.

Manning, P. K. (1980) 'Aspects of command and control in the West Midlands police' (Unpublished paper, Michigan State University).

——— (1983) 'Queries concerning the decision-making approach to police research', in J. Shapland (ed.) *Decision Making in the Legal System*, Issues in Criminological and Legal Psychology 5, Leicester: The British Psychological Society.

Martin, J. and Wilson, G. (1969) *The Police: A Study in Manpower*, London: Heinemann.

Mawby, R. I. (1979) *Policing the City*, Farnborough: Gower.

——— (1984) 'Bystander responses to the victims of crime: is the Good Samaritan alive and well?' (Paper given at Third International Institute on Victimology, Lisbon, 11–17 November 1984).

Maxfield, M. (1984) *Fear of Crime in England and Wales*, Home Office Research Study 78, London: HMSO.

Mayhew, P. (forthcoming) 'The effects of crime: victims, the public and fear', (Paper given to the Sixteenth Criminological Research Conference, Council of Europe, Strasbourg: Council of Europe).

Merry, S. E. (1981) *Urban Danger: Life in a Neighborhood of Strangers*, Philadelphia: Temple University Press.

——— (1984) 'Rethinking gossip and scandal', in D. Black (ed.) *Toward a General Theory of Social Control. Vol. 1: Fundamentals*, Orlando, Fla.: Academic Press.

Ministerie van Justitie (1985) *Society and Crime: A Policy Plan for the Netherlands*, The Hague: Ministerie van Justitie.

Morgan, R. (1987a) 'The local determinants of policing policy', in P. Willmott (ed.) *Policing and the Community*, PSI Discussion Paper 16, London: Policy Studies Institute.

——— (1987b) 'Police accountability: developing the local infrastructure', *British Journal of Criminology* 27: 87–96.

——— (1987c) *Public Disorder: an Analysis of Police Recorded Messages*, Report to the Home Office, Bath: University of Bath.

References 211

Morgan, R. and Maggs, C. (1985) *Setting the PACE: Police–Community Consultation Arrangements in England and Wales*, Bath Social Policy Papers 4, Bath: University of Bath.

NACRO (1982a) 'Flames Project: agreed action plan, Finch House Estate' (Unpublished paper, London, NACRO).

——— (1982b) 'Pepys Improvement Project: estate profile' (Unpublished paper, London, NACRO).

——— (1987a) *Proposals for Improving the Policing of Housing Estates*, London: NACRO.

——— (1987b) *Resourcing Tenant Participation*, London: NACRO.

National Consumer Council (1982) *The Neighbourhood*, Consumer Concerns Special Paper 5, London: National Consumer Council.

Newby, H. (1979) *Green and Pleasant Land? Social Change in Rural England*, Harmondsworth: Penguin.

Newman, O. (1972) *Defensible Space*, New York: Macmillan.

O'Connor, M. (1986) 'Policing in a country town, the 1860s and today' (Unpublished paper, University of New England, Armidale, NSW).

O'Dowd, D. (1987) Paper given to session on 'Information in Police Management', International Police Exhibition and Conference, the Barbican, London, 14–18 September 1987.

Osborn, S. (1987) *Towards a Community Safety Policy for Local Authorities*, London: NACRO.

Pate, A., Wycoff, M. A., Skogan, W. G., and Sherman, L. (1986) *Reducing Fear of Crime in Houston and Newark: a Summary Report*, Washington, DC: The Police Foundation and the National Institute of Justice.

Power, A. (1982) *Priority Estates Project 1982. Improving Problem Council Estates: a Summary of Aims and Progress*, London: Department of the Environment.

Poyner, B. (1983) *Design against Crime: Beyond Defensible Space*, London: Butterworths.

Pryce, K. (1977) *Endless Pressure*, Harmondsworth: Penguin.

Quayle, B. (1983) 'Centre and surround: images of place in contemporary Allendale' (Paper delivered at the British Sociological Association Conference, Cardiff, 1983).

Raban, J. (1974) *Soft City*, London: Hamish Hamilton.

Reiner, R. (1978) *The Blue-Coated Worker*, Cambridge: Cambridge University Press.

——— (1985) *The Politics of the Police*, Brighton: Wheatsheaf.

Riley, D. and Mayhew, P. (1980) *Crime Prevention Publicity: an Assessment*, Home Office Research Study 63, London: HMSO.

Rosenbaum, D. (1986) *Community Crime Prevention: Does it Work?*, Beverly Hills: Sage.

Scarman, Lord (1982) *The Scarman Report: the Brixton Disorders 10–12 April 1981*, Harmondsworth: Penguin.

Schafer, S. (1977) *Victimology: the Victim and His Criminal*, Virginia: Reston.

Shapland, J. and Hobbs, D. (1987) *Policing on the Ground in Highland*, Working Paper, Oxford: Centre for Criminological Research.

——— (1988) *Police Priorities and Chief Constables' Annual Reports*,

Working Paper, Oxford: Centre for Criminological Research.

Shapland, J., Willmore, J., and Duff, P. (1985) *Victims in the Criminal Justice System*, Aldershot: Gower.

Shaw, C. R. and McKay, H. D. (1942) *Juvenile Delinquency and Urban Areas*, Chicago: Chicago University Press (rev. edn 1969).

Skogan, W. G. (1984) 'Reporting crimes to the police: the status of world research', *Journal of Research in Crime and Delinquency* 21: 113–37.

—— (1987) *Disorder and Community Decline*, Final Report to the National Institute of Justice, Evanston, Ill.: Northwestern University.

Skogan, W. G. and Maxfield, M. G. (1981) *Coping with Crime*, Beverly Hills: Sage.

Slovak, J. S. (1986) *Styles of Urban Policing*, New York: New York University Press.

Smith, D. (1987) 'Research, the community and the police', in P. Willmott (ed.) *Policing and the Community*, London: Policy Studies Institute.

Smith, D. J., Small, S., and Gray, J. (1983) *Police and People in London*, 4 vols, London: Policy Studies Institute.

Smith, S. J. (1984) 'Crime in the news', *British Journal of Criminology* 24: 289–95.

Soetenhorst, J. (1983) 'Fear of crime as a policy problem', *Victimology* 8: 336–43.

Southgate, P. and Ekblom, P. (1984) *Contacts between Police and Public: Findings from the British Crime Survey*, Home Office Research Study 77, London: HMSO.

Sparks, R. F., Genn, H., and Dodd, D. J. (1977) *Surveying Victims*, London: John Wiley.

Spelman, W. and Brown, D. K. (1981) *Calling the Police: Citizen Reporting of Serious Crime*, Washington, DC: Police Executive Research Forum.

Stanko, E. (1987) 'Hidden violence against women', in M. Maguire and J. Pointing (eds) *Victims of Crime: a New Deal?*, Milton Keynes: Open University Press.

Steinmetz, C. H. D. (1983) *Initiative-takers, Aggrieved Persons and Witnesses of Aggressive Behaviour in a Youth-Clubhouse in the Dutch Metropolis "Randstad"*, The Hague: Ministry of Justice, Research and Documentation Centre.

—— (1984) 'Bystanders of crime: some results from a national survey' (Paper given at Third International Institute on Victimology, Lisbon, 11–17 November 1984, and forthcoming in *Victimology*).

Strathern, M. (1981) *Kinship at the Core: an Anthropology of Elmdon, a Village in North-West Essex in the 1960s*, Cambridge: Cambridge University Press.

—— (1982) 'The village as an idea: constructs of villageness in Elmdon, Essex', in A. P. Cohen (ed.) *Belonging*, Manchester: Manchester University Press.

Sykes, G. and Matza, D. (1957) 'Techniques of neutralization: a theory of delinquency', *American Sociological Review* 22 December: 664–70. Reprinted in M. Wolfgang, L. Savitz, and N. Johnston (eds) (1962) *The Sociology of Crime and Delinquency*, London: Wiley.

Thrasher, F. M. (1963) *The Gang*, Chicago: University of Chicago Press.

van Dijk, J. J. M. (1978) *The Extent of Public Information and the Nature of Public Attitudes Towards Crime*, The Hague: Research and Documentation Centre, Ministry of Justice.

van Dijk, J. J. M. and Steinmetz, C. H. D. (1983) 'Victimization surveys: beyond measuring the volume of crime', *Victimology* 8: 291–309.

van Dijk, J. J. M., Roell, A., and Steinmetz, C. H. D. (1982) 'Bystanders' intervention in a crime: a preliminary comparison between the results of questionnaire studies and a naturalistic experiment' (Paper read at 20th International Congress of Applied Psychology, Edinburgh, 25–31 July 1982).

van Dijk, J. J. M., Steinmetz, C. H. D., Spickenheuer, H. L. P., and Docter-Schamhardt, B. J. W. (1982) *External Effects of a Crime Prevention Program in The Hague*, Research and Documentation Centre Paper LI, The Hague: Ministry of Justice.

Warr, M. (1985) 'Fear of rape among urban women' *Social Problems* 32: 238–50.

Weatheritt, M. (1982) 'Community policing: does it work and how do we know? A review of research', in T. Bennett (ed.) *The Future of Policing* (Papers presented to 15th Cropwood Round-Table Conference, Cambridge, December 1982).

———— (1986) *Innovations in Policing*, London: Croom Helm.

Wild, R. (1983) 'Local government, resident action and social change: an Australian case study' (Paper delivered at the British Sociological Association conference, Cardiff, 1983).

Williams, R. (1976) *Keywords*, Glasgow: Fontana/Croom Helm.

Willmott, P. (ed.) (1987) *Policing and the Community*, PSI Discussion Paper 16, London: Policy Studies Institute.

Wilson, J. Q. and Kelling, G. L. (1982) 'Broken windows: the police and neighbourhood safety', *The Atlantic Monthly* March: 29–38.

Winchester, S. and Jackson, H. (1982) *Residential Burglary: the Limits of Prevention*, Home Office Research Study 74, London: HMSO.

Winkel, F. W. (1987) 'Response generalisation in crime prevention campaigns', *British Journal of Criminology* 27: 155–73.

Young, M. and Willmott, P. (1962) *Family and Kinship in East London*, Harmondsworth: Penguin.

Name Index

Subject Index

For Product Safety Concerns and Information please contact our EU
representative GPSR@taylorandfrancis.com
Taylor & Francis Verlag GmbH, Kaufingerstraße 24, 80331 München, Germany

www.ingramcontent.com/pod-product-compliance
Lightning Source LLC
Chambersburg PA
CBHW050427280326
41932CB00013BA/2017

*9 7 8 1 0 3 2 4 1 7 7 6 9 *